RICHMOND
After the War

RICHMOND
After the War
1865–1890

Michael B. Chesson

VIRGINIA STATE LIBRARY • RICHMOND • 1981

Library of Congress Cataloging in Publication Data

Chesson, Michael B   1947–
    Richmond after the war, 1865–1890.

    Includes bibliographical references and index.
    1. Richmond—History. I.   Title.
F234.R557C48   975.5′451   80-25833
ISBN 0-88490-085-1
ISBN 0–88490–086–X (pbk.)

Standard Book Number 0–88490–085–1 (case-bound)
                      0–88490–086–x (paperback)
©Virginia State Library 1981. All rights reserved.
Virginia State Library, Richmond, Virginia.
Printed in the United States of America.

Roony Lee says "Beast" Butler was very kind to him while he was a prisoner; and the "Beast" has sent him back his war horse. The Lees are men enough to speak the truth of friend or enemy, not fearing consequences.

Mary Boykin Chesnut

Contents

Illustrations

Plates 3, 7, and 12 are from the Library of Congress. Plate 5 is from the Virginia Historical Society, and plate 8 is from the Petersburg collection of the National Park Service. Plates 17 and 20 appear through the courtesy of Ebenezer Baptist Church, and plate 84 appears through the courtesy of Sixth Mount Zion Baptist Church. Plate 55 is from the Richmond Humanities Center, and plates 83 and 86 are from the Museum of the Confederacy. The Valentine Museum graciously supplied plates 13, 14, 18, 21 through 26, 29, 32 through 43, 48, 49, 51, 52, 56, 57, 63, 64, 67, 74, 77 through 80, 82, 87, and 89. All other illustrations are from the collections of the Virginia State Library.

Nonbiblical epigraphs are quoted from the following sources: Mary Boykin Chesnut (page v), *A Diary From Dixie*, ed. Ben Ames Williams (Boston, 1949), 396; Ellen Glasgow (page xiv), "The Dynamic Past," *The Reviewer* 1 (1921): 1–2; Frederick Law Olmsted (page 2), *The Cotton Kingdom* . . . , ed. Arthur M. Schlesinger (New York, 1953), 33; John W. Forney (page 116), *Richmond Daily Dispatch*, 29 April 1869; Records of the Richmond Common Council, 8 July 1867 (page 144), City Clerk's Office, Richmond City Hall, Richmond, Virginia; Colonel Albert Ordway, U.S.A. (ret.) (page 144), report of the James River improvement committee, 15 June 1870, City Clerk's Office; Robert L. Dabney (page 144), speech quoted in Allen W. Moger, "Industrial and Urban Progress in Virginia From 1880 to 1900," *Virginia Magazine of History and Biography* 66 (1958): 457; Ben Robertson (page 170), *Red Hills and Cotton* (New York, 1942), 89–92; Henry James (page 208), *The American Scene* (New York, 1907), 354–355.

Tables

Because I am a Virginian in every drop of my blood and pulse of my heart, I may speak the truth as I understand it. . . . At least the faults I deplore are my own faults, just as I hope the peculiar virtues of Virginians are my own also. . . . No Virginian can love and revere the past more than I do. No Virginian can find greater inspiration in the lesson that it teaches. To me Virginia's past is like a hall hung with rare and wonderful tapestries, or perhaps it would be truer to say that it is like a cathedral illumined by the gold and wine-colour of stained glass windows. It is a place to which we should go for inspiration and worship; it is a place from which we should come with renewed strength and courage; but it is not a place in which we should live and brood until we become like that ancient people whose "strength was to sit still."

Ellen Glasgow

Preface

POST–CIVIL WAR Richmond was neither Atlanta nor Charleston, neither a New South metropolis nor an antebellum fly-in-amber. Despite defeat and a devastating fire in 1865 the city remained until 1900 the South's second largest, after New Orleans. On the eve of the Civil War Richmond had been a major southern entrepôt, the center of culture and society for the Old Dominion and for part of the eastern seaboard. Even after four years of war, the former capital of the Confederacy had many advantages and an unusually bright future. In the decade of the 1870s Richmond showed significant signs of growth, whether measured in barrels of flour or in the attitudes of residents. Yet postwar Richmond fell dramatically short of its urban promise, surpassed by other American cities. Where once foreign and coasting vessels had carried passengers and freight to and from the James River and Kanawha Canal and the city's five railroads, by 1890 the canal lay in ruins and the deep-water port stood idle. Antebellum Richmond had depended on northern men and markets to a small degree, but the postwar city's railroads and tobacco industry were under northern control before 1890. As a regional entrepôt Richmond lost out first to Norfolk and then to Newport News and West Point. The Petersburg of William P. Mahone and the Alexandria of John S. Barbour were, in proportion to their populations, administrative centers as important as postwar Richmond. Richmond, of course, was the state capital, but the domination of Virginia politics had passed from the antebellum Richmond Junto to lawyers for northern corporations and rural leaders from the black-belt counties.

Before the war, slavery in heavily industrialized Richmond, where nearly 20 percent of the black residents were free, differed from the peculiar institution on southern plantations and farms. The immediate changes wrought by emancipation were not as stark in Richmond as in rural areas of the Deep South. But the first rule of postwar southern whites was to keep the region a white man's country, and the principal goal of most white Richmonders was to keep the capital a white-ruled city. They maintained power almost continuously after the war, but at a terrible cost. Able black workers left Richmond for better opportunities in northern cities far earlier than their counterparts elsewhere in the urban South. Conservative Democrats used tactics against Richmond Republicans, white and black, that brought corruption and one-party rule, but no end to party strife. In the last decade of the century, however, black voters lost their place in Richmond politics; their disfranchisement under the Virginia Constitution of 1902 merely ratified the status quo.

Various economic and geographic circumstances shaped Richmond's postwar decline, but Richmond stagnated chiefly because its leaders did not want nineteenth-century material progress—not badly enough, not with the alien things that accompanied it. The New South creed held that industry and scientific agriculture promised progress—prosperity, sectional reconciliation, and racial harmony—but it was a progress in which Richmond chose not fully to participate. Many Richmonders thought they could have both the Old South and the New, both the Lost Cause and the American dream. They made Richmond the old city of the New South. They preferred, perhaps without knowing it, the familiar cadence of decline. Tradition and the past were more powerful or attractive than progress. Beneficial at times, more often destructive, the city's enduring conservatism was the essential characteristic of Richmond after the war.

• • •

The absence of a modern history of Richmond during the post–Civil War era, noted by Charles B. Dew a decade ago,[1] was a puzzling gap in the historiography of one of America's most famous cities, for urban and southern historians recognize Richmond's importance in the nineteenth century. Until a comprehensive narrative account of postwar Richmond was available, many unanswered questions stood poised to ensnare the researcher who might attempt a statistically precise study of social mobility, or of residential patterns. Necessity dictated that this book be an urban history akin more to the city biographies

---

1. Charles B. Dew, "Critical Essay on Recent Works," in C. Vann Woodward, *Origins of the New South, 1877–1913*, 2d ed., in Wendell Holmes Stephenson and E. Merton Coulter, eds., *A History of the South*, vol. 9 ([Baton Rouge], 1971).

of Bessie Louise Pierce, Blake McKelvey, and Constance M. Green[2] than to the currently fashionable "new urban history."[3] The pressing need for a book on Richmond also precluded the comparative approach in which several cities are examined together. Excellent research of this kind has been, and is being, done.[4] In one sense, of course, the explanation of Richmond's postwar stagnation is implicitly a comparison of Richmond's development with that of other cities. Richmond was not the only southern city that declined. Don H. Doyle has shown that Charleston and Mobile fared more poorly.[5] The port of Savannah could not compete with the rail center that was Atlanta, nor could Natchez or war-shattered Vicksburg contend with New Orleans and Saint Louis. Yellow fever held Memphis back,[6] and Louisville was losing ground to Cincinnati even before the war. Comparison with the New South cities suggests that Richmond had some traits in common,[7] but again there is much research to be done. In

2. Bessie Louise Pierce, *A History of Chicago*, vol. 3, *The Rise of a Modern City, 1871–1893* (Chicago, 1957); Blake McKelvey, *Rochester: The Flower City, 1855–1890* (Cambridge, Mass., 1949); and Constance M. Green, *Washington*, vol. 1, *Village and Capital, 1800–1878* (Princeton, 1962).

3. Theodore Hershberg, "The New Urban History," *Journal of Urban History* 5 (1978): 3–40.

4. David T. Gilchrist, ed., *The Growth of the Seaport Cities, 1790–1825* (Charlottesville, 1967). For a comparison of two urban elites *see* E. Digby Baltzell, *Puritan Boston and Quaker Philadelphia* (New York, 1979).

5. Don H. Doyle, "Urbanization and Southern Culture: Economic Elites in Four New South Cities, 1865–1910," rev. ed. (Paper presented at the Forty-fourth Annual Meeting of the Southern Historical Association, St. Louis, Mo., 11 Nov. 1978).

6. Gerald M. Capers, *The Biography of a River Town: Memphis, Its Heroic Age* (Chapel Hill, N.C., 1939).

7. Sarah McCulloh Lemmon, "Raleigh—An Example of the 'New South?' ", *North Carolina Historical Review* 43 (1966): 261– 285. Lemmon lists four characteristics of New South cities: a theme of reconciliation with the North, an attempt to develop or attract industry, the start of public education, and the improvement and modernization of the city. Howard N. Rabinowitz, *Race Relations in the Urban South, 1865–1890* (New York, 1978). Rabinowitz defined three persistent characteristics shared by southern cities in the second half of the nineteenth century: increased size, but a failure to grow as rapidly as northern cities; economic importance based more on commerce or administration than on manufacturing; and, a strong desire on the part of white residents to control the black population.

recent years, scholars have not agreed about the essential characteristics of the South's post-Civil War experience.[8] Richmond seems to
add its weight to the side of those historians, such as W. J. Cash,[9]
who argue that continuity rather than drastic change marked southern
life in the nineteenth century.

The pages that follow portray not a city that succeeded (a common
American organism with limitations of its own) but rather a city that
failed. A city that failed, at least, at what late-nineteenth-century
American cities did, which was to grow rapidly. The sightseer or
resident in today's Richmond, of course, may argue that the city's
nineteenth-century stagnation held unexpected advantages: the am-
bience of a small city, the environmental benefits of limited growth,
or the charm of gaslit neighborhoods in the Fan District or on Church
Hill. It seems more appropriate, however, to evaluate the postwar
Richmond leadership by its own growth-oriented standard (repeatedly
expressed by the Chamber of Commerce, the city council, and the
leading newspaper) than to weigh its actions in a modern balance.
Richmond changed for the worse in many ways after the war. The
city in which sensitive young Ellen Glasgow grew up could not truly
share in the Progressive era. The advantages of life in provincial,

---

8. *See*, for example, Woodward, *Origins of the New South;* Jay R. Mandle, *The Roots of Black
Poverty: The Southern Plantation Economy After the Civil War* (Durham, N.C., 1978); Roger
L. Ransom and Richard Sutch, *One Kind of Freedom: The Economic Consequences of Emancipation*
(Cambridge, 1977); Dwight B. Billings, Jr., *Planters and the Making of a "New South":
Class, Politics, and Development in North Carolina, 1865–1900* (Chapel Hill, N.C., 1979);
Jonathan M. Wiener, *Social Origins of the New South: Alabama, 1860–1885* (Baton Rouge, 1978)
and "Class Structure and Economic Development in the American South, 1865–1955,"
American Historical Review 84 (1979): 970–992; commentary on Wiener's article by Robert
Higgs and Harold D. Woodman, *American Historical Review* 84 (1979): 993–1001; Peter
Kolchin, "Race, Class, and Poverty in the Post–Civil War South," *Reviews in American
History* 7 (1979): 515–526; and Michael Perman, "Sociologists as Historians and Planters as
Industrialists," *Reviews in American History* 9 (1980): 74–79.

For more traditional studies of the same problem *see* William J. Cooper, Jr., *The Conservative
Regime: South Carolina, 1877–1890* (Baltimore, 1968); Jack P. Maddex, Jr., *The Virginia
Conservatives, 1867–1879: A Study in Reconstruction Politics* (Chapel Hill, N.C., 1970); and
James Tice Moore, *Two Paths to the New South: The Virginia Debt Controversy, 1870–1883*
(Lexington, Ky., 1974) and "Redeemers Reconsidered: Change and Continuity in the Demo-
cratic South, 1870–1900," *Journal of Southern History* 44 (1978): 357–378.

9. W. J. Cash, *The Mind of the South* (New York, 1941).

postwar Richmond were largely restricted to upper-class males. Glasgow used the stench of industry as a symbol of moral decay in *The Sheltered Life*.[10] She found both in late-nineteenth-century Richmond.

• • •

This book could not have been written without the support and assistance of innumerable individuals. Some read or listened to portions of the work and supplied conscientious criticism. Many disagreed with my conclusions, and none is responsible for errors of fact or interpretation to which I may stubbornly have clung. My greatest debt, as always, is to my mother and father, Virginia Winborne Ramsey and W. E. Chesson, who from my beginning in the Fan District taught me to love history. My great-aunt, Mrs. Jesse Hill Crouch, fed and housed me on many occasions while I searched Richmond's archives. As a repository of oral history she·patiently reintroduced me to the folkways of the city of my birth. Colonel and Mrs. C. J. Rinker gave me their wholehearted support. Thomas J. Lanahan assisted me in many ways, as did Mark Winborne Chesson and his wife, Nancy. Richard McMurran gave me sound advice. I was fortunate to have had fine teachers, and I am particularly indebted to four gentlemen who were members of the history department of the College of William and Mary, 1965–1969: Harold Lees Fowler, Bruce T. McCully, Ludwell H. Johnson, and especially Richard Maxwell Brown.

In Richmond, Daniel P. Jordan, Jr., was generous with his time. I also received valuable comments from Alan and Penelope Briceland, Virginius Dabney, Scott C. Davis, Conley S. Edwards, William J. Ernst, Ernst-Ulrich Franzen, Joseph Goldenberg, Harold Greer, Allan K. Kulikoff, Edward J. Kopf, Susan W. Linden-Brooks, Robert Saunders, Philip J. and Janet Schwarz, Barry Westin, Harry Ward, David Boney, Jr., and James E. Scanlon—participants in the Richmond American History Seminar; as well as from members of the Historic Richmond Foundation and from my summer students at Virginia Commonwealth University. Tom Choate and others for whom I once worked at the Richmond, Fredericksburg and Potomac Railroad, Ray Carter, Roy Gaines, and Jane Sutherland shared their knowledge of Richmond, and Allen W. Moger warned me about the perils of writing Virginia history.

10. Ellen Glasgow, *The Sheltered Life* (Garden City, N.Y., 1932).

Louis B. Cei, John T. O'Brien, Jr., and Leslie Winston Smith, fellow students of Richmond, exchanged ideas with me. Stephen Botein and Peter Stanley, along with fellow graduate students Guy Land, John McCardell, and Bob Small, criticized a prospectus of this study. Rob Silverman took time from his own research to criticize my work, Stephan Thernstrom gave me guidance before I began my research. Frank Freidel expressed interest at an early stage and served as second reader of my dissertation. Two grants from the Charles Warren Center for the Study of American History enabled me to complete essential research that would otherwise have been beyond my resources. I am grateful to Donald Fleming, former director of the center, and to his colleagues for their assistance.

Andrew Buni, August Meier, Howard N. Rabinowitz, and Edgar A. Toppin sharpened my perspective on black leadership in Richmond, as did Don H. Doyle on urban growth in the postwar South. Curt and Flora Stith Lowe, Arnold Shankman, and especially Charles Michaud read my prospectus (and later the entire dissertation), criticized it in detail, and listened patiently to talk about Richmond, as have Curt and Diane Stallings. My colleagues and students at the University of Massachusetts in Boston have helped me, and I owe special debts to Jonathan Chu and to Michael Riccards, dean of the College of Arts and Sciences. David R. Goldfield, James Tice Moore, and Brent Tarter challenged me with stimulating questions and read the manuscript with keen perception.

I am grateful to Donald Haynes, state librarian of Virginia, who first expressed interest in publishing this work, and to Jon Kukla and Sandra Gioia Treadway; no author could ask for better editors. Henry G. Ecton and Emily J. Salmon located and secured the illustrations. I cannot adequately express my gratitude for the research assistance given at the Virginia State Library by John W. Dudley, Milton C. Russell, Robert Clay, Toni H. Waller, and others; at the Virginia Historical Society by William M. E. Rachal, Howson Cole, James Fleming, and Waverly K. Winfree; at the Valentine Museum by Elizabeth Grey Gibson, Eve Anderson, and E. M. Sanchez-Saavedra; at the Virginia Historic Landmarks Commission by Tucker Hill, Margaret T. Peters, and others; at the Richmond City Clerk's office by Clerk Edgar A. Duffy, Deputy Clerk Pete Martin, and Bernice Breeden; at the *Richmond Afro-American* by Robert W. Waitt, Jr.; and at the Earl Gregg Swem Library of the College of William and Mary by Pamela G. Boll. I am grateful as well for the courtesy extended by manuscript curators at the University of Virginia Library; the American Antiquarian Society; and the libraries at Emory University, Howard University, and the Mariners Museum.

I would not have begun this study without the inspiration of David Herbert Donald, or continued it without his profound patience. Except for my wife Anna, I would not have finished it. Only they know what I owe them.

Quincy, Massachusetts   MICHAEL B. CHESSON

RICHMOND
After the War

Richmond, at a glance from adjacent high ground through a dull cloud of bituminous smoke, upon a lowering winter's day [in December 1852], has a very picturesque appearance, and I was reminded of the sensation produced by a similar coup d'oeil *of Edinburgh. It is somewhat similarly situated upon and among some considerable hills; but the moment it is examined at all in detail, there is but one spot in the whole picture, upon which the eye is at all attracted to rest. This is the Capitol, a Grecian edifice, standing alone, and finely placed on open and elevated ground, in the centre of the town.*

Frederick Law Olmsted

1

Richmond on the James

RICHMOND is a city in thralldom to its past. Although its landscape and buildings have not always been preserved, only today's most callous visitor fails to sense that Richmond retains an unusual historical presence. Far from being the largest, or even the oldest, of the cities along the eastern seaboard, Richmond is a small city both because of the force with which it was hit in the 1860s and because change all but passed it by in the subsequent century. History happened here more than once, but never with greater intensity than during and after the Civil War. To some extent even today, because of its size and the memory of its inhabitants, the customs of Richmond's people are those of their ancestors.

During Reconstruction the old patterns of behavior were particularly important, for Richmonders had to adjust to great changes in their way of life. Richmond whites had suffered total military and political defeat. Most Richmond blacks enjoyed freedom for the first time. The experience of each group was without clear precedent, especially as untried members of either color, both natives and strangers, participated in the city's life in new ways. The customs and institutions that survived this decade gave the city a measure of stability, but they also retarded the development of Richmond after the war.

• 1 •

Richmond has remained the state capital for two centuries since the American Revolution, and its political importance as well as its location have contributed to its steady growth. In the early nineteenth century the city became headquarters for a group of Democratic-Republican leaders known as the Richmond Junto. But the city itself was a bastion first of Federalists, like John Marshall, and then of Whigs, like John Hampden Pleasants, until the eve of the Civil War.[1]

In the antebellum South, Richmond was a state capital as well as a major industrial center. In 1860, with nearly thirty-eight thousand people, it ranked twenty-fifth in size among American cities, but thirteenth in the value of its manufactures. In 1861, Richmond was the third-largest city in the Confederacy, but as a site of heavy industry it was more important than Charleston, which it soon surpassed in population. In manufactures it exceeded the far larger city of New Orleans. The commercial and social, as well as political and industrial capital of Virginia, Richmond was the place to which planters and small farmers came to sell their crops, to buy and sell slaves, to purchase seed, fertilizer, and tools, and to entertain themselves and their families. As the entrepôt and metropolis of Virginia east of the Blue Ridge Mountains, Richmond's important role in the conflict was assured.[2]

Geography had dictated that Richmond stand where the Atlantic coastal plain meets the piedmont, and geography shaped the city's growth and determined its later importance. In 1607, explorers from Jamestown first had visited the site, one hundred twenty-seven miles upriver from the Atlantic Ocean where, for seven miles upstream from Rocketts, the James is several hundred yards wide, interrupted by rapids and dotted with rocky islands. To the east the river and its tributaries drain sandy tidewater bottoms. Rolling clay hills rise to meet the Blue Ridge to the north and west, and red clay sprawls southward toward the Carolinas. Richmond became an entrepôt because it stood at the falls, on an east-west road (now state highways 5 and 6) that followed an old Indian trail parallel to the river. As the United States grew, Richmonders also found themselves on a north-south road, the Potomac path, which followed the fall line south from Baltimore and Washington, D.C., toward the towns and states of the Deep South.[3]

Seventeenth-century vessels sailing up the James River had been forced to unload passengers and freight at the fall line. Shipments broken here were carried into the backcountry by packhorse or oxcart. Produce, raw materials, and other goods from the interior were transported to the falls on primitive roads and loaded aboard ships. A fort built at the falls by William Byrd I, was the colony's westernmost line of frontier defense. But as western settlement had advanced beyond the falls a village had grown up around the stockade. This area, along the north riverbank just east of the mouth of Shockoe Creek at the foot of Church Hill, was variously known as the Falls, Shacco's, or Byrd's Warehouse. In 1737 William Byrd II, of Westover, had the land surveyed and named it Richmond. In 1742 the General Assembly of Virginia recognized Richmond as a town in Henrico County, and ten years later it became the county seat. In 1769 Richmond annexed the town of Shockoe, west of the creek, and nearly quadrupled its area. Eleven years later, while British ships plied the waters of the James and York rivers, patriot leaders moved the seat of the government there from its exposed location at Williamsburg.[4]

• 2 •

Richmond's oldest transportation problem, how to travel by water around the falls, was solved by the James River and Kanawha Canal, which was begun in 1784. The canal paralleled the James on the north bank and was designed for long, narrow canalboats with capacities of seven to ten hogsheads of tobacco. By 1795 the canal linked Westham, just above the falls, and Richmond. It was extended to the docks on the lower river near Rocketts by 1812. After a period of neglect, during which the parent James River Company was reorganized, the state supported a westward extension of the canal to Lynchburg that was completed in 1840. By 1851 the canal had reached Buchanan, its terminus west of the Blue Ridge in Botetourt County. Richmond's James River and Kanawha Canal could not duplicate the success of the Erie Canal, which virtually created metropolitan New York, because the Virginia project never crossed the Appalachian Mountains to establish a water link with the Ohio River and the Midwest. Midwestern commerce thus flowed along the Mississippi River and the Great Lakes-Erie Canal routes. Railroads also competed for the canal's freight and passenger traffic, although the James River canal in 1859 carried greater tonnage to Richmond than the total volume of the city's four railroads.[5]

In 1816 a Richmond steamboat navigated the James for the first time. Steam power transformed commerce at Richmond's port, Rocketts. Until the age of steam few city merchants shipped directly to Europe; they bought country produce and sent it downriver to Norfolk, the chief port of Virginia, to be exchanged for domestic and foreign manufactured goods. The advent of steam eliminated the Norfolk middlemen, because the new vessels could come directly up the James to Richmond.[6]

Like the rest of Virginia, early Richmond depended on its waterways for transportation and did little to improve its land routes. Because turnpike construction lagged in comparison with the northern states, and because the roads that were built often were poorly maintained, stages and wagons never rivaled the importance of the ships and canalboats that served Richmond.[7]

Nor could rural stages or wagons compete with the five railroads that terminated in Richmond by 1860. The Richmond, Fredericksburg and Potomac Railroad extended north to Aquia Creek, where it made connections with Potomac River steamships. The Virginia Central Railroad ran northwest through the piedmont to its junction with the Orange and Alexandria Railroad (which furnished antebellum Richmond's only rail link with Washington, D.C.) and then on to Charlottesville, across the Blue Ridge, and into the Valley of Virginia. The Richmond and Danville Railroad extended southwest to Danville, on the North Carolina border. Finally, two shorter lines that served Richmond were the Richmond and Petersburg Railroad, which ran south to the Appomattox River, and the Richmond and York River Railroad, which extended east to the York River at West Point.[8]

Each of these five railroads entered Richmond, but none was connected by tracks through the city. Such links could have improved service, lowered shipping costs, and attracted more business to the capital. Instead, urban teamsters reaped huge profits hauling freight between the depots—as did the hack drivers who carried passengers, and the hotel keepers who accommodated those who had missed connections.[9]

Antebellum Richmond's streets were unpaved, and travelers reported they were worse than those of other large cities, save only low-lying ones such as New Orleans. The capital's streets became quagmires in wet weather and dust bowls in dry. During the winter glare ice sometimes made steep hills impassable. Early Richmonders also were denied easy access to their nearest neighbors. No bridge crossed Shockoe Creek until late in the colonial period, and the valley was subject to periodic floods. Access to Manchester, on the south shore of the James, was even more difficult. The early inhabitants used ferries. In 1788 John Mayo built the first of many toll bridges that he or his descendants owned and operated, bridges on which the family fortune was based. Until after the Civil War the Mayos enjoyed an almost unbroken monopoly of traffic crossing the James at Richmond, although many of their bridges were destroyed by fires or floods. The lack of a free bridge retarded the growth of both Richmond and Manchester.[10]

Two late-antebellum improvements made local travel easier for the pedestrian who could afford the expense. An omnibus line started in 1856. Omnibuses, which had been used in northern cities since the early 1830s and were similar to large stagecoaches, carried about twelve passengers and usually were pulled by two horses. In Richmond, omnibuses carried passengers up Shockoe Hill from the steamboat depots at Rocketts, west on Broad Street to the R. F. & P. depot, and then along the Brook Road Turnpike to the north. In 1861 a horse-drawn street railway began service over a similar route. It did not survive the war.[11]

A visitor who came to the city, either up the James or on one of the two railroads from the south, met antebellum Richmond resting on the north bank of a gentle bend in the river, "spreading panorama-like over her swelling hills, . . . fringes of dense woods shading their slopes." Shockoe Creek split the city into two groups of hills. East of the valley rose the middle-class neighborhoods of Church and Union hills, and at their feet the ocean-port wharves of Rocketts landing. To the west of Shockoe Valley, Jefferson's classical white Capitol stood amid the grassy expanse of Capitol Square, surrounded by the dome of city hall, the Federal lines of the Executive Mansion, the spires and roofs of fashionable churches and hotels, and, south of Capitol Square, on Main Street at the foot of Shockoe Hill, the new United States Post Office and Customs House and the city's three largest banks. West from Rocketts landing, on a four-mile-long arc of flat land between Main Street and the river, stood the tobacco factories, flour mills, foundries, warehouses, and steamship depots. As visitors looked north across the James and moved their eyes up from the river, crossing the streets that paralleled its course, the city's variegated hillside revealed layers of industry, commerce, politics, and society.[12]

• 3 •

Tobacco, grain, and iron, both in raw and in manufactured forms, were Richmond's main exports. Tobacco came from the Maryland–Virginia–North Carolina tobacco belt. Wheat and corn came from the piedmont and the fertile Valley of Virginia. Lime and iron ore were brought to Richmond from western Virginia on canalboats. Less important exports were bituminous coal and granite, which came from deposits just west of the city.[13]

Because raw materials were abundant, manufacturing developed quickly in Richmond. Even before William Byrd founded Richmond, he had established two mills at the site, and milling operations continued on the same spot until the 1930s. During the 1790s the number of flour mills increased when the completion of the canal carried the James River's waterpower into the city itself. John A. M. Chevallié, James Dunlop, Joseph Gallego, and David Ross established mills in this period. The descendants of these early millers were active not only in milling, but in banking, railroads, and other activities, as well as in Conservative-Democratic politics. Men who had begun as clerks or office boys were trained to the family business. After the war many became full partners or inherited the companies.[14]

Joseph Gallego's legacy is an example of the way in which many of Richmond's oldest industrial firms were founded. Gallego, a native of Malaga, Spain, lived in Richmond as early as 1784 and built his mills by 1796. They passed in 1818 to Gallego's brother-in-law, John A. M. Chevallié. He left them to his son, Peter J. Chevallié, who died in 1837. From that year the younger Chevallié's son-in-law, Abram Warwick, operated the mills. He entered a partnership with the Barksdale family before the war and lived to sign Jefferson Davis's bail bond after the conflict.[15]

Business interests in Richmond were dynastic and conservative. In milling, in the iron and tobacco industries, and even in railroads, an industrialist without male heirs tried to keep the business in the family by willing it to a relative by marriage. This practice, which changed very little after the war, may help to explain the reluctance of Richmond's manufacturers to adopt technological innovations and their lack of aggressiveness in tapping new sources of grain, coal and ore, and tobacco. It may also be significant that not only in the city's earliest years but throughout the antebellum decades, many of Richmond's most prominent businessmen came from Europe or the northern states. The newcomers found a friendly reception in the city.[16]

Richmond's flour mills were not only the first industry to develop in the city, but the first to begin exporting their product in large quantities. The Gallego mill began shipping flour to Latin America during the 1840s, and it eventually gained a monopoly of the Australian and Brazilian markets because its flour maintained its quality during long voyages through the tropics. The Brazilian coffee that was exchanged for Gallego flour made Richmond the largest coffee market in the United States in 1860. In that year more than four hundred thousand barrels of flour, valued at more than $3 million, was milled in Richmond.

Most of it went to South America, in return for shipments of 4 million pounds of coffee.[17]

There were only seven flour mills in Richmond in 1859, but their combined production, together with that of a few mills in the surrounding counties, almost equaled that of the four to five dozen mills in and around Baltimore, the other great milling center of the Atlantic coast. Richmond's larger mills enjoyed economies of production. For years the Gallego mill was the largest in the world and occupied the biggest brick building in America. A fleet of three dozen large schooners and brigs, many of them owned by shipping magnate David Currie, carried Richmond's flour to distant ports around the world.[18]

Tobacco factories developed later than the flour mills, but the rise of the tobacco manufacturing industry was helped by the sharp increase in foreign prices in 1818. The 1819 city directory listed eleven factories, but most tobacco was still being exported without processing. During the 1830s less than a third of the tobacco shipped from Richmond was manufactured, plug chewing tobacco or smoking tobacco for pipes, but new factories soon made Richmond the greatest tobacco market in the world. Between 1830 and 1835, nearly three times as much tobacco as flour left Richmond, and, shortly after 1840, the value of the tobacco manufactured in Richmond surpassed the value of the raw leaf that was exported. By 1859 there were forty-three factories. Fifty, including two cigar manufacturers, were operating in 1860. Together with related suppliers, such as the makers of tobacco boxes and cutters, the industry grossed nearly $5 million in 1860.[19]

Richmond's iron foundries, rolling mills, and other metal shops comprised the city's third big industry, and the most vital one for the Confederacy. Although coal and iron ore had been mined in the area since 1619, the industry did not prosper until the nineteenth century. The real impetus for Richmond ironmakers was the development of Virginia's railroads in the 1830s. Iron rails were needed, and Richmonders soon realized the possibilities that the coal around Richmond and iron ore from western Virginia offered for local industry. The demands of new railroad lines and the expansion of old ones spurred production, especially during the 1850s, the peak period of railroad construction in the South. By the mid-1840s a secondary market emerged for the ornamental ironwork that became a popular feature of Richmond's houses. The Tredegar Iron Works was the most important foundry in the South and a mainstay of the Confederate arsenal under its president, Joseph R. Anderson. Richmond foundries turned out wrought and cast iron, cannon, and other finished products, such as steam engines. The industry employed a fifth of Richmond's labor force and grossed more than $2 million in 1860.[20]

Sales in another Richmond enterprise probably topped those of the flour mills and ironworks. After New Orleans, Richmond was the country's largest slave mart, although immediately before the war Charleston became a serious competitor. Travelers' accounts rarely fail to describe a visit to a slave auction or to one of Richmond's many slave depots. Some of the slaves worked in Richmond industries. More went elsewhere. As the chief city of a state that exported large numbers of surplus slaves in the antebellum decades, Richmond was the center of the trade for the seaboard South. The city's slave traders included men who operated interstate from Maryland to Louisiana. Richmond's transportation network brought slaves from all over Maryland, Virginia, and North Carolina. In the 1850s the largest slave trading firm reported annual slave sales of more than $2 million, and the total annual sales of the city's several dozen firms was estimated from $3 to more than $4 million in this period. The city netted more than ten thousand dollars annually from dealer licenses and taxes on slave pens.[21]

Contrary to the stereotype of the slave trader as a brute shunned by polite society, a dozen of the more than eighty Richmonders who dealt in slaves were among the most important businessmen in the city. Some were also socially prominent. All who continued to live in Richmond after the war retained their prestige and their fortunes. At least five had sufficient respectability and popularity to be elected to the common council, either before, during, or after the Civil War.[22]

Financial institutions supplied needed capital and insurance for businessmen in antebellum Richmond. By 1859 there were twenty-one banks in the city, the four largest having total assets of more than $10 million. This city's insurance companies were numerous, and four of the oldest and most prosperous survived the war. With its many banks and insurance firms in 1860, Richmond was incontestably the financial, as well as the industrial, capital of Virginia. Wholesale and retail trade was also important to Richmond's economy, and in 1860 the gross sales of the city's thousand merchants totaled $12 million. Commission merchants were particularly active, filling the needs of their country customers and the expanding market within Richmond.[23]

• 4 •

The characteristic social, cultural, and religious features of Richmond developed early in the nineteenth century. Richmond had four daily newspapers in 1860. Robert Ridgway, a staunch Unionist, edited the *Richmond Daily Whig*. He argued against secession until he was forced to resign in 1861, and thereafter the *Whig*'s policy was secessionist. O. Jennings Wise, eldest son of former governor Henry A. Wise, edited the *Daily Richmond Enquirer*, a loyal Democratic party organ that had long been controlled by the Ritchie family. The *Richmond Daily Examiner* was an extreme secessionist organ under both its editors, William Old and John Moncure Daniel. Daniel was later joined by Henry Rives Pollard and Edward A. Pollard. The *Examiner* and the *Whig* became bitter critics of the government of Jefferson Davis. The nonpartisan *Richmond Daily Dispatch* had a circulation equal to that of its rivals combined. It was ably edited by John D. Hammersley and music lover James A. Cowardin, who held their readers by concentrating on accurate reporting rather than harsh editorials. The *Dispatch* emerged as the city's most important postwar paper and Cowardin became influential in Conservative-Democratic politics. Few of the other editors, except the Pollards, played roles in Richmond after the war.[24]

Public education was virtually neglected in antebellum Richmond. The city council voted small amounts of aid to a few irregularly organized ward schools during the war, but there was no formal public school system until 1869. The city gave inadequate support to a Lancasterian school, which stood in an unsavory neighborhood near the city jail. Because it was a charity school, most parents refused to send their children to it.[25]

Whites who could afford to do so sent their children to one of the city's many private schools. By the 1840s Richmond had more than thirty-five private schools offering instruction at different levels, five private primary schools, and several charity institutions. The number of private schools increased to more than sixty in the 1850s, and at least ten of these survived the war. Some of them, particularly those for boys, had curricula comparable to the modern high school. Young men prepared to attend the University of Virginia or some other college. Young women, in the last formal education that they received, learned art, music, languages, and social graces. The tradition of exclusive private schools for whites grew stronger after the war, despite the development of a segregated public school system.[26]

Richmond had several institutions of higher learning in 1860, and all survived the war. The Virginia Baptist Seminary, now the University of Richmond, had been founded five miles north of Richmond in 1832. In two years the school had been moved to grounds just west of the

Table 1
Whites, Slaves, and Free Blacks in Richmond, 1820-1860

	1820	1830	1840	1850	1860
Whites	6,445	7,755	10,718	15,274	23,635
	(53%)	(48%)	(53%)	(55%)	(62%)
Blacks	5,622	8,305	9,435	12,296	14,275
	(47%)	(52%)	(47%)	(45%)	(38%)
Slave	4,387	6,345	7,509	9,927	11,699
Free	1,235	1,960	1,926	2,369	2,576
Total	12,067	16,060	20,153	27,570	37,910

SOURCE: U.S. census data in Richard C. Wade, *Slavery in the Cities: The South 1820-1860* (New York, 1964), 327.

city, where it was rechartered as Richmond College in 1840. Enrollment during the nineteenth century never exceeded three hundred, mostly southern, students.[27]

In 1837–1838 the faculty of Hampden-Sydney College, in Prince Edward County southwest of Richmond, organized a medical school in the capital. Classes were held in the Union Hotel until 1845, when the school moved to its new Egyptian-revival building, whose unusual architecture made it a city landmark. In 1854 the medical school faculty left to form the Medical College of Virginia. It profited from secessionist sentiment. In 1859 when 140 Southern medical students left Jefferson College in Philadelphia after John Brown's Raid, many transferred to the Richmond school. It was one of two medical schools in the Confederacy that continued classes during the war.[28]

The city's best schools for young women, while perhaps not of college level, provided more advanced classes than most of the other private schools. The Richmond Female Institute was the largest and most successful of several such academies. Its expensive new building opened in 1854 to accommodate 268 pupils from states as distant as Texas and Indiana in three departments: preparatory, collegiate, and ornamental. Classes resumed after the war and continued until 1916, when the school merged with the University of Richmond's Westhampton College for Women.[29]

For recreation Richmonders attended horse races and cock fights, or drilled with military clubs. Richmond had several racetracks, and thoroughbred races, as well as fox hunts, were well attended. Cock fights were perennial favorites. Fishing in the summer and ice skating in the winter were other pastimes.[30]

Though not a recreational activity, dueling was a social custom that numerous Richmond males felt compelled to practice as a test of manhood, particularly if they belonged to, or sought acceptance in, the upper class. The so-called code of honor was the most notorious feature of the bizarre southern system of etiquette. Richmond's first recorded duel was fought in 1800, over politics. During the following decades politics and rivalries over women were always the leading causes of duels. The code duello claimed its last Richmond victim in 1883, although public challenges to the field of honor were issued as late as 1893.[31]

The oldest and most prestigious of the city's private military organizations was the Richmond Light Infantry Blues, organized in 1793. Members of the Blues were an exclusive group in nineteenth-century Richmond, and their drills, balls, and suppers were popular events. The group continued to be an elite military and social unit long after the Civil War. Rival companies had been formed in the era of the War of 1812, but most had disbanded. Several new units had formed by the 1850s, and the Blues, the Richmond Grays, and others, served throughout the war.[32]

These antebellum military clubs were not just social organizations. In 1800, when the slave Gabriel organized an abortive revolt north of Richmond in Henrico County, the Blues had been called out for the first time. The threat of this attempted slave uprising led the state to organize the Public Guard, a paid militia with its barracks in Richmond. For the next sixty years the guard's members patrolled Capitol Square, the penitentiary, armory, and other public buildings. Visitors to antebellum Richmond were astonished to encounter guards with bayonet-tipped rifles around the Capitol. White Richmonders felt that such extensive security measures were necessary because of the city's large black population.[33]

The city government had responded to Gabriel's Conspiracy by enlarging the night watch, whose members walked the streets and sounded the alarm for fires or other disturbances. A loosely organized police force grew out of the watch, but these men had not worn uniforms and had had only limited authority. Their chief function was to control the city's black population (see table 1). The amount of money appropriated for the police department was directly related to the degree of insecurity that city whites felt about blacks. After Nat Turner's Rebellion in 1831 in Southampton County, the police force

Table 2
Sex Ratios of Richmond's Black Population, 1820–1860

	1820	1830	1840	1850	1860
Black males	2,703	4,125	4,813	6,382	7,778
Slave	2,171	3,288	3,953	5,307	6,636
Free	532	837	860	1,075	1,142
Black females	2,919	4,180	4,622	5,914	6,497
Slave	2,216	3,057	3,556	4,620	5,063
Free	703	1,123	1,066	1,294	1,434
Black females per hundred black males	107	101	96	92	83
Free black females per hundred free black males	132	134	123	120	125
Female slaves per hundred male slaves	102	92	89	87	76
Black females per hundred free black males	548	499	537	550	568
Black males per hundred free black females	384	367	451	493	542

SOURCE: U.S. census data in Richard C. Wade, *Slavery in the Cities: The South 1820–1860* (New York, 1964), 329–330.

was strengthened, and there were nineteen men serving on it by 1833. Then public support of the police declined, although ten men were added to the force in 1857.[34]

By 1830 slaves and free blacks composed 52 percent of Richmond's population, but in the decade after Nat Turner's Rebellion the city's black population grew more slowly. A small drop in the number of free blacks in Richmond reflected the belief of many whites that free blacks were dangerous and responsible for most of the crime in Richmond. By 1860 only 38 percent of Richmond's population was black. Despite this relative decline, black laborers were increasingly vital to antebellum Richmond. Slaves, whether owned by the corporations or employers for whom they worked, or hired from their masters, made up a large part of Richmond's work force. They did most of the work in the city's largest industry, tobacco manufacturing. They worked in the metal shops, particularly at the Tredegar works, where Joseph R. Anderson pioneered their use in heavy industry. And at least two of the largest flour mills employed many slaves.[35]

By 1860 the number of whites who owned slaves had declined markedly. City tax books show that nearly all who paid personal property taxes in 1840 kept slaves, while only one-third of the 1860 property owners reported slaves. Many of these individual owners used their slaves in their businesses, and a large individual owner was likely to be an industrialist. Forty-two of the city's fifty tobacco manufacturers paid taxes on 10 or more slaves in 1860, and sixteen of these men owned more than 95 slaves. At the same time the number of corporations that owned slaves increased greatly; by 1860 fifty-four held at least 10 slaves. Four of Richmond's railroads paid taxes on a total of 597 slaves; the Virginia Central alone owned 274 laborers. Although by 1860 more than two-thirds of Richmond's white families did not own slaves, industrial slavery flourished.[36]

Unlike most other Southern cities, Richmond had more male than female slaves (see table 2). Its industries required large numbers of young male slaves. But because there were more free black women than men, the sex ratio in the total black population was nearly even. However, the disparate sex ratio among enslaved blacks made it difficult to maintain conventional sexual relationships, even if the fact of slavery had not often made a mockery of Richmond slave marriages.

White males also outnumbered white females in Richmond, and many white men sought sexual partners among black women. Society imposed stronger sanctions against relations between white women and black men, which made them less common, although such liaisons were not infrequent. In 1859, for instance, the *Richmond Enquirer* reported at length about the arrest, trial, and imprisonment of two young white women convicted for prostitution with black males. Such articles were rare; similar occurrences were usually described briefly as events "too delicate to dwell upon."[37]

Racially segregated housing patterns became more prevalent in late-antebellum Richmond. Some blacks desired to segregate themselves from whites when possible. Free blacks tended to congregate in more or less separate neighborhoods on the perimeter of Richmond, or beyond the city line. They lived on both sides of Bacons Quarter, in Screamersville west of the city limits, in Penitentiary Bottom near the state prison, and along the river. Slaves, unlike free blacks, originally had to live on the premises of their masters, usually in brick-walled enclosures behind their owners' houses. As industries developed and the number of corporately owned and hired slaves increased, the slave population expanded beyond the capacity of these residential accommodations. By the 1850s, as the practices of boarding out and living out developed, of necessity, in industrial Richmond, large numbers of slaves had managed to move into the free black neighborhoods. It is doubtful that any of these areas were completely without white residents, as officials frowned on all-black districts, but the origins of some postwar black neighborhoods can be traced to the late-antebellum period. In some areas of the city, such as Oregon Hill, which was inhabited by stonecutters and Welsh ironworkers, the white residents' hostility kept blacks out. In other areas, such as Union Hill, free blacks lived among whites in integrated neighborhoods.[38]

Many blacks, both slave and free, risked heavy penalties by participating in illicit businesses. Some conducted cash or barter transactions; a few had their own stores, grog shops, or restaurants. Brothels and gambling halls in commercial buildings as well as private homes were run by blacks and patronized by both races. The most fashionable and daring blacks frequented "Taylor's Hotel," a luxurious spot run by a free mulatto in back rooms that he leased from the white owners of the respectable Exchange Hotel.[39]

When Frederick Law Olmsted visited Richmond in 1852 he thought there were more well dressed blacks on the main streets than whites, and he found that the Sunday dress and demeanor of some of the slaves compared favorably with the more rowdy whites. Samuel Mordecai, a chronicler of old Richmond, made a similar observation in the late 1850s, though with a different viewpoint:

> Like their betters, the negroes of the present day have their mock gentility, and like them, they sustain it chiefly in dress and pretension. In the streets on Sundays, plainness of attire is now-a-days rather an indication of gentility. . . . These gentry leave their visiting cards at each other's kitchens, and on occasion of a wedding, Miss Dinah Drippings and Mr. Cuffie Coleman have their cards connected by a silken tie, emblematic of that which is to connect themselves, and a third card announces, "At home from ten to one," where those who call will find cake, fruits, and other refreshments.

Those blacks who participated in such activities were often house servants.[40]

The strong separatist currents in the black community were nowhere more evident than in religious practices. Initially, slaves most often went to church with their owners' families and sat in a separate section, but some congregations urged blacks to establish their own churches and even aided them in the task. In the years immediately before the war, whites increasingly barred blacks from their church services— whether because of racial hostility or because of the increased number of industrial slaves who did not belong to white families—so the blacks petitioned for permission to establish their own churches. By 1856 there were four in Richmond, some of which had white ministers, and one black congregation was described as the largest in the world. Both the First and Second African Baptist churches were important centers of black life in postwar Richmond, along with the many new churches that sprang up following emancipation.[41]

Richmond whites devoted much attention to their own religious ceremonies, and by 1860 the city was a center of orthodoxy. Most Richmonders claimed some form of religious affiliation, and there were enough church members to support a variety of religious publications, schools, and orphanages. The capital had become the City of Churches that its boosters liked to call it. Episcopalians and Presbyterians comprised the more socially prestigious denominations, but Baptists and Methodists exceeded them in numbers. The city also had a sizable Catholic minority, chiefly of Irish and German descent, shepherded since 1841 by the bishop at the cathedral church, Saint Peter's. Jews had come to Richmond long before the Revolution, and Beth Shalome, one of the city's three synagogues, was the sixth oldest in the United States. By 1860 Richmond had a relatively small but important Jewish community, which included many immigrants from Poland and Germany. Although some of the most prominent men in the city had originally belonged to the Society of Friends, in 1860 there were only a few Quakers in Richmond. The city also had two Lutheran congregations and a Universalist church.[42]

Richmond had a separate burying ground for blacks, for the city enforced racial segregation in cemeteries, as did Raleigh and Nashville. Olmsted, after following a decorous funeral procession past the beautiful Shockoe Hill Cemetery to the black cemetery one Sunday afternoon, described the scene:

> the hearse halted at a desolate place, where a dozen colored people were already engaged in heaping the earth over the grave of a child, and singing a wild kind of chant. Another grave was already dug immediately adjoining that of the child, both being near the

foot of a hill, in a crumbling bank—the ground below being already occupied, and the graves advancing in irregular terraces up the hill-side.

The Richmond white community's lack of concern toward its black neighbors was shown, after the war, when the city graded both a street and viaduct through this historic black cemetery, and completely destroyed it.[43]

By 1860, Richmond's white cemeteries had come to represent a complex social hierarchy that regulated a person's status even after death. Shockoe Hill Cemetery, opened in 1826 on the extreme northern edge of the city, was the cemetery for most antebellum middle- and upper-class whites. Nearby was a potter's field for the city's paupers and for strangers. In 1841, Shockoe Hill was still being referred to as the new cemetery, in deference to the churchyard of Saint John's that had served as white Richmond's only quasi-public cemetery throughout the colonial and early national periods. The city gave land for a separate Jewish cemetery adjacent to Shockoe Hill. Roman Catholics were buried in Bishop's Cemetery on the Mechanicsville Turnpike outside the city limits. Beginning shortly before the war, whites who could not afford lots elsewhere were buried in Oakwood Cemetery, northeast of Church Hill.[44]

Hollywood, which became both socially and symbolically the most important of Richmond's postwar cemeteries, was located in rolling country just west of the city, overlooking the James. It was established in the 1840s by a group of prominent Richmonders who desired a rural cemetery like Mount Auburn, which they had seen on a visit to Cambridge. Initially, there had been enormous opposition to Hollywood. It blocked the city's westward expansion and occupied desirable real estate on the river, and because of these and other objections, the General Assembly did not charter the cemetery company until 1856. Lots sold slowly, as Richmonders did not believe Hollywood would be permanent, and not until the Civil War did the grounds begin to fill. In 1858 the body of James Monroe was reinterred in Hollywood, and John Tyler was buried there four years later. Their graves and Hollywood's beautiful landscaped grounds assured the future success and social prominence of the cemetery, which became one of the most exclusive spots in postwar Richmond, the resting place for the city's heroes and heroines.[45]

• 5 •

Richmond became the capital of Virginia in 1779, although work on the Capitol did not begin until after the Revolution. In 1782 Richmond was incorporated as a city in the commonwealth of Virginia. Alexandria, Norfolk, and several other larger towns had better claim to the name city, as the new capital had barely one thousand residents and fewer than three hundred houses. Thomas Jefferson chose Shockoe Hill for the classical structure whose design he adapted from that of the Maison Carrée, a Roman temple in Nîmes, France, and in 1784 state officials picked lots for the site. Locating the Capitol on the habitable terrain beyond Shockoe Creek spurred the city's westward growth, but the General Assembly did not hold its first session in the building until 1788. The state armory in Richmond, begun after Gabriel's Conspiracy and completed in 1809, was destroyed in the 1865 evacuation fire, although it was not operated continuously during the antebellum era. As early as 1806 armory workers manufactured more than thirty-five hundred firearms and edged weapons annually, supplementing the work done in the privately owned foundries.[46]

The Virginia State Penitentiary was begun in 1796 in a valley west of the city between Gamble's and Belvidere hills, overlooking the James, a location that affected Richmond's growth because it precluded respectable residences in the immediate area. Planned as a model penal institution, it was designed by Jefferson and Benjamin Henry Latrobe. Public executions at the prison, a source of free entertainment for antebellum Richmonders, continued for some years after the war. The convicts made shoes and other items, which were sold at low prices to city customers. Most of the inmates were black males, and the chain gang, which cleaned Capitol Square and the streets, was all black.[47]

In 1803 the General Assembly amended the city charter and gave Richmond's municipal government its basic antebellum form. The legislature ended the at-large election of city councilmen and aldermen and divided Richmond into three wards, east to west, their boundaries perpendicular to the James: Jefferson, Madison, and Monroe. The freeholders in each ward elected eight councilmen. (After 1861, the voters of each ward elected five councilmen for one-year, and after 1872 two-year, terms). These twenty-four councilmen chose from among themselves a mayor, recorder, and seven aldermen, who also acted as magistrates. The other fifteen men formed the Common Hall, or council. These changes significantly increased the length of tenure among city officials. Men were more willing to serve in government because of the changes, it became rare for an incumbent to resign, and officials increasingly specialized in one job. One of the two major changes in Richmond's government between 1803 and the Civil War came in 1851, when the newly revised Virginia constitution provided for more elected officials. After 1851 Richmond's mayor, recorder, and some other officials were chosen directly by the people in a city-wide election. Manhood suffrage was also granted in 1851. As a result, the number of Richmond's voters in the 1852 election was more than double that in 1848. Balloting was still viva voce, however, and the old habits of deferential politics prevailed, because a laborer's boss was usually present when he publicly announced his vote to the election judge.[48]

The council passed all city ordinances and appointed almost all the nonelected city officials, including superintendents of the almshouses, cemeteries, waterworks, and gasworks; weighmasters and clerks of the markets; chiefs of police and fire; and harbor masters, grain inspectors, and others. The council's various committees laid streets, ordered sidewalks built, and directed the clearing of obstructed thoroughfares. Councilmen supervised the construction of bridges and the enlargement of cemeteries. They considered requests for building permits, received petitions from merchants who wished to erect signs, granted licenses to businessmen and tradesmen, and assigned market stalls to butchers, fishmongers, and grocers. The council administered public charity, distributing wood and coal to those unable to afford winter fuel, and granted money to assist private charities as well. It supervised the city's scavengers and the doctors on the city's board of health, levied taxes, set the tax rate, and heard requests for tax remissions.[49]

Richmond's officeholders in 1860 included Joseph Mayo, who had served as mayor since 1853 and on the common council for thirteen years before that. Most of the common councillors were prominent lawyers and businessmen, but a few were wealthy tradesmen. Most had served before, and continued to be elected during, the war.[50]

Early in the nineteenth century the capital gained added importance with the formation of the Richmond Junto, a political ring that eventually controlled Democratic-Republican politics in Virginia as completely as the later organizations of Thomas S. Martin and Harry F. Byrd, Sr. The Junto leaders included Judge Spencer Roane, who served on the Virginia Court of Appeals from 1794 to 1821 and was a bitter antagonist of John Marshall; Thomas Ritchie, Roane's cousin, editor of the *Richmond Enquirer* from its founding in 1804 to 1845; and Dr. John Brockenbrough, who founded the Bank of Virginia and was its president from 1805 to 1843.[51]

Although the Democrats generally carried Virginia in state and national elections, after 1836 the Whigs usually won in Richmond by large margins. In the gubernatorial and presidential elections of 1855 and 1856 most Richmond Whigs voted for the candidates of the American, or Know-Nothing, party, who exploited native Richmonders' hostility toward the city's large immigrant population. In 1860 the Constitutional Union candidates received nearly five hundred more votes than the combined totals of the southern and national Democrats.[52]

The temper of Richmond politics was, then, conservative. As John S. Wise, a son of the Democratic governor Henry A. Wise, recalled:

notions about manhood suffrage, public schools, the education and elevation of the masses, . . . did not suit the uncompromising views of people in places like Richmond. It was the abode of that class who proclaimed that they were Whigs, and that "Whigs knew each other by the instincts of gentlemen."[53]

As the capital of Virginia, Richmond was the meeting place for the east-west sectional interests that polarized the state and contributed to its dismemberment during the Civil War. The state constitutional conventions of 1829–1830 and 1850–1851 met there, as did delegates to the General Assembly's slavery debates of 1831–1832. Though it was the state capital, Richmond had interests different from those of important regions of the state. Situated in the heart of the slaveholding area, Richmond had little in common with the western counties where antislavery sentiment was strong, and where natural transportation routes led to Baltimore or to the Ohio Valley. But Richmond's interests also conflicted with the coastal counties around Norfolk. Richmond, Petersburg, and other fall-line towns engrossed most of the southwestern commerce because their legislators both blocked passage of railroad charters to connect Norfolk with the interior and defeated appropriations for improvements to Norfolk's harbor. Residents of the Norfolk area held bitter memories in the postwar years; even in the 1850s they had stronger commercial ties with Baltimore, Philadelphia, and New York than with Richmond, and some talked of seceding to become the chief port and city of North Carolina.[54]

After Abraham Lincoln's election in 1860 and the secession of the states of the lower South, secessionist sentiment grew in conservative Richmond. The city sent three attorneys as delegates to the first session of the Virginia secession convention, which was held in the city from 13 February to 1 May 1861. Two of the three—Marmaduke Johnson, a successful criminal lawyer and commonwealth's attorney, and William H. Macfarland, a prominent railroad president and banker—were former Whigs. Both were elected as conditional Unionists, or moderates, who demanded greater protection for slavery, as opposed to the outright antislavery position of nationalistic Whigs like John Minor Botts. The third delegate was George Wythe Randolph. A Democrat and a grandson of Thomas Jefferson, Randolph favored secession although he was not a leading fire-eater, and he served in the Confederate cabinet and army, in the Virginia Senate, and on Richmond's common council.

Another Richmond lawyer and former Whig, Williams Carter Wickham, represented Henrico County but is sometimes considered a part of the Richmond city delegation. He voted against secession twice, but changed his vote after the final ballot. Wickham served the Confederacy as a cavalry brigadier and congressman. Like his fellow Whigs, Johnson and Macfarland, he played an important role in postwar politics, albeit as a Republican, and like them, he provided a measure of continuity amidst the change of Reconstruction.

The convention took two votes on secession. The Richmonders voted two to one against secession on the first ballot, but all three voted for it on the second. The city had strong business and social ties with both the North and South. The two Unionist delegates, who were members of the city's professional elite, changed their votes after popular sentiment in Richmond shifted toward the Confederacy following the cannonfire at Fort Sumter and Lincoln's call for troops.[55]

Virginia seceded on 17 April 1861, but a month passed before the convention's action was submitted to the people for approval. When Richmonders voted on the Ordinance of Secession on 23 May 1861, only four voted for the Union. Events had overtaken reason. Richmonders hoped that their city would be chosen as the permanent capital of the Confederacy. It would then take its place with London and Paris among the capitals of the world.[56]

Some Unionists supported Virginia and the Confederacy against their better judgement, as was the case with Wickham. Others, including a number of old Whigs like Botts, sat out the war. Some of the latter, despite their politics, retained their standing in Richmond society through acts of charity for poor Confederate families. More daring Union sympathizers ran the busy underground movement in Richmond. Some of them continued as Republicans after the war. Others, like the Irish grocer John M. Higgins, successfully switched political affiliations. Higgins was so adept a politician that he represented Jefferson Ward on the city council for eighteen years.[57]

The nearly unanimous Richmond vote for secession did not reflect the real diversity of private opinion on the issue. Richmond's traditionally conservative leaders, like many of Virginia's, had strong and genuine love for the Union. But emotional ties to the seceded states also were strong, even among many Unionists, as was the readiness to resist "coercion" on the part of the Lincoln administration.

• 6 •

When Frederick Law Olmsted first came to Richmond he was critical of what he saw, not only because he disliked slavery but also because Richmond compared poorly with New York and Philadelphia, the cities that he had just left. Olmsted returned to the Virginia capital after touring much of the South, and was more favorably impressed, but his criticism on this visit, as the old city drifted into war, was especially significant:

> Richmond . . . somewhat surprised me by its substance, show, and gardens. . . . Richmond is a metropolis, having some substantial qualities, having a history, and something prepared for a future as well. Compared with northern towns of the same population, there is much that is quaint, provincial and excessively slovenly. . . . It is only the mills and warehouses, a few shops and a few private residences and hotels, that show real enterprise or real and permanent wealth. . . . [Richmond] is plainly the metropolis of Virginia, of a people who have been dragged along in the grand march of the rest of the world, but who have had, for a long time and yet have, a disposition within themselves only to step backward.[58]

If this is an accurate description of the prosperous, booming Richmond of the 1850s, it is all the more a true depiction of Richmond after the war. As the blacks and whites of old Richmond looked back, the members of each group had their own set of memories. When they died, their children remembered what had been told to them—tales of slavery, the Lost Cause, and life before the war. Two ghosts, the black and the gray, haunted the streets of Richmond and mingled truth and falsehood in its history.

Except the Lord keep the city,
the watchman waketh but in vain.

Psalms 127:1

Now Jericho was straitly shut up because of the children of
Israel: none went out, and none came in. And the Lord said
unto Joshua, See, I have given into thine hand Jericho, and the
King thereof, and the mighty men of valour . . . the seventh day
ye shall compass the city seven times, and the priests shall blow
with the trumpets . . . and it came to pass, when the people
heard the sound of the trumpet, and the people shouted with a
great shout, that the wall fell down flat, so that the people went
up into the city, every man straight before him, and they took
the city.

Joshua 6:1–2, 4, 20

2

The Conservative Citadel

1861–1865

FROM June 1861 until April 1865 Richmond was the capital of the Confederacy, the citadel of the South, and the goal of the North. During the Civil War the city's fame and power reached a level never again attained. More has been written about wartime Richmond than about all other periods of the city's history combined. Most of the accounts focus on the gallant defense of the capital by General Robert E. Lee and the Army of Northern Virginia. They describe the gay society in the city in sharp contrast to the widespread hunger of the poor and the suffering of the sick and wounded, but few tell in detail the impact that war had upon Richmond's political and economic life. Richmond's leaders proved unable to deal efficiently with the many problems that war thrust upon them. Their conservative traditions and whiggish principles were useless baggage as the city made a violent transition from antebellum to wartime conditions. In their dealings with the Confederate and Virginia governments, and in their discussions of difficult issues, the city fathers showed themselves to be singularly inept, and even corrupt. Richmond's wartime experience cast a shadow over the postwar years and profoundly affected the way in which its black and white inhabitants dealt with the problems of Reconstruction.[1]

· 1 ·

Richmond's mayor and city council shared governmental authority during the war with the city's tenants, Virginia and the Confederacy.

25

As the city and state governments had coexisted in Richmond for eighty years, there were precedents for cooperation, and relations between city officials and Virginia's legislature and war governors were generally good.

The city's first necessity was to provide for its own defense, and at this task the municipal government failed. Early in May 1861 a council committee met with General Robert E. Lee, who had recently accepted command of all state troops, to plan fortifications for the capital. The aged mayor, Joseph Mayo, was to furnish laborers from among the unemployed free blacks in Richmond. The council issued currency to pay for war costs and appropriated $30,000 for defense construction. Within a few weeks the mayor reported that he had been unable to find enough workers to build earthworks. Slaves from the tobacco factories had proved of little use in construction, and the only work accomplished was that done by free black volunteers from Danville and a few state penitentiary inmates. Not a single free black in Richmond had offered to help build the city's defenses, and the mayor and city council did nothing to coerce those who were idle on street corners. After further urging from General Lee, the mayor used the threat of impressment to induce over one hundred free blacks to volunteer, but the work done was of limited value.[2]

Next the city turned to private enterprise to erect the fortifications. The council advertised for builders, and Leroy P. Walker, Confederate secretary of war, promised that the Southern government would share construction costs with the city. Some work eventually was accomplished during the summer and fall of 1861, but no cannon were supplied for the redoubts that were built. In December, Charles Dimmock, a West Point graduate, captain of the Public Guard, and former superintendent of the state armory, told the council that unarmed batteries were useless. Since it would take months to manufacture the necessary gun carriages and place the cannon, he urged the council to begin at once. His advice was ignored.[3]

Richmond was unable to defend itself. In the fall of 1861 the Confederacy assumed sole responsibility for the construction of the city's defenses. A Confederate official spent most of the $50,000 specially appropriated by the council on poorly located batteries, and failed to build necessary fortifications along the turnpikes leading into the city and on the James River below Richmond. After the battle of Seven Pines late in May 1862, when the Confederate army withdrew to the eastern suburbs of the city and Lee took command from the wounded Joseph E. Johnston, the army built additional earthworks around Richmond. The soldiers, and thousands of slaves and free blacks under the direction of the Confederate Engineer Bureau, constructed three lines of breastworks, which would have required three hundred thousand soldiers to man fully. Lee never had that many men, or means to supply them during a siege. These fortifications, built by the Confederate army and black laborers, not the city, helped local forces to repel several raids on Richmond during the war. The city council did support many of the more than forty companies of regulars in which about three thousand men served. It also supported units of volunteers who were too young or too old to fight, or whose jobs kept them from being full-time soldiers.[4]

The first of the newly organized local forces was the Richmond Home Artillery, three eighty-man companies of mounted militia formed in July 1861. Its members joined with the understanding that they could not be ordered beyond the immediate vicinity of Richmond except for "some special occasion of attack or defense, and then only to a convenient distance and for a short time." The council voted $11,000 to supply the companies with horses, harness, and stables, but in August the state seized their cannon for the Confederate army and attempted to muster the men into regular service. The budding artillerists refused to report for duty, Governor John Letcher disbanded the unit after an exchange of insulting letters with its commander, and the council sold its horses to the Confederacy at cost. After the passage of the first Confederate conscription act in April 1862, other men joined the local forces as a way of avoiding the war.[5]

Some local defense force clearly was needed, sufficient not to repel a major attack but to meet enemy raiding parties and to reinforce the city's dozen overworked policemen. In May 1862 the capital was threatened by General George B. McClellan's Union army. A prominent city attorney, John H. Gilmer, foresaw chaos if events required that the Confederate government evacuate the city. There was no force to maintain order and protect life and property from the city's criminal element in the interim between a Confederate withdrawal and the arrival of Union troops. Gilmer proposed that the state's second-class militia, consisting of boys and old men, be armed. The defense committee of the city council authorized the creation of a city battalion to keep order and guard public property, persons, and bridges in the "present emergency," but Governor Letcher, jealous of his prerogatives, opposed this plan and called the second-class militia out for state service. When McClellan's army was repulsed in June, the emergency passed. The council's plan was then approved by George Wythe

Randolph, the new Confederate secretary of war and a Richmonder. The city battalion's five companies were mustered for six months' service in August 1862 and manned the city defenses along with regular troops that fall. Early in 1863 they enlisted in the Confederate army for the duration of the war.[6]

The first city battalion was not very effective. After General George Stoneman's May 1863 cavalry raid on Richmond, the council voted to create another unit to defend the city "from sudden and unexpected assaults of the enemy." Randolph, who had recently resigned as secretary of war and been elected to the council, was appointed to command the new unit, which was to have companies of fifty to seventy-five men, who drilled and mustered on a voluntary basis and were not to serve beyond the outer line of city defenses. Since Governor Letcher again declared his determination to call these volunteers into state service in the militia, however, it was impossible to form a city force.[7]

After Stoneman's raid, the Confederate Congress created a local defense brigade for Richmond, separate from the militia and composed of five companies, one each from the Confederate armory, arsenal, navy yard, Tredegar works, and the government departments. The brigade successfully defended Richmond against a large cavalry force led by General Judson Kilpatrick and Colonel Ulric Dahlgren that reached the outskirts of the city in February 1864. It evacuated Richmond with the rest of the rebel army in April 1865.[8]

The council's few further attempts to create its own military force were unsuccessful. In January 1864 the chairman of the police committee proposed that companies of volunteer mounted police be raised to guard the city, but the idea was not adopted. After Cold Harbor, in June 1864, the council and mayor met with Governor William Smith and the commanders of the 19th regiment of Virginia militia and the second-class militia, but no city security force was formed. Finally, in mid-March 1865, frightened by General Richard S. Ewell's warning that Richmond might be evacuated, the state legislature allowed the city to raise an armed volunteer force of more than fifty men, to get weapons from the state or Confederate government, and, when two hundred had volunteered, to organize companies and elect officers. When only one man volunteered, this last attempt to protect the city failed.[9]

After nearly four years of argument in which nothing had been done to provide a city-controlled military force, the flight of the Confederate and Virginia governments was followed by mob violence and a disastrous fire, as Gilmer had foreseen. In the waning days of the war, few Richmonders had the courage or character necessary to deal with hungry, drunken mobs, and few militiamen cared to risk capture or death at the hands of the invading Yankees. Order was not restored until soldiers occupied the city. The council lacked the ability and imagination to provide for Richmond's safety, but it also felt that it lacked any real power to act. Its efforts were hindered by the state's overlapping authority and the regular Confederate army's tendency to absorb forces organized for local duty.

In defense of Richmond officials, it has been argued that American cities were incapable of military organization and of providing adequate labor to erect fortifications—an observation not applicable to European cities, which had defended themselves for centuries. Perhaps modern artillery had made such defense impossible. In some other Southern cities, where local government did not share authority with both state and Confederate governments, municipal defense efforts were more successful. Still, Richmond's city council minutes show that the councilmen and the mayor had authority to impress the more than one thousand free black males in Richmond, as well as slaves from idle factories, and to put them to work under the direction of leaders such as Captain Dimmock. While many black Richmonders realized that the construction of fortifications was not in their best interest, had the council chosen to marshal black laborers to build defensive works at well-chosen strategic points, much could have been accomplished, and less time and money wasted. The councilmen's inaction was not because of respect for personal rights, for they had few scruples about the rights of blacks later in the war. The council's assumption, the minutes suggest, was that black Richmonders, although skilled at the difficult tasks of the city's factories, were incapable of wielding picks and shovels in the construction of fortifications—a notion that seems absurd, as black laborers eventually did the construction work.

Perhaps the best solution to the problem of a city security force might have been a greatly enlarged police department, with the extra men, if necessary, armed with rifles and serving part-time. City workers usually were exempt from conscription, and the council should have been able to find recruits, not volunteers, who were looking for a second salary or a relatively safe job, provided that they were not sent outside the city. But, as in peacetime, the "businessmen-politicians seemed to move only when crisis was at their doorsteps."[10]

Nonmilitary affairs also caused disputes between the city and state. In April 1861 the council began to issue its own currency against the city's credit in order to pay military and other expenses. This course was held to violate state law. City officials were threatened with prosecution, and in November a grand jury ordered that the issuance of notes be stopped. The council pled military necessity, and Richmond's delegates persuaded the General Assembly of 1861 to permit the city to issue notes for less than one dollar. An 1862 act authorized larger denominations.[11]

A more important, and long-lived, cause of conflict between the city and state was railroads. Richmond was served by five railroad lines, but, like most American cities, it had no central railroad depot. The city government, supported by merchants, hotel owners, and draymen, had always opposed the construction in the city of tracks that would link the five terminals. But in an April 1861 burst of patriotism, the council granted the state permission to lay connecting tracks if they were necessary for state and Confederate use. The north-south tracks of the Richmond, Fredericksburg and Potomac and the Richmond and Petersburg railroads were linked that August, and remained connected until after the war. In May 1862 the Virginia Central Railroad joined to the R. F. & P. so that equipment could be moved out of danger from the Union army, but these rails were taken up in January 1863. The city council required the state and the railroads, separately, to seek permission each time a train was to run over the connecting tracks, and in February 1863 the council successfully opposed a bill in the legislature that would have given the railroads "unlimited and uncontrolled use of the streets of the city."[12]

• 2 •

With the far larger and more powerful Confederate government the city's relations were more troubled than with the state. The city had no precedent for the situation; perhaps the closest earlier model was the experience of Philadelphia's city government and the Continental Congress during the American Revolution. Richmonders always were ambivalent about their city's status as the Confederate capital. While the coming of the Confederate government from Montgomery, Alabama, had been generally welcomed in 1861, genteel Richmonders commented about uncouth strangers from other parts of the Confederacy and soon learned to resent an expanding government bureaucracy and its autocratic agents. Discontent increased as the war dragged on and problems multiplied. The city's 1860 population of thirty-eight thousand more than tripled. There was a shortage of housing and of food, and the latter became even scarcer as the Confederacy's needs strained the inadequate transportation system supplying the city. Crippling inflation damaged Richmond's economy, and crime and vice threatened security and health.

Before Jefferson Davis arrived late in May 1861, the council bought an elegant three-story townhouse at 1203 East Clay Street as the official residence for the Confederate president. There was some argument among the council members over the price, $35,000, for the lot, house, and furnishings, and when the Confederacy refused to accept the house as a gift the city leased it. Until the mansion was ready for occupancy, the Davis family stayed at the city's newest and finest hotel, the Spotswood. When the $3,289 bill for their room and board was presented to the city council in October, it was paid without recorded comment, but there was criticism in the press.[13]

More important, and more persistent, were the conflicts between the municipal and Confederate governments over the maintenance of law and order in the capital. Initially the city fathers assumed that they would be responsible for policing the city. Following Virginia's secession on 17 April 1861 the city had increased its security by passing an ordinance "Concerning Suspicious Persons," which gave the police broad authority. Another law "Concerning the Good Order of the City of Richmond" required all places serving liquor to close at ten in the evening, and a later amendment required Sunday closings. The mayor was authorized to buy four horses for the police, who began to patrol carrying muskets loaded with buckshot. In May the council ordered that rail and steamship depots, bridges, mills, arsenals, and other critical locations be well lit. A committee was appointed to determine if a law was needed to forbid the sale of "newspapers and other improper publications" disseminating anti-Southern sentiments. In July the mayor told the commanders of units camped around Richmond that when coming to the city their men were to leave their weapons in camp. Unable to maintain law and order in Richmond, the council asked the Confederacy to put the city under martial law, and many inhabitants were pleased when the Confederate Congress did so on 1 March 1862. A Marylander, General John H. Winder, was appointed provost marshal of Richmond and the area ten miles around the city.[14]

Until the spring of 1864 Winder ruled the capital through his feared gang of detectives, who were popularly known as Baltimore plug-uglies. The city council praised the positive results of Winder's harsh regime (although some Richmonders complained of corruption in his administration), but conflict did arise when Winder impressed food destined for the city's markets. Less than two months after the imposition of martial law, the council's committee on markets complained to the war department about Winder's decision to tax farm produce because farmers were refusing to bring food into the city and civilians were suffering. Throughout the war the council fought with Winder and other Confederate officials who attempted to impose regulations that caused shortages, or who seized city food supplies.[15]

Other disputes with the Confederate government in 1862 included the council's refusal to give up its chambers so that the judge advocate could hold courts-martial. Council members claimed that the city had already given up every other room in its possession to either the Virginia or the Confederate government. When a major in the commissary corps claimed he was not a city resident and was therefore exempt from city taxation, the council ordered him to pay. Later the point at issue was resolved by a council decision that only civil, not military, officers were subject to muncipal taxation.[16]

The Confederate government's reaction to the city's lack of cooperation came when it refused to exempt city officers and employees under the second conscription act, of December 1862. City council members shuttled frantically between the offices of President Davis and the new secretary of war, James A. Seddon, a Virginian. Neither Davis nor Seddon would grant exemptions. Only by getting temporary exemptions from Confederate enrolling officers did the council manage to avert the wholesale conscription of the city's fire department and the important employees at its gasworks and waterworks. Richmond's council responded by asking the Confederacy to remove its soldiers and other prisoners from the overcrowded city jail, and by imposing or raising the rents for various buildings used as hospitals. When Josiah Gorgas, the Confederacy's capable chief of ordnance, asked for control of the city's powder magazine, the council promptly refused. The controversy continued until January 1863, when Congress finally granted the city's petition for exemptions.[17]

The two-year dispute over control of the city almshouse is an example of the struggle between the city and the Confederacy for space in crowded Richmond. Just before the war the city had built a new poorhouse for white paupers. In June 1861 the Confederacy rented it to serve as General Hospital No. 1. Early in 1863, after the Confederacy had rented sufficient hospital space in other buildings, including the municipal tobacco warehouse, the city tried to regain the almshouse. The Confederate surgeon general acknowledged the council's request but took no action on it. Then, an agreement was made allowing the government to rent the almshouse for $7,000 per year. In October 1863

Provost Marshal Winder asked that the almshouse be turned over to him to house political prisoners from Castle Thunder, as he needed Castle Thunder to accommodate an expected shipment of fourteen thousand Union prisoners. His request provoked debate in council: most members felt that the city's paupers, lodged in temporary quarters, would suffer during the coming winter, and that if the Confederacy no longer needed the almshouse for a hospital, it should be returned to the city to be used for its intended purpose. After the council heard a plea from the city's overseers of the poor, Winder's request was denied.[18]

The city council soon had cause to regret its decision. Early in 1864 the Confederacy began paroling large numbers of Union prisoners. Those who stayed in Richmond contributed to the crime problem. A Confederate officer told a grand jury that there were six hundred released prisoners in the city; the mayor learned that four hundred had been released in January alone. They were said to be of "a very vicious class. Not one of them . . . was worthy to be trusted where there were slaves." The parolees appeared frequently in the city courts, charged with various crimes. President Davis expressed surprise at the parole policy and promised to stop it, but did nothing. A council committee asked the war department to stop releasing prisoners, but Secretary Seddon refused to heed the request and told the council that it should punish the men for their crimes and "hang them if necessary."[19]

Before the council regained its poorhouse, General Ulysses S. Grant began his great offensive in 1864. In June the council agreed to allow the Confederacy to retain the building as a hospital because of the military emergency. In August the government asked to keep it to house wounded officers during the winter, and after some argument the council said yes, but raised the rent to $12,000. Apparently the Confederacy did not need the building badly enough to pay the higher rent, and Virginia officials intervened. In November the state took over the poorhouse, and the council agreed to rent the building for $15,000 as a barracks for the cadets of the Virginia Military Institute, which had been burned during General David Hunter's raid on Lexington.[20]

The burial of soldiers was another source of conflict between the municipal and Confederate governments. In July 1862 the Hollywood Cemetery Company, a private corporation, acting on the authority of the secretary of war, began burying soldiers on city land adjacent to its own. As the city's permission had not been obtained, and as the land in question was the only space available for a new city reservoir, the council protested. Another problem concerned the city's newer, less prestigious Oakwood Cemetery, where sixteen thousand Confederate soldiers eventually were buried. After major battles the gravediggers fell behind in their work. Shallow graves and unburied bodies caused complaints from nearby residents during the summer of 1863, but the council avoided legal action by declaring that it was not liable for property damages committed by its tenant, the Confederate government.[21]

The quarrel that eventually had the most serious consequences for Richmond was about the war department's plan to destroy the valuable stores of cotton and tobacco if the city were evacuated. The three-year dispute began in May 1862, when McClellan's army was within sight of the steeples of city churches. The Confederate government's plan was to burn all these stores in a warehouse near the center of the city. The council protested. McClellan went away, but the problem remained. Late in February 1865 Lee ordered General Ewell, commander of troops around the city, to burn all military stores, cotton, and tobacco. The holocaust of the evacuation fire was the result.[22]

• 3 •

The war had little immediate effect on Richmond politics. Former Whigs retained the majority on council, but a single party system began to evolve after secession. Most politicians considered themselves to be good Confederates, but they tended to coalesce into pro- and anti-Davis factions. Unionist influence in the city government was weak; several Unionists ran for the council, but none was elected during the war.[23]

More men sought city jobs. When the city treasurer retired in December 1861 five candidates scrambled for the job. They were nominated by various councilmen and supported by groups of real estate agents and merchants who wanted to influence the choice of the city's chief revenue officer. The city's bureaucracy grew as the war continued, and as the conscription age was raised, in September 1862, to forty-five. Although there were several attempts to economize by cutting the number of city officials, only one office was ever dropped: assistant inspector of the gasworks, in March 1865.[24]

Nepotism involving council members, and the desire to escape army service, protected old positions and created new ones. The office of measurer of wood was revived at the request of citizens, but awarded to the son of a councilman in September 1864. For the sake of appearances, the father did not vote. That same month the post of city scavenger, arguably necessary in a city overcrowded since 1861, was created, at the request of a political hack who was then given the job. In marked contrast to the competition for the office of city treasurer, there were no other candidates for either of the lesser posts, probably because the vacancies were not publicized, or because the council had already let its choices be known. The city jailer and the keeper of the powder magazine repeatedly asked for special fees for the performance of their routine duties. A member of a prominent family was allowed to remain as clerk and weighmaster of the Second Market, despite obvious incompetence and apparent theft of city funds; to make his job easier and to double the number of positions exempt from conscription, the office was split into two separate positions. Some of these may have been needed offices simply filled through political logrolling, but the timing of the creation and filling of others seems more than coincidental.[25]

Members of the city council did not always take their duties seriously. Frequently the council failed to meet as scheduled because it lacked a quorum. On 9 June 1862, for instance, most of the members were at a fish fry rather than city hall. Although the council was not reluctant to raise the salaries of top city officials, it often resisted the demands for higher pay from city workers. Inflation was not seriously felt until the summer of 1862, when requests from the day police and the superintendent of the waterworks led to an average salary increase of 17 percent for almost all city officers. Another raise in November affected a smaller number of positions. The pace of inflation quickened in 1863; there were three general pay raises, each averaging 22 to 25 percent. The salaries of the mayor and hustings court judge were raised for the first time since secession, from $3,000 to $3,500, but neither matched the $6,000 earned by Confederate cabinet members. The city's last two wartime salary increases came in November 1864 and February 1865; each averaged 60 percent. Throughout the war, the salaries of city officers had been increased by a total of more than 200 percent, but as these pay raises were cumulative, the rate of actual increase had been far higher.[26]

Employees with menial jobs did not get comparable wage increases, and the council often used black labor to lower salary costs. To replace white workers at the gas plant in the fall of 1862, the council voted $30,000 to buy as many slaves as were needed. Two blacks were hired for the fire department early in 1864. When gravediggers at the city's Shockoe Cemetery struck for higher wages in the fall of 1864, the city replaced them with blacks. The white workers attacked the black substitutes, drove them off, and returned to work without a pay raise. At times the council did grant the workers' requests. In January 1864,

when employees at the waterworks asked for a pay raise proportional to
that given to other workers the previous autumn, the council gave them
a raise.[27]

The Richmond city government printed its own currency during the
war years to pay both for military necessities and the municipality's
usual budget items. In April 1861 the council authorized the issuance of
$300,000 in small bills. Even after the state declared the city's currency
legal, there was a shortage of money in circulation, as companies and
individuals hoarded city notes and banks refused to issue them.

To raise more revenue, new taxes were adopted. A fee system,
known as the class tax, was instituted, which placed every firm and
businessman in a category determined by annual earnings. In 1862, and
each subsequent year, the class tax was revised upward to provide
greater revenue. City licenses were required before persons could
engage in trades or practice professions. The city charged a seal tax of
two dollars for stamping legal papers. In 1862 the council passed a
comprehensive tax ordinance that imposed a 1 percent tax on all real
and personal property, except slaves. Slaves were taxed at three dollars
each, as were all free adults. Interest income was taxed at 10 percent,
bank and insurance company dividends at 5 percent, and bank stock at
8 percent.[28]

Richmond loaned the Confederate government $300,000 in July
1862, and in the spring of 1863 the council reinvested half that money
in Confederate bonds. By the end of 1863, however, finances had
grown so weak that the council tried to sell the bonds. The city's credit
was impaired in February 1864 when President Davis signed a law that
devalued Confederate currency and authorized the issuance of new
notes and bonds.[29]

Forced to adopt stern measures to support the city's budget, at the
end of 1862 the council considered selling all its railroad and canal
stock, but its finance committee opposed the plan, which was reconsidered and again rejected in the spring of 1863. When the city was unable
to pay a $57,000 debt due in January 1864, the council sold all the city's
stock in the Virginia and Tennessee and the Southside railroads. That
September a finance committee report suggested three ways to meet all
budget demands through June 1865: sell city stock, levy additional
taxes, or sell the remaining railroad bonds. The council voted to sell its
Virginia Central and Richmond and Danville railroad bonds. The council also negotiated two $50,000 bank loans in 1864. But despite its
growing financial problems, the council decided that the city did not
have authority to tax investments made outside the state.[30]

The common council's actions during the war demonstrate that the goal of its fiscal policy was to do nothing that would increase the city's funded debt. Consequently, the costs of all city services—water, gas, and others—rose, while the quality of services such as police and fire protection deteriorated. This trend was most evident in the production of gas. In 1861 Richmond had two gasworks, which provided light for street lamps, homes, and public and commercial buildings. In the spring of 1862 the works reported a profit of $75,744.50. As the cost of coal, lime, tile, and fire brick increased, and as the retorts used in making gas wore out and could not be replaced, the amount of gas manufactured declined and costs went up, while the smell of the gas was compared to that of a skunk. The council had to increase gas rates repeatedly during the war. The price went from $6 per thousand cubic feet in November 1862 to $50 in February 1865. The gasworks deficit grew from $122,268.17 in October 1863 to $610,634.33 in March 1865 when the committee on light made its final report.[31]

The city waterworks operated more sucessfully than the gas plants, as costs were lower and broken machinery could be more easily repaired. Yet the old reservoir and pump houses were inadequate to the needs of Richmond's swollen population. The pumps shut down when the James flooded and the pipes occasionally ran dry during droughts. City water never lacked a trace of mud. To supplement the water supply in the summer of 1862 the council voted $3,000 for new wells and offered to maintain private wells that were opened to public use. The water committee reported its first deficit of $9,457 in February 1864; as a result rates went up 50 percent that summer, and the police were told to enforce the ordinance against wasting water. In March 1865 the water rate was increased by 100 percent, and the water committee reported receipts of $5,477 in excess of costs.[32]

The Richmond fire department was weakened both by inadequate appropriations and by wartime mismanagement. The city's six-company fire brigade had a chief engineer, six commanders and foremen, and 108 firemen. When the antebellum council had refused to buy a new steam fire engine to protect the business district, five insurance companies bought the engine and gave it to the city. In 1862 the council voted funds to enlarge an engine house and to buy the necessary fittings for its new engine. But later it decided that the city could not afford twelve thousand dollars for a team of horses to pull the new engine; the council members reasoned that one team could pull two engines to a fire almost as quickly as it could pull one. Scandal touched the department in 1864 when a company commander attempted to sell the new fire engine to a Confederate quartermaster at Raleigh, North Carolina.[33]

The council also cut fiscal corners with the police department, which had been woefully undermanned and underpaid even in the quieter antebellum era. Whenever the police committee tried to enlarge the eleven-man day police force, or add to the night watch, a majority of the council rejected the proposal. No police could be spared to ring the city alarm bell in Capitol Square in the event of riot, enemy attack, or fire. Fires for which no alarm was rung caused extensive damage. The entire police force spent much of its time on duty attending the mayor's court.[34]

Basic city services became more expensive during the war. Burial rates at the city cemeteries quadrupled between June 1863 and March 1865, when it cost from fifteen to twenty dollars to bury a white adult, and ten to fifteen dollars to bury a black adult. The city saved some money by neglecting street improvements, although city engineers claimed that more might have been done to improve the streets had not city personnel been continually used to cart coal and wood to the poor. Flood damages suffered by property owners near Shockoe Creek were neglected. The council did spend more than six thousand dollars in 1862–1863 on poorly considered repairs and enlargements of the city jail, which was a perennial cause of expense. Except for an armory, the municipal government erected no new buildings during the war.[35]

Despite the council's fiscal restraint and policy of raising the prices of city services while at the same time cutting services back, the finance committee warned in February 1865 that city credit was in danger. Expenses for 1865 were estimated at 1.5 million dollars, and the tax rate would have to be tripled to keep up with inflation. City salaries were barely staying ahead of inflation. Most city departments had to spend more because the currency had depreciated, and the city also had to maintain land and water defenses, support military units from Richmond, and assist the families of soldiers. The council authorized the sale of $200,000 in thirty-year bonds to finance the new budget, and the finance committee boasted that, despite wartime inflation and costs, the city's funded debt had not increased since 1861.[36]

• 4 •

The city council's most effective measures, and greatest innovations, were to support soldiers and their families and provide general relief for the city's poor. To their credit, the council members undertook experiments in social welfare that they would not even have considered before the war. These projects consumed the largest part of the wartime municipal budget.

In the summer of 1861 the council arranged for druggists to bill the city for all prescriptions given to the families of Virginia soldiers. The wounded in private homes and hospitals also received free medicine. Families with men in state service got free water. After the battle of First Manassas, city hospitals were set up in various buildings. At first the council proposed to supply them with free water and gas, but later it decided to charge a special low rate for lighting. The council voted $5,000 for soldiers' families in the spring of 1861, and $50,000 to buy winter clothing for Richmond volunteers. Another $10,000 was spent on families in the spring and fall of 1862. After 1864 most of the support for these women and children came through a charitable organization from private donations. Various Richmond units requested assistance, and during the war the council voted more than $179,000 for clothing, weapons, and horses. In general, Richmond troops seem to have been adequately supplied, although the minutes record several council discussions of improper disposition of blankets and overcoats.[37]

More than four hundred thousand dollars was appropriated for general poor relief. The largest amounts went to the Board of Overseers of the Poor, which administered the almshouse and cared for paupers, and to the Union Benevolent Society and the Citizens Relief Committee, which distributed charity throughout the city. The council gave generous amounts to the Richmond Soup Association, the Female Humane Association, and the Male Orphan Society, and to hospitals run by groups of ladies and gentlemen. It also gave ten thousand dollars to support Fredericksburg refugees after that town was evacuated in 1863.[38]

The council did put some restrictions on its aid. At the end of 1863 it refused to supply the poor with free medicine. It rejected requests for aid from nonresidents. Soldiers' families received the most benefit, whites were favored over blacks, and known Unionists often were denied aid. The editor of the *Richmond Enquirer* advocated giving no aid to the families of deserters, who should be "sent away." On 20 March 1865 the council sent a committee to confer with the Confederate government about the expulsion of such families from the city and into enemy lines. Between five and six thousand of these women and children were reported to be in Richmond.[39]

The quality of medical care varied widely. In January 1864, when the council raised the rates at the city hospitals, most of the patients were blacks who could not have paid anything. Of the thirteen whites who had been patients during 1863, all had come to the hospitals from jail or the poorhouse. Most whites were nursed at home, but civilian medical care was affected by the shortage of doctors, many of whom were serving with the army. In February 1865 the city's physicians, troubled by the growing legions of indigent, petitioned the council to appoint a doctor in each ward to treat the poor and be supplied with free medicine. The council took no action.[40]

The plight of Richmond's poor was critical by early spring in 1863. Heavy snow in March kept many farmers from the city, and the Confederate forces impressed the crops of others. Poor people could not afford to pay the high prices speculators asked for the food that was available. Apparently they were too proud to beg. Diarist John B. Jones continued to be amazed that there were no beggars in the streets. Governor Letcher tried to increase the amount of food reaching the city by asking the Confederate government to stop its impressments, but the Confederate bureaucracy did not act upon his request. By the end of March observers such as Robert Garlick Hill Kean, head of the Confederate Bureau of War, saw signs of famine in Richmond.[41]

The Richmond bread riot grew out of these conditions, but no incident in the wartime city has been more frequently misrepresented. On Wednesday, 1 April 1863—city election day—several hundred women from working-class neighborhoods and the counties around Richmond met secretly in the Belvidere Baptist Church, on Oregon Hill, to discuss their grievances. The meeting had been organized by a forty-year-old huckster, Mary Jackson, who sold meat in the Second Market and who was married to a prosperous painter. Mrs. Jackson was by all accounts a striking woman, with a "vixenish eye." She was a natural leader. For two weeks she had been telling all who would listen that the women were going to meet and demand bread at the prices paid by the Confederate government rather than the higher rates charged private citizens.[42]

Early Thursday morning the women marched downtown to Capitol Square, led by Mrs. Jackson, who reportedly brandished a bowie knife and a six-barreled pistol, and six-foot-tall, "rawboned and muscular" Minerva Meredith, waving a revolver. Many of the women carried hatchets, as they had agreed to do. They confronted Governor Letcher, who spoke to them outside the Capitol. When their demands were not met, they headed toward the business districts, intending, according to participants, either to ask for food or to seize it. A witness later testified that by the time the women left Capitol Square, Mrs. Jackson had lost control of her followers. The crowd had become a mob.

The women first broke into stores in the area of Fifteenth and Cary streets, seizing bread, flour, bacon, ham, sugar, coffee, and butter, along with "candles, silk, cloth, brogues, balmorals, cavalry boots, ladies' white satin slippers, children's embroidered dresses, wash tubs, men's shirts, pocket handkerchiefs, bowie knives, stacks of felt hats, clothes pins, unfinished tailors and shoemakers work, etc." Some carried their loot away, and others seized vehicles to haul their booty. They were helped in many instances by men, including patients from military hospitals, local regiments, and members of the city battalion. The men broke open store windows and doors with axes, helped the women through the openings, or entered themselves and threw goods outside.

Governor Letcher called out troops (which were identified as the Public Guard or the city battalion) to disperse the mob. Mayor Mayo, standing on a stool on the sidewalk, read the Riot Act to those who would listen. The crowd, angered when firemen turned hoses on them, drifted up to Main Street and continued the looting. About this time President Davis arrived. Both he and the governor later claimed that they ordered the troops to load their muskets and fire on the mob if its members did not disperse in five minutes. After tense moments while the politicians eyed their watches, the crowd broke up, carrying away stolen goods and looting stores on Franklin Street as it retreated. Witnesses later testified that Mayor Mayo had been warned in advance of the protest and again just before the trouble started, but Mayo denied it.

The portly mayor, the plump governor, and the haughty president did not distinguish themselves in their scramble to claim chief credit for putting down the rioters. The Confederate war department tried to impose a news blackout after the riot, but wild reports reached Danville and Lynchburg by telegraph before noon. Business stopped and civilian morale fell. News was carried north by refugees and by a group of exchanged Union prisoners who left after the riot. The newspapers, with the notable exception of John Moncure Daniel's *Examiner*, ran no stories on the riot. The *Examiner*, however, began extensive coverage the next day and continued it throughout April. Daniel and his editors were bitter critics of the Davis administration, and they blasted not only the president, governor, and mayor, but also the merchants for not shooting the looters. The paper, which had often labeled Davis a tyrant, called for a Napoleon to suppress lawlessness.

But the *Examiner*, and later other newspapers like the *Dispatch*, conspiring with the authorities in the best Know-Nothing tradition, blamed the disturbance on the Irish, Germans, and other "foreigners" in the city, as well as blacks and outside Yankee agitators. The *Examiner*, in its famous editorial of 4 April, called the mob "a handful of prostitutes, professional thieves, Irish and Yankee hags, gallows-birds from all lands but our own." This version was quickly accepted by most people, and by many historians. Soldier Fred Fleet, writing to his father on 7 April 1863, called the riot "a disgraceful affair . . . no doubt . . . concocked by Yankees, and aided by their assistants in Richmond, the Dutch and the Irish." For the *Examiner*, similar disturbances in Mobile, Atlanta, Petersburg, and Salisbury, North Carolina, were proof enough that Yankee troublemakers had made their way north to Richmond.

As always, the truth was not so simple. It is difficult to estimate either the size or composition of the mob, but Richmond's small police force, aided by merchants and prominent citizens, managed to arrest at least twenty-five men and forty-five women. The mob probably numbered several hundred or more; many others escaped and only the leaders, the greedy, the slow of foot, and the unlucky were caught. There is no evidence that any slaves or free blacks were involved. While there were some Irish and Germans among those arrested, as well as a fourteen-year-old prostitute and a twelve-year-old orphan boy (one of several youths), there were also many with such names as Bell, Blake, Brown, Goode, Hampton, Henry, Johnson, Radford, Smith, Williams, and Woodward. The culprits included "old Mrs. Taliaferro . . . well-to-do in the world, and . . . the owner of real estate," who had been caught with a load of bacon and brooms, and freed on bail because of her age and property. Margaret A. Pomfrey owned a farm and slaves in New Kent County and was brought to court by a policeman sent there to arrest her. She was charged with looting Pollard & Walker's. Mary Jacobs, a Jewish lady, was arrested for receiving from three women at her husband's large store on Main Street, stolen goods that may have been taken from Minna Sweitzer, another Jewish merchant. Thomas Samani, a native Richmonder from a wealthy family, was charged with breaking into the Sweitzer store.

Most of the women eventually were tried for misdemeanors. Those who were young, pretty, and "genteel," or who were wealthy and represented by counsel, often were discharged without trial in the mayor's police court, or acquitted by juries in Judge John A. Meredith's circuit court. The judge and jurors were lenient, especially with mothers and pregnant women, usually sentencing them to no more than thirty days in the city jail and a $75 fine. Minerva Meredith, who

1. View of the city of Richmond, about 1856. Mayo's Bridge, in the center, was the only passenger bridge across the James River to Manchester. Also visible are ships at the canal *(center right)*, flour mills along the river *(center left)*, and the Capitol.

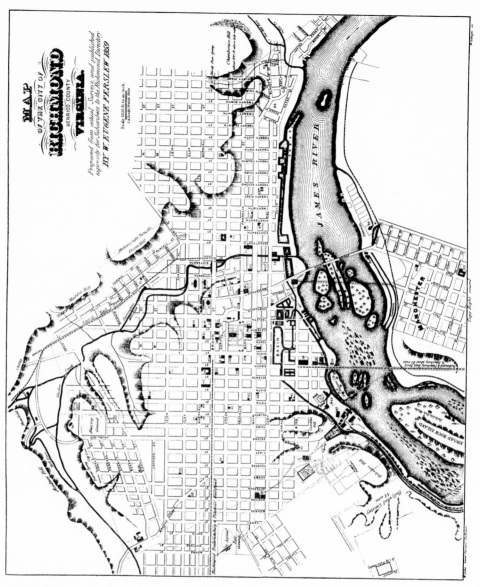

2. W. Eugene Ferslew's 1859 map of Richmond

3. Richmond skyline in April 1865 photographed from the river by Mathew Brady. The United States Post Office and Customs House *(center)* and the Capitol *(upper left)* escaped the flames.

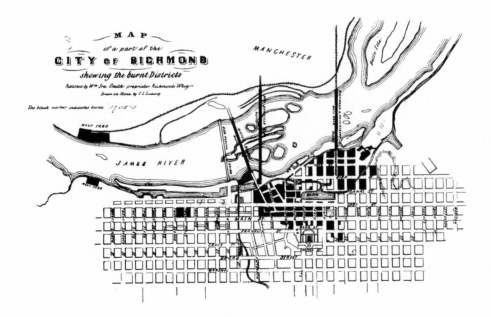

4. Confederate forces evacuated the city in April 1865 and destroyed military supplies and war materials as they left. Fire raged out of control, burned most of the business district *(blackened areas)*, and caused $30 million damage.

5. Black families living in makeshift quarters on canalboats immediately after the fire. Subsequently many found temporary shelter on Chimborazo Hill in facilities run by the Freedmen's Bureau.

6. Capitol Square seen from Ninth and Main streets. The evacuation fire destroyed eight to twelve hundred buildings—including numerous homes, more than two hundred businesses, and every saloon and bank in the city.

7. Richmond and Danville Railroad bridge ruins, the Dunlop flour mill, and Haxall-Crenshaw mill ruins, seen from the south. The bridge was not rebuilt until May 1866.

8. The evacuation fire, which did not cross Eighth Street, spared Saint Paul's Church *(right)*. Eighth Street carried the Richmond and Petersburg Railroad tracks from the river to Broad Street.

9. The Freedmen's Bureau office at Tenth and Broad streets was the central point for the distribution of government rations to hungry Richmonders of all races.

10. "High-toned Southern ladies," pictured in *Harper's Weekly*, on their way to the Freedmen's Bureau to receive government rations. Thousands of Richmonders, regardless of race, received rations and help from the bureau.

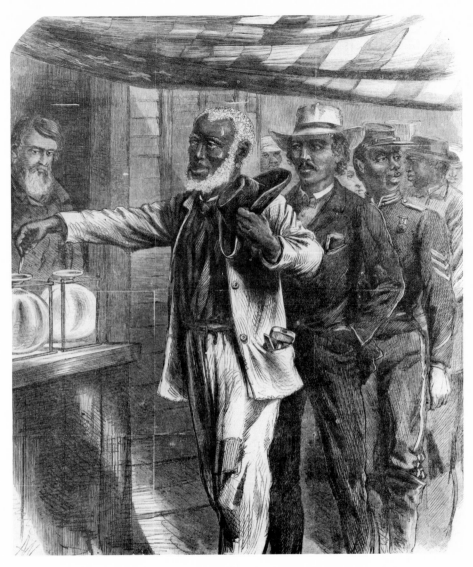

11. With the passage of the First Reconstruction Act in 1867, black voters became a political force in Richmond for the first time. This illustration from *Harper's Weekly* depicts balloting in 1867 for a state constitutional convention. The convention met from 3 December 1867 to 17 April 1868 and drafted the Constitution of 1869, or Underwood Constitution, which was ratified by popular vote on 6 July 1869. The Underwood Constitution remained in force until 1902.

12. Robert Mills's city hall in 1865

13. Robert Mills's city hall in 1865

Photographs by Mathew Brady in 1865 (plates 12 and 13) show the Richmond city hall designed by Robert Mills and built in 1816. After the 1870 disaster in which a balcony collapsed in the Capitol across the street, city leaders decided to tear down the city hall lest a similar accident occur. Only too late did demolition crews (plate 14, *above*) discover that Mills's edifice was well built and difficult to raze. Until 1894 when the new gothic Victorian city hall (see plate 90) was completed, city offices were housed in a low building in the 900 block of East Broad Street (plate 15, *below*).

16. Ralza M. Manly coordinated Freedmen's Bureau educational activities in Richmond in 1865 and 1866.

17. The Reverend Peter Randolph was pastor of the Ebenezer Baptist Church from 1865 to 1869 and a conservative leader.

18. Lewis Lindsay was one of Richmond's radical black leaders after 1867.

19. Joseph Mayo was mayor of Richmond before, during, and after the Civil War.

20. The Reverend Richard Wells was a black leader and pastor of Ebenezer Baptist Church from 1870 to 1901.

21. Judge John C. Underwood presided over Virginia's Convention of 1867–1868.

22. John N. Van Lew represented Marshall Ward on the city council during Reconstruction.

23. Albert P. Brooks was a leading black businessman active in Republican politics.

Several prominent Richmonders can be identified in these photographs of the petit jury selected to try Jefferson Davis for treason. On plate 24 *(above)* are: Martin M. Lipscombe, standing fourth from left; Barnham ("Born Ham") Wardwell, Albert P. Brooks, and Lewis Lindsay, seated second, third, and fourth from left. On plate 25 *(below)* are Joseph Cox, standing fourth from left, and John N. Van Lew, foreground. In May 1867 Judge John C. Underwood postponed Davis's trial, and Davis was released from his two-year confinement at Fort Monroe.

26. The Richmond Male Orphan Asylum, established in 1846, was located at Broad and Mayo streets and supported by the Board of Overseers of the Poor. Richmond citizens were acutely aware of social needs during the Civil War.

27. The city almshouse, on Hospital Street adjacent to Hebrew and Shockoe Hill cemeteries, was the place of last resort for Richmond's poor.

28. Pratt's Castle, or Pratt's Folly, was built in 1853 by William A. Pratt on Gamble's Hill, immediately east of the state penitentiary. The house had a wood frame overlaid with iron plates. It was destroyed in 1958.

29. Members of the Richmond Boating Club posed in the 1890s. Across the river is the Dunlop flour mill, the city's only flour mill that survived both the evacuation fire and the nineteenth century.

Richmond's Spotswood Hotel, one of the finest in the city, played host to Presidents John Tyler and Jefferson Davis. Completed in 1860 at Eighth and Main streets, the hotel (plate 30, *above*) survived the evacuation fire of 1865 but burned on Christmas Eve 1870 (plate 31, *below*) with a loss of eight lives.

32. Fulton and Rocketts, on the James River in the 1870s. Fulton's working-class German, Irish, and black residents walked more than two miles to their jobs in Richmond industries.

33. Richmond in 1873, a photograph taken from the Richmond and Petersburg Railroad bridge looking north toward Eighth Street. The Capitol is visible at the right.

34. Pupils at the Leigh Street School in the 1880s

35. William G. McCabe's school at 405 East Cary Street

36. Night class, Leigh Street School

Education was important to postwar Richmonders, white and black. The Leigh Street School, for example, at First and Leigh streets, served white children by day in the 1880s (plate 34). At night, adult classes were conducted there, too. Plate 36 records an adult class attended by seventeen Richmond plasterers.

Headmaster William G. McCabe's private school for boys was highly regarded among white Richmonders. In the 1880s the school occupied the former home of Lewis Ginter (second building from left in plate 35). Immediately after the war, the Freedmen's Bureau opened schools for black children (plate 37), and early in the 1870s the city council established a system of segregated public education in Richmond.

37. Freedmen's Bureau schoolchildren

38. The Lancasterian school at Fifteenth and Marshall streets

39. Bellevue Special School at Twenty-second and Broad streets

40. Lillie Logan's art class at Moldavia in the 1880s

The Lancasterian school (plate 38), founded in 1816, was the first public school in Richmond. After the Civil War it was used as a public school for blacks, the Valley School. The Bellevue Special School served white children of Richmond's west end. Plate 39 records Bellevue pupils engaged in craft activities on Friday, 2 June 1882. Women who sought classes in the fine arts during the 1880s often took them under Lillie Logan. These classes (plate 40) met at Moldavia, the former home of John Allan. For other Richmond women, however, the 1880s brought new forms of employment. The Southern Bell Telephone and Telegraph Company began operations in the city in 1882, and began using women operators (plate 41) in 1883.

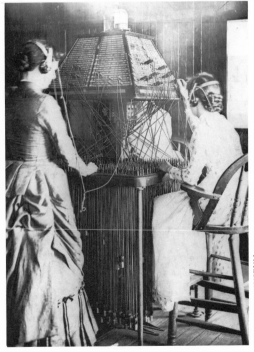

41. Richmond telephone operators

42. Completed in 1845, the first building of the Medical College of Virginia is a monument of antebellum Egyptian-revival design. This photograph was taken about 1870.

43. Hunter Holmes McGuire *(right)* and his staff at Saint Luke's Home for the Sick, which had opened in 1883. The leading surgeon in the postwar South, McGuire held the chair of surgery at the Medical College of Virginia from 1865 to 1881.

44. Plans to extend the James River and Kanawha Canal west to the Ohio River were pressed by the Richmond leadership until 1878, when it became apparent that the canal would never be completed. This scene along the canal in Richmond was published in 1872 to illustrate William Cullen Bryant's *Picturesque America*.

45. This 1888 map of Richmond shows the city's six wards as they existed from 1871 through 1892.

46. The Virginia State Agricultural Fair in October 1877 gave Richmond an opportunity to demonstrate that it was a city of the New South. Displays at the fair emphasized the New South's move to modern farm machinery.

47. Visitors to the 1877 State Agricultural Fair gave a warm welcome to President Rutherford B. Hayes, who spent two days in Richmond.

48. Late in the 1870s, Company F of the Richmond Fire Department posed proudly with their horsedrawn hose reel and steam engine in front of their station on North Twenty-fifth Street.

49. George A. Ainslie was chief of the Richmond Fire Department from 1870 to 1880.

In 1887 *Harper's Weekly* printed a romanticized view of the Tredegar Iron Works at night (plate 50, *above*). Plate 51 shows the Tredegar plant in 1865 immediately after the evacuation fire. The ironworks had been the Confederate government's primary arms supplier, and it was one of the few Richmond industries that survived the evacuation fire. Plate 52 records the Tredegar Iron Works in 1890, with Oregon Hill in the background.

51. Tredegar Iron Works in 1865

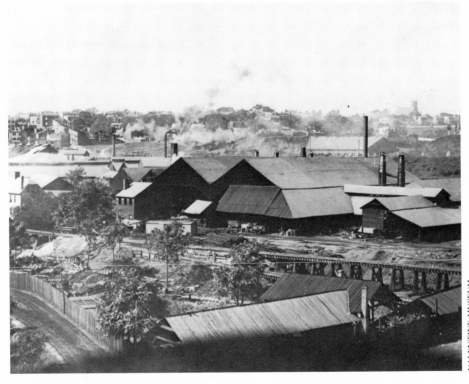

52. Tredegar Iron Works in 1890

53. Joseph Reid Anderson owned the Tredegar Iron Works until his death in 1892.

54. Ellen Glasgow (photographed about 1882) grew up in Richmond and won the Pulitzer prize for literature in 1942.

RICHMOND HUMANITIES CENTER

55. John P. Mitchell, Jr., a member of city council, published the *Richmond Planet* until his death in 1929.

56. Williams Carter Wickham was active in the Baltimore and Ohio Railroad and built the Church Hill tunnel.

57. Joseph Cox, a Richmond business-man, was a moderate Republican politician and a member of the Convention of 1867–1868.

58. John S. Wise, Republican candidate for governor in 1885, actively organized black voters in Jackson Ward.

59. Moses Drury Hoge was a prominent Presbyterian clergyman in mid-nineteenth-century Richmond

60. Episcopalian clergyman Charles Frederick Ernest Minnegerode was pastor of Saint Paul's Church.

The Knights of Labor held their national convention in Richmond in October 1886. Reports in national newspapers (such as plate 61, *above*, from *Frank Leslie's Illustrated Weekly*) emphasized the group's national commitment to the equality of all workers, a position that caused conflict in Virginia. Governor Fitzhugh Lee refused to allow former Richmonder Frank J. Ferrell to introduce him to the convention. Plate 62 *(below)* shows Ferrell introducing Knights president Terence V. Powderly, who in turn introduced the governor.

63. Richmond, with Mayo's Bridge in the foreground, 1889

The Main Street business district flooded frequently. Plate 64, above, records flooding in 1886 near the city market *(at the right)* at Seventeenth Street. The market building, shown about 1890 in plate 65, below, was built in 1854.

Employees (plate 67, *below*) at the Richmond Locomotive Works (plate 66, *above*) in Shockoe Valley could produce two hundred locomotives a year. In 1890 northern business interests purchased the factory, and it was closed before 1910.

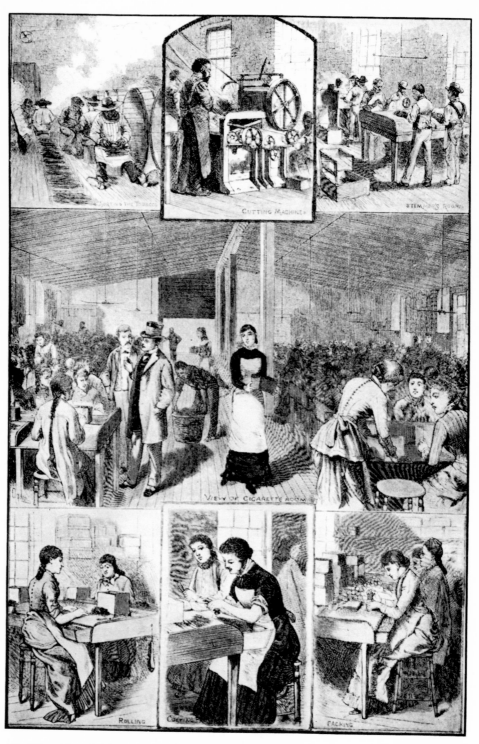

68. The title of this 1880s illustration, "Cigarette Manufacture at Richmond—Old Style," reflects the fact that Richmond's cigarette manufacturers initially were reluctant to adopt technological advances.

Richmond's tobacco industry was dominated by the Allen and Ginter Company. Early in the 1880s, America's leading cigarette manufacturer, Lewis Ginter (plate 69, *left*), chose not to install James Bonsack's patented cigarette-making machine. James B. Duke, of North Carolina, began using Bonsack's machines in 1883. In 1890 Duke's new American Tobacco Company, head-quartered in New York, bought the Allen and Ginter Company (plate 70, *below*).

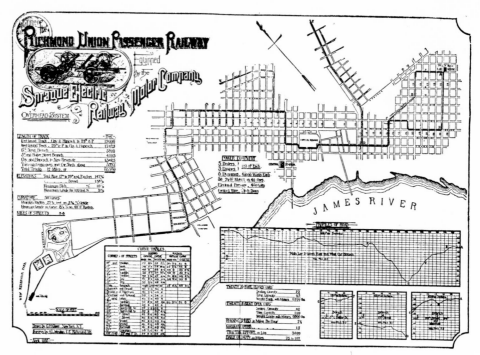

71. Map of the Richmond Union Passenger Railway, April 1888

72. John Thompson Brown published the *Richmond Progress* and was president of the Richmond Union Passenger Railway.

73. Frank J. Sprague, of New York, designed Richmond's pioneering electric streetcar system.

74. Workers near First Street in 1888 preparing to lay new streetcar lines. By 1890, Richmond had eight competing streetcar lines.

75. Richmond Union Passenger Railway cars 28 and 29 passing on Franklin Street near Thirteenth in an 1888 snowstorm

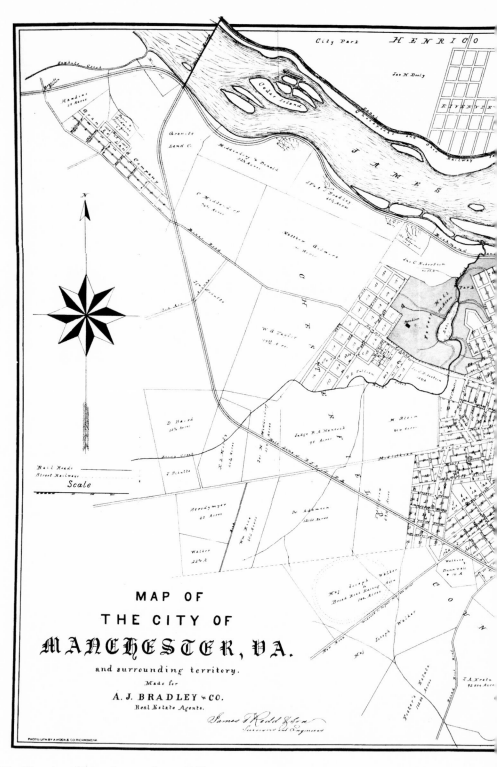

76. The city of Manchester about 1893

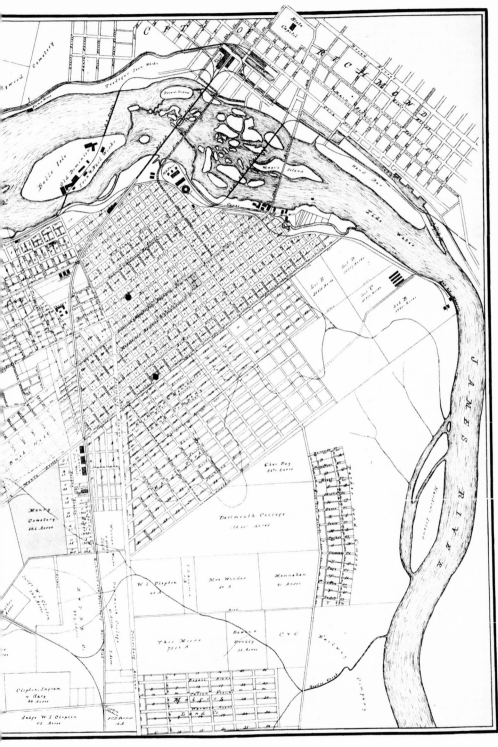

Manchester was annexed in 1910.

In 1873 Page McCarty (plate 77, *above left*) and John Brooke Mordecai (plate 78, *above right*) fought Richmond's most famous postwar duel over a published insult to Richmond belle Mary Triplett (plate 79, *below left*). Mordecai died, and the wounded McCarty spent the rest of his life in grief for his late friend. Triplett married Philip Haxall (plate 80, *below right*), coowner of the Haxall-Crenshaw flour mills.

81. The city waterworks shown in this 1890s photograph was located on the James River near William Byrd Park, which was then known as New Reservoir Park.

82. A store on East Main Street decorated for Emancipation Day, which was celebrated in Richmond throughout the 1880s

83. The Robert E. Lee statue was unveiled on 29 May 1890.

84. John Jasper was minister of the Sixth Mount Zion Baptist Church for thirty-four years.

85. Josiah Crump was a highly respected member of the city council at the time of his death in 1892.

86. The Lee statue soon after its unveiling

87. During a flood in 1889, Richmonders used carriages, horsedrawn streetcars, and small boats to negotiate the waters of East Main Street between Fifteenth and Seventeenth streets.

88. Discernible in this photograph of the Richmond skyline (seen about 1890 from Church Hill near the intersection of Marshall and Twenty-third streets) are, from left: the Capitol; the spire of Saint Paul's Church; city hall under construction; Monumental, First Baptist, and Broad Street Methodist churches on Broad Street; and the Egyptian Building of the Medical College of Virginia.

89. The city market building at Seventeenth and Main streets was built in 1854 to replace an earlier structure. A large meeting room on the second floor was used for political events.

90. Capitol Square at the turn of the century. Richmond's gothic city hall was completed in 1894. Ford's Hotel, now the site of the Virginia State Library, stood east of city hall. Early in the twentieth century the Capitol was expanded by the addition of House of Delegates and Senate wings completed in 1906.

lacked these desirable attributes, was found guilty by a jury that fined her the maximum of $100, and the judge gave her six months in jail, though it was open to question whether she had actually stolen any goods. The fate of Mrs. Jackson, who was refused bail and held for a felony trial despite her husband's attempts to free her, is unknown, but probably it was even more severe. Trials were held until March 1864. Male rioters were given stiffer sentences, including the maximum $100 fine and a year in jail for a misdemeanor conviction. Several of the male rioters were tried on felony charges in the Richmond hustings court by Judge William H. Lyons. Their sentences ran up to three years and eight months in the state penitentiary.

The role played by men in the bread riot may have been somewhat understated. Although the organizers and leaders were women, the riot had widespread support. Dr. Thomas Palmer, a middle-aged surgeon at the Florida hospital, who had stood on a corner in his blue uniform and urged the women on, had been unaware that the gentlemen standing next to him were Governor Letcher and Mayor Mayo. Palmer observed that there was a power behind the throne greater than the throne, and when asked what that power was, he replied "the people." He was arrested and charged with refusing to help suppress the riot and refusing to leave the scene when ordered, but later released.

Following the *Examiner*'s lead, modern historians have criticized the "plump rioters," who allegedly stole more jewelry and clothing than bread.[43] Yet, contemporary accounts do not mention any theft of jewelry, while there is ample evidence that large quantities of food were taken. Some on-the-scene observers put the women in more favorable light. The wife of a former United States congressman who was then a Confederate colonel described one of the women as "a pale, emaciated girl, not more than eighteen, with a sun bonnet on her head and dressed in a clean calico gown." As they talked, she said, the girl's loose sleeve "revealed the mere skeleton of an arm." The girl said that they had a right to live and were going to the bakeries where each woman would seize a loaf of bread, and the colonel's wife wished her luck. John B. Jones, the peppery diarist who hated food speculators but had no love for "foreigners," met "a young woman, seemingly emaciated" in the crowd, who told him that she was going to get something to eat. Jones said he hoped she would "and I remarked they were going in the right direction to find plenty in the hands of the extortioners."[44]

Fortunately for the colonel's wife and diarist Jones, their kind words were not overheard. A Mrs. Lane from Henrico County and Isabella Ould, a British subject, were arrested the day after the riot for voicing similar sentiments. They were standing on the steps of city hall just as the preliminary hearings were about to end in the mayor's court when some heard them express approval of the riot and sympathy for the looters. They were immediately taken before the mayor, who charged them with the use of incendiary language.[45]

Richmond's city council, shaken by the event, met that afternoon and adopted resolutions condemning the "disgraceful riot . . . in our favored and quiet City" and attributing the cause to "devilish and selfish motives." The council noted that generous amounts were set aside for relief and that no recent requests for aid had been made, and discussed methods of riot suppression. The council paid a claim from the city hospital superintendent for 310 pounds of beef that had been stolen, but, on the advice of the city attorney when two merchants presented claims totaling twenty thousand dollars, said that it had no legal obligation to pay for private losses.[46]

The city council moved quickly after the riot to improve food distribution in Richmond—action that cast further doubt on its claim that relief had been distributed in sufficient quantities before the riot. A new law provided free food, for which the poor were issued tickets, one day a week at the city markets. The Board of Overseers of the Poor administered the system, and the assessor and tax collector determined eligibility. No food was to be given to able-bodied men or known participants in the bread riot.

While there were similar disturbances in other Southern cities during the war, the Richmond incident was the Confederacy's most serious. The bread riot was a sign of unrest among urban poor whites similar to the discontent of small farmers in the rural Confederacy. Like their country cousins, many of the city's poor were convinced that "it was a rich man's war and a poor man's fight." For some months before the bread riot the council had been trying to ensure that a sufficient quantity of food reached the city's markets. Various food supply plans had been discussed in the previous two years. The council in the summer of 1862 had arranged to have half a ton of salt shipped to the city each month from the works at Saltville, Virginia. Later it regulated salt prices.[47]

Months after the riot, as the 1863 harvest season approached, a plan was proposed to buy food in quantity in the country and sell it in the city markets at prices below the normal retail levels. Richmond lacked food not because of scarcity in surrounding counties, but because farmers feared that Confederate agents would impress their produce as it was being transported to the city and because city buyers risked being charged for interfering with the effort to feed the army. The council created a Board of Supplies, composed of councilmen and private citizens, and the board secured warehouses, appointed purchasing agents, and arranged for transportation. The council with some misgivings, also decided that hucksters again be allowed to act as middlemen, buying food from farmers and selling it in the city.[48]

In June 1864, Thomas B. P. Ingram, a butcher and meat speculator, offered to supply the city with live beef cattle. He and the city were each to put up $50,000. The meat would be sold at a 20 percent profit. The city would distribute its half of the meat to the poor and the speculator would sell the rest at retail prices. The proposal was tabled after one councilman attacked profiteers, but the offer continued to be debated during the summer of 1864. Some members thought the Board of Supplies was securing adequate quantities of meat, but on 19 July 1864 a majority of the supply committee voted to accept the plan. The Confederate secretary of war promised not to impress beef on its way to Richmond, and the speculator was given a stall in each city market to sell his beef. When he began to offer meat at $3.00 and $3.50 a pound, the competition forced other merchants to lower their prices by several dollars. By September a scandal had developed, however, as other butchers reported that the city's partner had proposed illegal deals to them. After a bitter debate, the meat contract was canceled.[49]

Bread prices rose rapidly during the war. While bakers paid $325 for a barrel of flour in the summer of 1864, they could get $700 or more for the bread made from it, depending upon the size of their loaves. A citizens' petition asked the council to regulate the size of loaves of bread—a practice that had strong legal precedents—but instead of regulation, the city subsidized two bakeries that sold a loaf of bread twice the normal size for the usual price. The city's subsidized bakers supplied the capital and materials and got 15 percent profit on their sales; the city guaranteed a supply of grain and flour, and promised that the bakers would not be subject to Confederate impressment.[50]

In the fall of 1864 the council prepared to supply Richmonders with wood and coal for the winter. The newly created committee on fuel purchased a canalboat to haul fuel into the city. In March 1865 the council protested the Richmond and Danville Railroad's theft of wood that the city had purchased for the poor. The railroad had contracted to deliver the wood, but as the council had sold all the city's stock in the line and no longer had that leverage, the company never surrendered a single cord. A comparison of Richmond prices for food and fuel in 1862 and in the last nine months of the war (see table 3) shows the extent of

Table 3
Commodity Prices in Richmond, 1862, 1864–1865

Commodity	Unit	Price in 1862	Price(s) in July 1864 and/or March 1865
Milk	quart	$ .25	$ 2.50
Butter	pound	.50	20.00
Flour	barrel	16.00	1,500.00
Bacon	pound	.25	20.00
Beef	pound	.13 to .30	12.00 to 15.00
Sugar	pound	.80	10.00
Firewood	cord	8.00	150.00
Coal	25 bushels	9.00	90.00

SOURCE: J. B. Jones, *A Rebel War Clerk's Diary at the Confederate States Capital*, ed. Howard Swiggett, 2 vols. (New York, 1935).

inflation, the scarcity of goods, and the lack of effective government regulation of speculation.[51]

Despite the pressures of war and the demands of its myriad relief activities, the council tried to provide Richmond's white children with an education. Although the city generally is not credited with having a public school system until 1869, the council appropriated funds for the salaries of teachers in various ward schools in the political subdivisions. They also increased their support of the long-established free Lancasterian school after the state withdrew its subsidy. In 1863 and 1864 alone, the council voted almost seventeen thousand dollars for public schools. Many of the city's famous private schools continued to operate, sometimes intermittently, during the war years.[52]

• 5 •

The war had an enormous impact not only on the activities and expenses of city government but on Richmond commerce and industry as well. Secession and the Union blockade ended Richmond's career as Virginia's largest port. Near the end of 1861 the *Richmond Dispatch* reported that sixty-eight fewer ships had docked in the city than in 1860. Canal tolls fell to almost half the previous year's receipts. The city's five railroads either were in enemy hands or strained by heavy military usage. Still, as in other cities, north and south, the commercial spirit was strong in Richmond. Business thrived in the capital during the first years of the war. In private as well as government circles enterprising men managed to ship goods to and from Richmond. While such illegal trade was not necessarily treasonous—as both Union and Confederate officials winked at some of it—there were many critics, John B. Jones among them, who blasted the merchants for cursing the Yankees and trading with them at the same time. On 8 June 1863 Jones reported that cargoes from blockade-runners were arriving at the rate of one a day, and that most of the goods were of Northern manufacture.[53]

While the profits of war made some men rich, as is indicated by the higher ratio of coaches and carriages to taxpaying males, the total value of personal property rose only $200,000 from 1860 to 1861, despite the large increase in the city's population. Three of Richmond's four antebellum industries were seriously damaged by the war. The tobacco factories all but shut down, as they gradually were cut off from farms and the Northern and foreign markets. Richmond's huge flour mills operated below full capacity because they were unable to obtain sufficient grain. The city's millers were shut off from their traditional South American markets as the ships of Richmond's flour fleet were either captured by the Yankees or sunk by the Confederates to block the James River channel. Slaves continued to sell for high prices at least as late as August 1864, but of course the Union victory ended Richmond's prosperous slave trade.[54]

Iron manufacture and other metalworking was the capital's only booming industry. In addition to Joseph R. Anderson's Tredegar Iron Works, Richmond had the Bellona Arsenal, the Confederate arsenal and armory, and numerous lesser concerns. The Tredegar was the South's only rolling mill in 1861, and only good foundry after the loss of Leed's in New Orleans in April 1862. Together with the Tredegar company, the Confederate armory and arsenal made about half of the total ordnance supplied to the Confederate armies. Lee's battered men fought the last year of the war as much to defend this huge industrial complex as to protect the Confederate capital. The Confederacy did not long survive the loss of Richmond's capacity to forge the tools of war.[55]

The war had come just as Richmond industry was beginning to diversify. A sugar refinery with a capacity of 150 to 200 barrels a day had been about to begin operations in 1860. In the same year Richmond also had had a shipyard, a railroad car spring factory, a woolen mill, a sewing machine company, a plant to manufacture patented building block, and a plaster mill. None of these firms survived the war. The city had forty-three manufacturing plants in 1859 and only sixteen in 1866. Of these, all but one was either a foundry or a book-and-job printer.[56]

• 6 •

The transfer of the Confederate capital to Richmond brought people from all over the South, as well as exiles from the North. Thomas C. DeLeon, a writer who followed the government to Virginia, found that the little city of forty thousand that he had visited earlier was filled with perhaps one hundred twenty thousand persons, including refugees, politicians, government workers, officers, and their families. To DeLeon it seemed that the entire population between Montgomery and Richmond had come to the city on the James.

In addition to resident civilians and officers, ten to fifteen thousand soldiers were always stationed in or passing through Richmond. Texas Rangers dazzled even the horse-loving Virginians with their equestrian feats, while brawny frontiersmen from Arkansas and Missouri jostled slim Richmond gentlemen. The butternut uniforms of Georgia troops and the colorful garb of the Zouave regiments contrasted with the plain gray of the Richmond units. The men from New Orleans, such as Rob Wheat's Louisiana Tigers, terrorized the city by burglarizing houses, stealing chickens, and assaulting and robbing pedestrians. They entered restaurants and "charged" expensive meals to the Confederate government. A South Carolinian rode his horse into a bar. The proud soldiers from the Palmetto State were rebuffed when they announced to the city's matrons that they had come to fight Virginia's battles and expected to win Richmond brides.[57]

The seamier side of city life could be found in Shockoe Valley, especially in the neighborhood of Cash Corner, the "notorious . . . sink-hole of iniquity." Here was Richmond's equivalent of New York's Five Points. Here the criminal class congregated. Bars, brothels, and gambling dens, or hells, attracted the high and the low of the Confederacy. With so many men in the city, it quickly became the prostitution capital of the South. Vice had not been an unknown feature of antebellum Richmond life, but it had never thrived in such abundance. In August 1862, writing to his son Fred, Dr. Benjamin Fleet referred to the city as "that *Hog hole*, Richmond. I never supposed I could ever have been so thoroughly disgusted with any place this side of Yankeedom." The massive influx of population and rough, wartime conditions changed the tone of Richmond society. It did become a "city of strangers," albeit Southern ones.[58]

The small police force could do little to control the crime rate. At first the rigors of martial law had some impact on criminal activity, but there were always many complaints about crime. Early in 1864 a councilman said that "frequent robberies" were causing "much alarm among citizens" and were "seldom . . . detected." Juvenile crime was also on the rise. Several women were seriously injured, and the marble statue of Henry Clay in Capitol Square was badly damaged, because the authorities were unable to prevent the frequent rock battles between rival youth gangs. One reason that the council wanted the Confederacy to return the almshouse was because it planned to use it as a juvenile house of correction.[59]

Richmond was the goal of the Union armies in the east for four years, but it seems to have been in the most danger during the first year of the war. The first Union advance was stopped at Bull Run, near Manassas, in July 1861. In the Peninsula campaign of March through July 1862, General McClellan's army extended itself halfway around Richmond and almost captured the city. Many members of the Confederate Congress, along with Mrs. Jefferson Davis and other prominent residents, fled. Lee drove McClellan away in the Seven Days' Battles and Richmond was not again threatened until Grant's Wilderness campaign in 1864.

Richmonders reacted with considerable naiveté to the early battles of the war. They exaggerated the importance of each victory or defeat, such as the skirmish at Big Bethel, won by the Confederates in June 1861, or the defeat suffered at Rich Mountain, West Virginia, in July. Each little victory tended to encourage enlistments, and lent credence to the view that the war would be a short one. Richmonders were unable to comprehend the defeats. They blamed such setbacks on poor leadership or bureaucratic bungling. Each early engagement meant only a few dead officers and men.

After the first big battle, near Manassas, Richmonders began to understand war and the price of victory. The bodies of prominent officers, such as General Barnard Bee and Colonel Francis Bartow, came back to the city along with hundreds of dead and wounded men. But many Richmonders still hoped for a short war. Their army continued to win, but the enemy was never destroyed, and the war did not stop. Richmonders waited with growing frustration for the foe to be crushed, but their hopes were denied, at Second Manassas in August 1862, at Fredericksburg in December, and even at Chancellorsville in May 1863. In his first invasion of the North, Lee lost at Sharpsburg in September 1862, and failed to win Maryland for the Confederacy. Richmonders could not admit defeat, since Lee escaped to Virginia with most of his army, but Gettysburg was a more terrible blow, and after July 1863 many in the city gave up hope of ultimate Southern victory.[60]

Many of the wounded men who survived these battles were carried in railroad cars and ambulance wagons to Richmond. The capital was also the hospital center of the Confederacy. The city had sixty or seventy private and government hospitals of varying size, including Camp Winder, the largest, to the west of the city, and the best-organized and most famous, Chimborazo, set on a healthy elevation east of Richmond. This complex of buildings and tents was almost self-sufficient, with its own herd of cattle and goats, a large bakery, brewery, and other facilities, under the capable surgeon-in-chief Dr. James B. McCaw. Chimborazo treated more than seventy-six thousand patients and had a relatively low mortality rate of 20 to 25 percent. Areas around the hospitals smelled of sickness and death, however, and the streets were crowded with convalescing veterans and amputees.[61]

Muffled drums and the "Dead March" from *Saul* were familiar accompaniments to life in Richmond. Military funerals were an almost daily occurrence. Occasionally there was a great state ceremony of the kind given Stonewall Jackson in 1863. More often, the impressive funerals were for men from one of the city's prominent families—such as O. Jennings Wise, the captain of the crack Richmond Light Infantry Blues and eldest son of former governor General Henry A. Wise, who was killed at Roanoke Island in 1862—whose bodies were carried from Saint Paul's Episcopal Church to Hollywood. Hundreds of more obscure Virginians were buried with no attendants save a minister (not always of their denomination), a nurse who had known them, the gravedigger, and passing strangers. And thousands of Confederates, from all over the South, were buried in mass graves in Oakwood without religious services of any kind after each great battle. Their bodies were stripped of garments, for the Confederacy could ill afford to clothe its dead. After Jackson's death in 1863 people had little heart, or time, for elaborate funerals, even for the most famous generals. J. E. B. Stuart was buried without the usual honors in May 1864 because General Philip Sheridan was just outside the city. And at the 1865 funeral for A. P. Hill, killed in the final Union attack at Petersburg, the funeral cortege almost collided with Lincoln's carriage and escort on the day the president visited Richmond.[62]

Tradition is that sick and wounded Confederates were nursed back to health by the devoted women of Richmond. White women of all ages and classes did visit the patients, bringing food and comfort, but most of the nursing was done by black men. At Chimborazo, for instance, 256 blacks and 76 white soldiers served as nurses. The hospital also had 123 laundresses, 54 cooks, and 4 bakers, all black.[63]

During the war Richmond blacks were closely regulated and often mistreated, despite the vital services they performed in hospitals, on fortifications, in ironworks, and in the city's departments. Some concern was occasionally shown for their rights, as when the mayor suspended a police captain for a week after he hit with his nightstick a small black boy who had been firing "popcrackers." More typical, however, was the city council's concern for restricting blacks. Free blacks were forbidden to enter the city without a certificate of good character signed by a justice of the peace in their home county. The mayor's signature was also required, although presumably one had to enter the city to get it. Negroes without this document could be arrested by the police or market clerks and flogged at the mayor's discretion. Antebellum laws regarding slaves were stiffened, although the council permitted owners or hirers of slaves to give them passes that protected them from overzealous policemen.

Blacks were blamed for much of the crime in Richmond. In January 1865 the mayor accused black hack drivers of complicity in the city's many burglaries. He urged that "Negroes of suspicious character" be denied city licenses for their vehicles. Yet some blacks prospered. The free black cobbler who repaired John B. Jones's shoes made more money than a Confederate congressman. Some few slaves ran away to the Yankees, taking clothing, money, and other property with them; a house servant in the Davis mansion was one of these fugitives. But there were also many instances in which whites, such as Mary Boykin Chesnut, entrusted slaves with large sums of money and considerable responsibility.[64]

At first, social activities in Richmond were limited by the war. But Richmonders inevitably sought outlets for tension, despite the disapproval of ministers and glum souls who thought frolic unseemly. By December 1861 many city residents were enjoying "danceable teas" and other diversions unlike any Richmond had ever known. Aristocratic families entertained lavishly until their money ran out. Then powerful Confederate officials, blockade-runners, and speculators stepped in to fill the void. Mrs. Chesnut enjoyed a luncheon of "gumbo, ducks and olives, *supreme de volaille*, chickens in jelly, oysters, lettuce salad, chocolate cream, jelly cake, claret cup, champagne, etc." at the

Davis mansion in January 1864. Extravagant menus could still be found in a few places in the last months of the war. Supply rather than inflated prices was the problem for the rich.

"Starvation parties," at which no refreshment was served except muddy James River water, became popular among the younger set. Unmarried middle- and upper-class women entertained Confederate officers and men alike at these informal affairs. A custom in Richmond noted by visiting observers was that belles who married, no matter how beautiful, retired from parties to devote themselves to domestic duties. Thomas Jefferson had declared in 1818 that "the French rule is wise, that no lady dances after marriage. This is founded in solid physical reasons, gestation and nursing leaving little time to a married lady when this exercise can be either safe or innocent." The democracy of the camp extended to the parlors, for many sons of the most prominent families went in the army as private soldiers, and some served in the ranks throughout the war.[65]

The poor had little entertainment and were kept busy trying to survive on government charity. In some ways the middle-class government workers had an even harder time, as they were ineligible for relief and had to survive on meager salaries. City rents were so high that some workers lived in distant villages, such as Ashland, and commuted by train. There was little new housing built in Richmond during the war, despite the crowded conditions, because labor and building materials were in short supply. Families in houses often lived in one room, forced into the smaller quarters by their landlords or, if they owned the house, renting the extra space themselves to tenants. In hotels and boardinghouses, several lodgers slept in each bed. Criminals actually stole a house, demolishing it in one night and carrying away everything of value.[66]

Anti-Semitism was prevalent in wartime Richmond. Jews were not often attacked directly in the newspapers, but much of the torrent of abuse heaped on Judah P. Benjamin, who held three successive posts in Davis's cabinet, stemmed from the fact that he was Jewish. Wartime diaries and postwar memoirs are filled with criticism of Jews. Government clerks, young soldiers, and aristocratic ladies blamed Jews for the high prices in Richmond, for the lack of food and housing (although most of Richmond's Jewish merchants were either jewelers or clothiers), for security leaks, and even for Confederate defeats. Despite these prejudices, many of Richmond's Jewish families had one or more sons in the Confederate army, and they proudly set aside a section of the Hebrew Cemetery for their war dead.[67]

Most Richmonders faced the war bravely. They rushed to defend their city on 21 April 1861, popularly remembered as *Pawnee* Sunday, because a Union gunboat by that name was said to be coming up the James to shell Richmond. When the vessel failed to appear, the people laughed at themselves. Union raiders under Generals Stoneman and Kilpatrick almost reached the city in 1863 and 1864, and ladies with antique weapons prepared to defend their homes, waiting patiently for the hoofbeats of Union cavalry. Mrs. Chesnut, on the other hand, was so frightened that, on the advice of one of her slaves, she burned a portion of her diary.[68]

Women pale with worry for their own loved ones tried to follow the admonition to "rend your heart but not your garments." Though some of the gayest society women felt ashamed of their frivolity, Lee himself approved of any activity that gave his men a respite from war. In the final months the social pace became frantic as men and women sensed that the Confederacy was dying. Weddings and funerals followed each other in a macabre procession. The gallant General John Pegram married the beautiful Hetty Cary, of Baltimore, in Saint Paul's and was buried from the same church three weeks later. When the Confederate lines at Petersburg were broken and Richmond had to be evacuated, Colonel Walter Taylor of Lee's staff rode back to the city, married his sweetheart and dashed off to join the retreating army. He survived the march to Appomattox; others were not so lucky.[69]

Not all Richmonders were heroic Confederates until the end, or even at the beginning. Strong Unionist sentiment existed in Richmond throughout the war. There was an active Union underground with such leaders as Elizabeth Van Lew, the famous spy, and Samuel Ruth, an R. F. & P. superintendent who delayed beef shipments to Lee's army. These indomitable men and women smuggled messages out of the city to Union generals, disrupted communications and transportation, and tried to weaken morale by setting fires, by chalking Union slogans on walls and fences, and by helping slaves and Union prisoners to escape.[70]

A decline in Richmond's Confederate spirit was evident by 1865. Few Richmonders wished to sacrifice their city in the death struggle of the Confederacy. There were women who would not help the cause. The ladies of Monumental Episcopal Church, many of them wealthy, refused to knit socks for the soldiers in the last bitter months. And many men had decided that the Confederacy was a lost cause. After packing government documents for shipping during the evacuation, Philip Whitlock, one of postwar Richmond's most successful tobacco manufacturers, and other clerks in one building found that a sentinel had been posted to keep them inside until they could be mustered into a company to join Lee's retreating army. "This *did not suit* me," Whitlock recalled, and he escaped through a basement door and went home to his wife.[71]

When Governor Thomas Jefferson had abandoned Richmond during the American Revolution, Benedict Arnold's British raiders sacked and burned the town. Richmonders never forgave him. They were equally angry at Jefferson's namesake when, as they saw it, Davis and the Confederate government left them to the mercy of the Yankees without putting up a fight. Lower-class women jeered at the retreating Confederates as they passed through Rocketts. Not satisfied with an abject retreat, the Confederates burned the city behind them. Richmond's attitude toward Davis did not change until after his release from prison, when he was brought back to Richmond by the Federal government and indicted for treason in 1867. This event won Davis the sympathy of Confederate Richmonders.[72]

When the war's end came, blacks rejoiced at their emancipation. Many residents were glad that the war was over. But those who had ardently supported the Confederacy suffered from an almost unendurable weariness. They had not bent under the strain of war, but they had finally been broken. The capture of Richmond on 3 April 1865 and the final Confederate surrenders in the following weeks were convulsive shocks to a spirit that was already dead.

Babylon is fallen, is fallen, that great city.

Revelation 14:8

And the smoke of their torment ascendeth up for ever and ever: and they have no rest day nor night, who worship the beast and his image.

Revelation 14:11

And a mighty angel took up a stone like a great millstone, and cast it into the sea, saying, Thus with violence shall that great city Babylon be thrown down, and shall be found no more at all.

Revelation 18:21

3

The Desolate City

1865-1870

AT the close of the Civil War in the spring of 1865, a mass of humanity traveled the roads to Richmond. Thousands of freedmen from all parts of Virginia sought relatives in the city. Frightened white civilians moved to the capital from the surrounding countryside. Both groups desired the food and shelter provided by the Union army. Hundreds of men who had fought in the Confederate army returned to their homes in the city, accompanied by thousands of veterans who lived elsewhere in Virginia and the South but who found temporary quarters in Richmond. Northern tourists wanted to see the rebel citadel, and reporters seeking stories for eager northern editors came up the James River on steamships. Ten thousand Union soldiers stationed in and around the city vainly tried to limit access to it and attempted to control Richmond's varied inhabitants.

• 1 •

The city did not look like its wartime self, and it bore even less resemblance to the Richmond of bygone days before the war. The business district was a smoking nightmare of tottering walls and piles of rubble. Tall brick chimneys stood isolated amid the ruins of the city's industrial might. Travelers who came from the south gazed across the river and the piers of three burned bridges, to the gutted factories, mills, warehouses, and stores that lined a mile or more of the river-bank.[1]

Richmond had been evacuated by the Confederate government on

2–3 April 1865. During the night, retreating Confederates set fire to warehouses full of tobacco and cotton in the center of the city and ignited arsenals stocked with munitions. They left timed charges to destroy the Confederate navy's rams in the James River and to blow up the city's powder magazine on the northern outskirts of Richmond. The terrific explosions that followed in the early morning hours broke most of the windows and mirrors in the city and killed more than a dozen inhabitants, including some of the inmates of the city almshouse, which was located near the powder magazine.[2]

City officials were unable to prevent the Confederate army from lighting the fires or igniting the explosives, but they did take other precautionary measures. Responsible men in each of the city's three wards were entrusted with the job of destroying all the wine and liquor stored in their neighborhoods. The mayor also asked for men to help the small guard of Confederate convalescents police the city, but only one man volunteered.[3]

While liquor barrels were being broken open and their contents dumped into the streets, the explosions began. Hundreds of people awoke and hurried outside, thinking that retreating Confederates or advancing Federals were shelling the city. When the terrified Richmonders discovered that the gutters were awash with whiskey, rum, and brandy, they scooped it up in hats and buckets, or lapped it up while lying on their stomachs. Bold from drink, they burned and looted stores in the business district, breaking windows and smashing doors. The drunken, looting mob included Confederate deserters and stragglers, escaped Union soldiers from Libby Prison, blacks, poor whites, and impoverished aristocrats.[4]

Fire engulfed block after block. Hundreds of panic-stricken dogs and cats ran the streets, ignoring the squeals of thousands of rats scurrying from building to building and the cries of those trapped in the flames. Many Richmonders stood guard on their rooftops, frantically trying to quench airborne embers with buckets of water and wet sheets. Mrs. Robert Stanard, a beautiful Richmond hostess famous for her wartime receptions, sat outside her magnificent home in her best clothes and quietly watched the mansion burn to the ground. Above the roars of the mob and the flames, explosions that seemed continuous shook the air. No Richmonder who lived through the evacuation fire was ever able to forget it.[5]

Nor were the Union soldiers who advanced from the east to occupy Richmond. They approached the city along the various turnpikes that converged at the eastern end of Main Street. Smoke obscured all but the church steeples and houses on the highest hills. Spears of flame shot through the blanket of smoke, and the explosions became louder as the Army of the James neared the disaster.[6]

Urged on by eighty-year-old mayor Joseph Mayo, who surrendered to Union forces just outside the city, the soldiers quickly occupied Richmond, raised the American flag over the Virginia state Capitol, and tried to control the fire. Their job was difficult, because the hoses of Richmond's small fire department had been hacked to pieces, either by the mob or by escaped state penitentiary inmates. Union forces arrested some arsonists and looters, and civilians helped the soldiers form bucket brigades to wet down structures adjacent to those already burning. Buildings, including the Traders Bank patronized by Jefferson Davis, were blown up to create firebreaks, and as the wind lessened the flames subsided. By late afternoon of 3 April 1865 the blaze was under control, although small fires continued to smolder beneath huge piles of debris until the end of June 1865, nearly three months later.[7]

Richmonders of every class suffered losses in the fire. Wealthy tobacco magnate John Stewart, who owned the house where General Lee and his family lived, lost a fortune when thieves stole bonds from the Exchange Bank before it burned. Major Lewis Ginter, of the Confederate army, returned to Richmond to find the ruins of his dry goods store, once the largest south of Philadelphia. He despaired of rebuilding and left the city to try a new career in New York. Tom Griffin, a free black restaurant owner locally famous for the cuisine at his Congress Hall, saw it and his other saloon destroyed by fire. Griffin decided to stay in Richmond. The candy stores of Kate Taylor and Mary Kumpner burned, as did the groceries of Catherine Botto and Mrs. E. Ryan.[8]

Before the Union forces of young Brigadier General Edward H. Ripley could control the fire, it had consumed an area of more than twenty blocks. Between eight and twelve hundred buildings were destroyed in what came to be known as the Burnt District—an area of the city that included nine-tenths of the business district and four-fifths of the food suppliers. More than two hundred twenty-eight businessmen lost goods and merchandise to the fire or to looters. The value of the property destroyed is impossible to assess accurately. An early estimate put the figure at just above $2 million. Later claims of damage ranged as high as $30 million.[9]

The evacuation fire devastated Richmond's business community. Every bank in the city burned, as well as the offices of nine brokerage houses, and more than twenty law firms. More than two dozen groceries burned, along with the premises of more than three dozen commission merchants. Only one church burned, but temperate citizens noticed that fire had consumed every saloon in the city. Their destruction was particularly distressing to Richmonders because the saloons had not only sold liquor but doubled as restaurants.[10]

Factories and shops suffered less damage than the premises of the retailers, wholesalers, and professionals. Ironworks sustained the most severe losses. The Tredegar Iron Works survived because the company's president, Joseph R. Anderson, had armed his workers, who repelled attempts to ignite the plant. Seven smaller firms burned, including a stove foundry, a machinist's shop, and the office of the Old Dominion Iron and Nail Works. Two carriage factories, two paper mills, a tin shop, a pottery, two tobacco factories, and several flour mills also burned.[11]

The offices and printing shops of most of Richmond's commercial and religious press were destroyed, including those of the *Dispatch*, *Enquirer*, *Examiner*, *Illustrated News*, *Southern Literary Messenger*, *Central Presbyterian*, and the Methodist *Christian Advocate*. Only the offices of the *Sentinel* and William Ira Smith's *Whig* survived the fire, but Charles H. Wynne was able to resume publication of the *Times* on 21 April 1865. Seven other printing shops burned, as well as seven book and stationery stores.[12]

The depots and train sheds of the Richmond and Danville and Richmond and Petersburg railroads burned along with their bridges over the James River, as did Mayo's toll bridge, the sole span across the river for horsedrawn vehicles and pedestrians.[13]

Both the state Capitol and Richmond's city hall were saved because of their location on Shockoe Hill above the main area of the fire, but the buildings of the General Court of Virginia and the Henrico County Court burned. These two structures had contained many valuable records, which were destroyed, and the Henrico courthouse had had custody of the official papers of several eastern Virginia counties, which had been carried to Richmond for safekeeping during the tidewater campaigns.[14]

In all, more than sixty different professions, trades, businesses, and industries suffered damage in the fire. Most of the businessmen and women who lost their stores and merchandise during the evacuation never recovered. Only about 35 percent of the merchants burned out or looted in April 1865 were back in business by 1871. When the work of reconstruction began, Richmonders concentrated on rebuilding offices, banks, and stores. Few mills or foundries were rebuilt during the first two years after the war.[15]

• 2 •

The initial recovery of Richmond after the fire was swift. Some Richmonders were depressed by the magnitude of the task that lay ahead, but most reacted as people generally do after a disaster: they went to work. They worked with the Union soldiers to restore order to the city. After they had controlled the fire, teams of men began to clear debris from the streets. They began at Main Street, where the damage was worst, and had it open for traffic by the afternoon of 3 April, but some side streets remained blocked for weeks, or even months, at first by the rubble, and later by building materials.[16]

Richmond's utilities had suffered damage in the fire. Tons of falling brick and mortar had broken gas lines beneath the streets and prevented access to valves. All gas service in and west of the Burnt District had to be shut off because of the leakage. Service was not resumed until mid-May, and then not enough gas could be manufactured to light all the streetlamps. Fortunately, most Richmonders had running water because the waterworks, in the western part of the city, had been unaffected by the fire, although the pumps and other equipment were in poor condition.[17]

The rebuilding of the Burnt District was accomplished relatively quickly and the resurrection of Richmond's economy began in 1865 almost as soon as the streets were cleared and the fires extinguished. Northern men and their money played a part in this process, but the details of their participation are often hard to document, and the importance of their role is difficult to gauge. The first arrivals from the North were army sutlers who came to Richmond behind the Union troops. Some of the sutlers opened stores on Broad Street, which became the temporary center of retail trade. Others leased vacant lots in the Burnt District from Richmonders who did not yet have the money to rebuild their own stores. The sutlers' prices were generally uniform throughout the city and their arrival was welcome, as they were the only source for most goods in the early days of the military occupation. After a few months nearly all the sutlers left Richmond because the people did not have enough currency to buy their goods. For months a currency shortage retarded business. When the money situation began to ease with the opening of new banks that could make loans, Richmond's white inhabitants preferred when possible to deal with businessmen who had long resided in the city, rather than with the sutlers.[18]

Men from outside Richmond worked with prominent local businessmen to form new banks. Hamilton G. Fant, a Washington, D.C., supporter of President Abraham Lincoln, received a charter for the First National Bank of Richmond on 17 April 1865. His associates were another Washingtonian; a New Yorker; eight men from Alexandria, including Governor Francis H. Pierpont, leader of the Restored government of Virginia; and six Richmonders. Of the Richmond men involved in the First National Bank, three were native Virginians, one only recently had arrived in the city and was related to the New Yorker, and the last two were born in Vermont and Connecticut but had been prominent in Richmond's antebellum business circles for decades. Of the five antebellum Richmonders, three had been Unionists—two of them had been imprisoned during the war for their sympathies. The First National Bank opened on 10 May 1865 in the former United States Post Office and Customs House building. The federal government made the bank an official depository—a sign that its incorporators had friends in Washington—but Robert E. Lee was one of the first to open an account.[19]

On 29 April 1865 the National Bank of Virginia was chartered by S. T. Suit, a partner in the New York firm of Ford, Suit and Company. Suit was elected president and the bank opened on 15 May 1865. Like the First National, Suit's bank was located in the customhouse and was made a government depository. It was also an agent of Jay Cooke and Company for the sale of United States securities. A third institution, the National Exchange Bank, opened in June 1865. German-born A. Vance Brown, the president, was from Washington, D.C. His National Exchange Bank merged with the First National Bank in December 1867.[20]

Although a number of other banks were established in Richmond during Reconstruction, by July 1867 these three banks—the First National Bank, the National Bank of Virginia, and the National Exchange Bank—held 80 percent of the total bank deposits in Richmond. All three had been founded by men from outside the city, yet the outsiders apparently did not continue to play an active role, at least in public, in the management of the banks that they had helped to establish. For example, as early as January 1866 the board of directors of the First National Bank consisted largely of men who had been active in Richmond before the war. The two exceptions were Hamilton G. Fant and A. Vance Brown, both of whom resigned their banking positions in January 1869 and left Richmond to resume their careers in the North. Money from these banks helped local businessmen rebuild stores and factories. Loans to merchants enabled them to grant their customers credit. The banks performed a vital function by injecting cash into a tight economy. They loaned money to the city and state governments, bought the city's revenue bonds, and generally strengthened Richmond's financial structure.[21]

Inflated property assessments and the exorbitant rents demanded by property owners made the rebuilding of the Burnt District difficult, however, even with the help of the banks. The owners of vacant lots who were themselves unable to build, often placed unrealistically high prices on their property that deterred northern men from investing in Richmond during the summer and winter of 1865–1866. At a meeting of real estate agents and property owners in Richmond in June 1865, J. A. Martin, a land agent from Rahway, New Jersey, outlined a plan for rebuilding the Burnt District. He had already talked to Governor Pierpont, to General Edward O. C. Ord, military commandant of Richmond, and to William H. Macfarland, president of the city council and, later, head of the Planters National Bank. Martin, who had consulted with Alexander T. Stewart and other prominent businessmen before coming to Richmond, said he would go north and find men willing to supply bonds for the mortgages necessary to begin rebuilding. But Martin urged Richmond real estate owners to put fair values on their lots, and he warned that current prices were far too high. For instance, a Main Street lot that had sold for $750 before the war was being offered at $4,000. Peter W. Grubbs, of the prominent city real estate firm of Grubbs and Williams, supported Martin's statements.[22]

The other difficulties that faced Martin and the Richmonders were the threat of confiscatory legislation by the Radical Republicans in Congress, and uncertainty about President Andrew Johnson's policies. The president's pardon and amnesty proclamation of 29 May 1865 did not extend amnesty to persons owning property worth more than $20,000, and the attorney general ruled that persons who had not been pardoned, or who had not taken the loyalty oath, could not sell property, negotiate bills of exchange, execute promissory notes, or raise money by mortgaging property. Grubbs reported that potential real estate buyers always asked whether title to the property was clear, or whether it was liable to confiscation. They wanted to know if the seller had ever served in the Confederate army and if his total worth exceeded $20,000. Grubbs found no one willing to buy property from former rebel officers of the rank of brigadier general or higher.[23]

Local businessmen could not agree with Martin and other northern speculators on a plan to rebuild the Burnt District, but the process of restoration somehow got underway by the autumn of 1865. Since there was little capital in Richmond or Virginia, northern money must have financed much of the new construction, but the exact sources and amounts of this investment are unknown. Some of the funds were funneled through the city's newly established banks.[24]

High rents continued to prevail for both commercial and residential buildings. Landlords of buildings untouched by the fire felt that, with so few stores available, they could charge whatever they wished. If one tenant could not pay, another could always be found. Owners of the few new buildings also charged high rents, as they wanted quick returns on their investments. The high rental market drove some old merchants out of business.[25]

Richmond also had a shortage of housing at prices that the working class could afford. This shortage was not a result of the fire. Only two hotels had burned in the evacuation fire, the residential sections of Richmond had been largely untouched, and spare rooms were for rent in many private homes because the former occupants had fled the city or had been killed in battle. Yet with the huge influx of northern officers and tourists, rooms were at a premium, and the freedmen who came to Richmond occupied many of the cheaper rooms.[26]

In January 1866, with rents at exorbitant levels, angry tenants and worried city officials protested the high prices in a series of meetings, while property owners angrily rejected demands for lower rents and talked of class legislation. Politicians sympathized with the poor and said that they should be helped, but not by pulling down the rich. Within a month, business rents began to fall, as the supply of stores grew, and as building owners began to realize that a slackening demand for store sites foretold a diminished rate of business expansion.[27]

Feelings between landlords and tenants remained bitter. In 1866 the General Assembly passed legislation that made it harder for landlords to evict tenants, and set a higher limit on the total amount of a tenant's furnishings that were exempt from seizure. In February 1867, John Turpin, then living in Augusta, Georgia, wrote a sympathetic letter to his friend William Orville George, who was one of the largest property owners in Richmond:

> I am truly sorry to hear of the bad state of feeling . . . existing in Richmond at this time. It fills my mind with many apprehensions as to the future prosperity of Richmond . . . there is no encouragement, for those who have the means, to build such houses as are most needed; consequently the legislature which was so very liberal to the tenant, in allowing him a much larger amount of

property; free from *distraint*, than many of them possess, should have been at least sufficiently just to the *landlord* to allow him some little priviledge in dispossessing a non paying tenant, on a reasonable notice, and with out the trouble, cost, and delay now necessary, in order to obtain possession of his property. . . . You speak of leaving Sodom & Gamorrow [*sic*]—where will you find a land of Canaan? As you have no strong family ties to bind you to Richmond, I will recommend this city [i.e., Augusta] to you.

But George stayed in Richmond and died in 1869. By that time, despite the fears of his friend, a number of enterprising contractors and businessmen had found sufficient inducement to erect many fine stores and some new tenements in the Burnt District.[28]

The buildings of the new Richmond were more sturdily and safely built than those of the antebellum city. Because the danger of fires was fully apparent, the city council prohibited wooden buildings in the blocks adjacent to Capitol Square and merchants frowned upon the construction of wooden stores in the commercial district. Some did erect temporary frame structures, but most businessmen chose to build substantial edifices for their permanent stores. Many were of brick, often with ornamental lintels made of stone or of brickwork that was painted to resemble stone. Iron fronts were a popular addition to brick buildings in postwar Richmond. This architectural form had been well known in the North before the war, but it had not appeared on many business buildings in antebellum Richmond. Ornamental iron fronts were bolted to the inner frame of a store, adding beauty as well as a degree of strength to the building and allowing the installation of large windows for lighting and display. An iron front was easily maintained with paint, whereas a brick or stone building became increasingly dirty in the urban air. Proponents also claimed that iron front buildings were fireproof. Other buildings were of masonry, of stucco, or of mastic, a mixture of oil and sand noted for durability, resistance to water, and fireproof qualities that were reputed to be almost the equal of iron. Mastic got harder and more beautiful as it aged.[29]

Critics differ on the aesthetic merits of Richmond architecture of this period, but all agree that a great change occurred in the appearance of the downtown area. The buildings of the antebellum business district had been erected as residences, and when merchants or artisans converted them to business use they often continued to live above their shops. Most of the prewar buildings had been two or three stories high with steep roofs. The new structures often rose four or five stories above the street, with sheer walls and fronts, flat roofs, and the

Table 4
Retail Stores on Broad Street and Main Street, 1860–1871

	Main Street Stores		Broad Street Stores		Total City Stores	
	1860	1871	1860	1871	1860	1871
Boots and shoes	14	24	16	18	42	56
Clothing	26	15	8	5	60	24
Dressmakers	7	2	4	8	24	12
Druggists	14	14	9	13	26	41
Fancy and variety goods	22	16	21	18	70	44
Furniture dealers and cabinet makers	1	7	3	4	10	16
Hardware and cutlery	9	8	2	3	16	13
Hats, caps, and furs	9	7	3	—	14	7
Jewelry and watches	17	10	5	3	22	13
Milliners	9	3	14	8	26	11
Tailors and merchant tailors	13	15	11	6	49	32
Total	175	143	134	107	487	339

SOURCES: W. Eugene Ferslew, comp., *Second Annual Directory for the City of Richmond . . .* (Richmond, 1860); [B. W. Gillis, comp.], *Richmond City Directory . . . , 1871–2* (Richmond, 1871).

maximum available display and storage area on a lot. The effect was no longer quaint, but modern—similar to what visitors saw in northern cities or the newer towns of the West. Whatever the costs of the fire—and they were great—Richmond benefited from the evacuation blaze in that within a few years it acquired a modern business district filled with new and vastly more efficient buildings.[30]

The building boom furnished many Richmonders with jobs. It supplied a market for several new brickyards and lumberyards, and business for the foundries that had survived the war and for new metalworking shops. Unemployed blacks and whites, including many unskilled young men of prominent families, spent their daylight hours in the Burnt District. They picked bricks from the rubble, chipped mortar from them, and sold them to contractors.[51] Junkyards did a profitable business, buying metal collected from battlefields and vacant lots, and reselling the scraps to foundries, blacksmiths, and machinists. As the fields were picked clean of lead and iron and as the Burnt District began to yield fewer pieces of metal, those in search of junk turned to theft, stealing iron fences, iron stopcocks from the gas streetlamps, and even the lead pipes from the kitchen of Richmond's Roman Catholic prelate, Bishop John McGill.[31]

The junk trade became a scandal, which led to an investigation by the city council and an attempt to regulate it with stringent taxes. In a letter published in the *Dispatch* entitled "The Junk Dealers of the City of Richmond *vs.* Their Royal Highnesses, The Council of Said City," the owners of the junk firm of Corey and Lubbock protested the new tax, threatening that they would refuse to pay it and claiming that big foundries were as guilty as junkyards of buying stolen metal. It was not wise to tax out of existence a trade that supported more than two thousand people, they thought, and in a sly reference to a member of the city council, the junk dealers reported that "we have heard of Charles D. Yale, Esq., buying lead; but don't know whether he used it in his regular business or whether it was made into cartridges with the powder he made for the Confederate government." Corey and Lubbock defended junk dealers in their closing jibe, that in northern cities the junk trade "is carried on by some of the most worthy and excellent men to be found, and we know of several, each of whom could not only buy and sell, but buy and keep the City Council of the city of Richmond."[32]

Because it was difficult to build on lots covered with rubble or tottering ruins in the Burnt District, the center of trade shifted temporarily three blocks north from Main Street to Broad Street. There, uphill from the ruins of the fire, many of the United States Army sutlers opened shops, and in mid-May 1865 the *Richmond Daily Whig* reported that "stores are opening by scores, and merchants, large and small, seem to be driving a thriving trade."[33]

The unprecedented activity on Broad Street did not continue, however, for the sutlers soon left town, and Richmonders began a conscious effort to rebuild Main Street and the rest of the Burnt District so that it would be a more attractive business location than ever before. By the end of Reconstruction, Main Street had regained its reputation as the place of commercial leadership that it had been before the war (see table 4). But since the total number of stores in the downtown district in 1871 was 30 percent lower than before the war, it cannot be said that the rebuilding of Main Street brought a return of prewar prosperity, although photographs of Richmond show that even in the early postwar years Main Street was filled with people and vehicles. It resembled the main street of any other American city of comparable size, while Broad Street, only partly because of its greater width, was not as built up and appeared to be uncrowded. Several large clothing and dry goods stores

on Broad Street advertised frequently in the local papers; their advertisements indicate that these stores sold inexpensive goods to a mass
market. The sales volumes of these stores may have been higher than
some on Main Street, but clearly in 1871 Broad Street was still uptown,
not downtown.[34]

Despite the great strides made in construction on Main Street, other
parts of the Burnt District remained unredeemed for years after the
evacuation fire. In 1872 John R. Thompson, a local literary figure,
surveyed the new city with a romantic eye and wrote in *Appleton's
Journal* that "the broken walls of the warehouse (destroyed by the fire of
April, 1865, and never rebuilt) are more picturesque than would be the
smooth front of a factory that might give occupation to five hundred
operatives." A few such ghostly ruins cast long shadows across the face
of the new Richmond, reminding civic boosters of an April night that
all tried hard to forget.[35]

• 3 •

While the evacuation fire had its indirect benefits for Richmond's
Main Street business district, both the conflagration and the preceding
years of war had severely damaged the city's transportation network.
Inspired at least in part by the demands of military logistics, the Union
army did much to restore Richmond's lines of communication with the
outside world. Confederate forces were scarcely clear of the city before
army engineers had erected a temporary bridge to connect Richmond
with the town of Manchester on the south bank of the James River. The
bridge was necessary not only to allow food supplies and travelers to
reach Richmond from the south but also to ensure quick access if
military reinforcements were needed by the Union commander in
Richmond. Within two days of the occupation Union troops erected a
pontoon bridge with two lanes across the river. The army also rebuilt
Mayo's Bridge, and before the end of June a new covered span was
opened to traffic and the pontoon bridge was removed. The stone piers
of the Richmond and Danville Railroad bridge had remained standing,
and within a short time the bridge was rebuilt and opened to rail traffic.
Rebuilding the Richmond and Petersburg Railroad bridge was a more
difficult task, and it did not open until 26 May 1866. Telegraph
communication to Washington, D.C., and to the south of Richmond
was available by 19 May 1865. Two commercial and press lines
between Richmond and Washington were ready by July, with another
in preparation.[36]

However, Richmond's most vital transportation link was, unfortunately, its most neglected. In the years immediately after the war, the James River channel was not dredged, because of the absence of federal aid, limited city and state funds (although Petersburg dredged the Appomattox River and Norfolk improved its harbor with state aid in 1866), insufficient technical ability, and an apparent lack of willpower, or foresight, among Richmond's leaders. Many of the obstructions in the James River, including the wrecks of the Confederate rams destroyed in the evacuation and of other vessels sunk to prevent the Union navy from launching an upriver attack, were blown into pieces small enough to be carried to the surface and removed. The demolition of these barriers to navigation opened the river to steamers from City Point, Fort Monroe, Norfolk, and northern cities. The vessels brought needed food and supplies, as well as tourists.[37]

But the United States government did nothing to deepen the James River channel, and city resources proved inadequate to the task. The city council did not keep pace with the constant silting of the channel, nor did it remove bars of solid rock (although, given available technology, perhaps nothing could have been done about the rock even with unlimited funds). During the summer months low water compounded the city's problem: the channel was too shallow for many of the new commercial iron vessels.[38]

Weather made things worse. The Richmond Board of Trade, and its successor, the Chamber of Commerce, claimed that Richmond was a year round, warm-water port, but the James froze over several times in the five years after the war. Ice caught ships at Rocketts and in the ship locks, and trapped others on their way upriver or down. Still other vessels remained downriver at City Point (now Hopewell, at the confluence of the Appomattox and James rivers below Petersburg), unable to come upriver to Richmond. Freshets in the spring and fall damaged docks and warehouses. Some port facilities were so poorly built or maintained that they simply fell into the river. Underwater obstructions, either from the war or from subsequent accidents, endangered navigation. In August 1867, for example, the city council's committee on the improvement of the James River was trying to determine how much it would cost to remove the wreck of the steamer *West Point* from the channel, but two years later the hulk was still a barrier to navigation.[39]

The James River and Kanawha Canal, which stretched beyond the Blue Ridge Mountains to Buchanan, in Botetourt County, had been Richmond's western water route and only direct line of transportation to western Virginia. By 1865 many of the canal locks were broken, and most of the canalboats had been burned, sunk, or occupied as makeshift housing by freedmen. At the western end of the canal Union cavalry raiders had done serious damage when their horses trampled the towpath and caused breaks that lowered the water level, breaks that never were repaired.[40]

Portions of the canal did open before the end of April 1865, but passengers and freight were delayed by transshipments at the canal's unopened sections, and much cargo was damaged. Operations over the canal's entire two hundred miles did not resume until mid-1869, but by then competition from railroads was too strong, and the canal never recovered the position it had held in 1859, when it had carried more tonnage into Richmond than the total freight brought by four railroads. The canal suffered from many of the same natural forces that impeded transportation on the lower James. Frequent low water, floods, and freezes put the canal out of service for long periods. Long after the canal's obsolescence had been demonstrated, there were many Richmonders who, despite these facts, continued to dream of the fabled all-water link with the Ohio River, and it was not the last time that Richmond would cling to an outmoded form of transportation.[41]

Of the five railroads terminating in Richmond, four had resumed at least partial operation by 28 April 1865. Those to the south resumed full service more quickly than the lines leading northward. Although hindered by the damage to its bridge across the James, which was not reopened until 26 May 1866, the Richmond and Petersburg Railroad operated trains between the two cities. The Richmond and Danville carried passengers as far as Bakersville, and its service reached Danville in May 1865. By mid-February 1866 the line was extended to Greensboro, North Carolina, and by the end of March it had connections with the lower South.[42]

The tiny York River Railroad remained out of service for most of Reconstruction. Its thirty-eight miles of track to the village of West Point, at the head of the deep channel of the York River, had been completed in June 1860, but the damage caused by the repeated passage of warring corps of infantry and artillery made it necessary to rebuild the railroad almost from Richmond. Through travel by rail to West Point again became possible only in January 1869.[43]

The rebuilding of the Richmond, Fredericksburg and Potomac Railroad was also a tedious process, primarily because its many bridges had to be repaired. In June 1865 spans over the South Anna and Little rivers and Hyde Run still had to be built. Connections with Washington, D.C., by Potomac River steamers, an arrangement that meant transshipments and winter ice blockages, resumed in early 1866. The Potomac was frozen over for seven weeks after Christmas 1866, and for a month's time in January and February 1868. A direct all-rail route between Richmond and Washington, D.C., was not completed until 1872.[44]

The Virginia Central Railroad, which became the Chesapeake and Ohio Railroad Company in 1867, was rebuilt promptly. Extended to Shadwell, four miles from Charlottesville, its connections with Washington, D.C., via the Orange and Alexandria Railroad, which it joined at Gordonsville, were in service by 20 May 1865. The entire antebellum 204-mile right-of-way was rebuilt by the spring of 1866. Despite this early progress, the C. & O. did not cross the crest of the Allegheny Mountains until mid-1869, and it did not reach the Ohio River until 1873.[45]

With its meager revenues, the city could do little to hasten the rebuilding of the railroads. And when the city council sold most of its remaining railroad stock to speculators and northern rail interests after the war, it sacrificed that means to influence railroad company policies. However, the funds that the council appropriated for work on the obsolete canal might have supported rail improvements. Connections between the city's railroads remained inadequate or nonexistent. In antebellum Richmond the hotel keepers, teamsters, and others who profited from the transfer of freight and passengers from one railway's station to another had prevented the completion of permanent, efficient connections. After the war, with many horsedrawn vehicles on the city streets, Richmonders remained hostile to the prospect of sharing their streets with steam locomotives, although they were welcomed in other, larger cities than Richmond.

In 1867 the Richmond and Petersburg and R. F. & P. railroad lines were connected through a recently annexed, sparsely inhabited section of the city (in the vicinity of present-day Belvidere Street). The *Dispatch* announced that the connection made it possible to travel from Weldon, North Carolina, to Aquia Creek on the Potomac, without changing cars. The railroad men were not able to build connecting tracks through the center of the city as easily as they could on its perimeter, however. Late in 1867 the Richmond and Danville and York River railroads petitioned the city council for permission to connect the two lines. The request caused a bitter controversy, for imagination was a rare commodity in Richmond's postwar business circles. The *Dispatch*, the city's most progressive and energetic booster, argued for the connection because through rail traffic meant progress. Such connections were common in cities such as Baltimore, Wilmington, and Newark: no grass grew in their streets; no trains ran in Richmond's. The council finally allowed the lines to lay a circuitous connecting route through narrow side streets, provided the locomotives ran no faster than four miles per hour during daytime. The connection was not yet completed in the spring of 1870.[46]

Although the various turnpikes leading to Richmond had suffered from poor maintenance and heavy military use during the war, which had made parts of them impassable in wet weather to all but the hardiest farmers, no consistent plan of road improvement was undertaken in the five years following the war. By 1865 the roads were in such condition that few had mules or horses strong enough to carry loads on them. The bridges over many creeks and rivers had collapsed or were unsafe. Of the four major routes out of Richmond leading to the east and north, three—the Mechanicsville and Williamsburg turnpikes, and the Brook toll road—were in poor condition during most of Reconstruction. Only the Hermitage toll road was fairly well maintained. It is evident from this brief examination of postwar Richmond's external transportation routes that the road to the city was not an easy one, but then the Yankees already knew that.[47]

• 4 •

The most critical needs after the Confederate evacuation were food, shelter, and clothing for Richmond's impoverished black and white residents. The federal government did far more to relieve the suffering of Richmonders than did the municipal government. Union forces gave rations to freedmen, certified Unionists, and all those who would take an oath of loyalty. They set up a soup kitchen, and they distributed fuel, and in some cases, clothing. Medical care was provided for veterans of both sides in the Confederate hospitals, which were taken over by Union doctors.[48]

Among the needy were the estimated twenty thousand blacks in Richmond in April 1865, at least half of whom had come from the country. Most of these freedmen had no way to support themselves. Nor did the five thousand white women who had been employed making clothing for the Confederacy have any means of livelihood.[49]

Within a week of its arrival, the Union army established a seventy-member civilian relief commission under the supervision of an officer and two white Richmonders, divided the city into thirty districts, and appointed to the commission two or three prominent men from each district to certify the needy cases in their neighborhood. William P.

Munford, the head of the commission, belonged to an old-line Richmond family and during the war had directed the work of a relief committee under Confederate authority. He and the other commission members, who were mostly prominent white businessmen and city officials, were to distribute food provided by the army. Federal officers chose to ignore the warnings of Richmond Unionists that during the war blacks generally had been excluded from relief. From 8 to 15 April 1865 the commission's rations supported 86,555 persons. The editor of the *Whig* said that this figure probably represented the entire population of the city. By the end of April thirteen thousand rations were being given daily to persons of both sexes and races.[50]

The army's attempt to restrict access to the city, both to prevent large numbers of Confederate veterans from congregating in Richmond and to reduce the strain that white and black migrants placed on the relief effort, was a failure. In June 1865 General Henry W. Halleck estimated that there were thirty to forty thousand blacks, the same number of white civilians, and ten to fifteen thousand paroled Confederate soldiers in Richmond. On 3 May 1865 the army stiffened its policy of keeping blacks out of Richmond: it began to turn back incoming black men as well as women and children, and it attempted to force the black men who were already in the city to return to the country, where their labor was needed. This policy was administered through a stringent pass system, which proved controversial, and which caused blacks to distrust the army and the Freedmen's Bureau. The military tried to remove as many white and black migrants as could be encouraged to leave. Army wagons and ambulances carried refugees back to their rural homes, and the army also arranged for special, low railroad rates for this purpose.[51]

General Ord and General Halleck, commander of the newly created Division of the James to which the Department of Virginia was attached, worked to prevent the distribution of free rations from becoming a "permanent evil." Ord devised strict guidelines that limited the number qualified to receive rations. By June there were only eleven thousand people on the relief rolls, drawing thirty-nine thousand rations weekly. The army forced many of these people to work. Although the demand for free rations did not really decline, some proud Richmonders chose to buy eighteen-ounce loaves of government bread for 6¼ cents rather than accept federal charity.[52]

Private benevolent associations from the North supplemented the government's relief effort. In the first months of the occupation, the United States Christian Commission distributed fifteen hundred rations in a few days, supplied a total of five hundred barrels of flour to 10,721 persons, and dispensed free soup. During April and May the American Union Commission distributed eighty thousand pounds of flour and gave soup to 800 people each day. This group also sold plows, shovels, and spades at cost, and donated peas and garden seeds to those who were unable to pay for them. The policy of the head of the Union commission, C. Thurston Chase, was to refuse to help secessionists or members of leading Virginia families, and to aid the relatively small number of white Unionists in Richmond and, particularly, the German population.[53]

The Union army, through the civilian relief commission, and these private charitable organizations provided all Richmond's relief during the first two months after the occupation of the city. Not until the end of May 1865 did General Orlando Brown arrive in Richmond as the assistant commissioner of the Freedmen's Bureau for Virginia. Brown appointed Halstead S. Merrell as superintendent of the bureau's third Virginia district, which embraced Richmond, Manchester, and Henrico County. On 13 June 1865 the army surrendered to the bureau its authority over freedmen, and the next day General Alfred H. Terry replaced General Ord as commandant of Richmond. Ord had not been sympathetic to the blacks' plight. Terry was more helpful, and his cooperation with the Freedmen's Bureau agents gained him the enmity of Richmond whites.[54]

Now the government worked to eliminate racial discrimination in the relief effort. General Brown endorsed the bureau's concepts of self-help and self-reliance in dealing with freedmen, but in June 1865, when he learned that the relief commission had distributed only 942 rations among the city's estimated twenty thousand blacks but 8,498 rations among the same number of whites, he decided that if labor was scarce then whites would be forced to work for their rations as well as blacks. Brown also found that nutritionally sound rations of soup and bread (instead of the flour, beef, pork, and fish that had been given out) were cheaper to supply as well as more inconvenient and less palatable to the relief recipients. He made soup and bread the staple.[55]

For a short time after the surrender the Union army assumed most of the functions of the city government. The city council was allowed to resume its deliberations, but only under military supervision. At first, infantry details patrolled the streets and guarded private homes. Later a mounted provost guard kept order. Soldiers prevented blacks from gathering on street corners, blocking sidewalks, or entering the grassy expanse of Capitol Square, an area to which access also had been denied them as slaves. The provost guard also tried, unsuccessfully, to stop fast riding in the streets. Before the end of April, the military prohibited the sale or consumption of alcohol in public buildings, but within a week its order was modified to allow the sale of bottled beer and wine by hotel keepers and druggists. Military police enforced the law in Richmond until 20 December 1865, when General Terry finally ordered the city to resume this duty. The army would have relinquished this authority even earlier, but the city council was reluctant to pay for this expensive government responsibility.[56]

General Halleck reported that there were fewer than ten thousand Union troops stationed in Richmond in June 1865. Except for one black cavalry regiment and a black military band, black units had been kept out of Richmond as the Union army occupied it. Black soldiers were mostly stationed around the outskirts of the city. In response to complaints from the United States military authorities that the presence of black troops instilled notions of their own independence and importance in the freedmen and made them more difficult to control, General Grant ordered all black troops removed from Virginia at the end of April 1865.[57]

In contrast to the generous relief efforts of the army, the Freedmen's Bureau, and northern charities, Richmond's city officials were tight-fisted in their provisions for the poor. White conservatives criticized the activities of the northern benevolent associations and called them to turn over their charity to local churches and the Young Men's Christian Association. The city council contended that its own meager efforts on behalf of the indigent were more than ample. Council members denied aid to blacks and Unionists, and even to some whites who had supported the Confederacy. The pattern of neglect was not a new one, however, for, as the *Richmond Whig* admitted, the city "had long been criminally negligent of its poor." When the distribution of free government rations ended in mid-December 1865, the *Dispatch* called for private charity to supply the needs of three to four thousand destitute people who had been completely dependent on the United States authorities for food. Yet the paper's figure probably was a conservative one, limited to whites.[58]

As in most American cities, there was no clear distinction in postwar Richmond between the deserving and the undeserving poor. The city almshouses were run with military discipline by a Confederate veteran who had lost a limb in the war, until 1867, when a Republican replaced this conservative Democrat. At that time the almshouses had only 89 inmates (all white women except for one recently arrived black woman)

—fewer than the 426 paupers who had been supported in 1860, but close to the late-antebellum average of 125.[59]

Even with its limited funds, the council might have made life in the almshouses more pleasant. There were not enough beds. Sanitary conveniences and heating were often inadequate. Although the main poorhouse dated only from 1860, because the council failed to appropriate enough money for maintenance, both it and a new structure built in 1867 were in disrepair. Most poor people tried to avoid the almshouses' strict regimen and went there only as a last resort, during cold weather or when they were sick or hungry. Yet, despite the council's neglect, there were more paupers in the city's almshouses at the end of Reconstruction than before the war, an increase that is partly explained by the transfer of the care of blacks from the federal government to the city. In 1870 Richmond spent twenty-nine thousand dollars to support 753 native-born paupers (of whom 268 were white) and 79 foreigners.[60]

Richmond's government also made inadequate provisions for the health care of city dwellers. Four hospitals had operated in the city of 1860: the Medical College facility, Bellevue Hospital on Church Hill, one administered by a Roman Catholic order, and a slave hospital. All had been privately supported, and none had survived the war, although the Medical College did continue to function as a dispensary. Whites who could afford a doctor's care were treated at home, and they died or recovered in their own beds. There was no hospital for the general white population until 1877.[61]

Howard's Grove, a Confederate hospital northeast of the city, was taken over by the Union army and used as a smallpox hospital. In December 1865 it became a hospital for blacks, and it was the most important of the medical facilities established in Virginia by the Freedmen's Bureau. In 1866 the bureau had a ward for the insane at Howard's Grove and, nearby, a home for aged and infirm blacks. After 1868 Howard's Grove was the only hospital the bureau operated in Virginia. It continued under the bureau's administration until March 1870, when the remaining patients were transferred to the city's black almshouses. City officials, who recognized no responsibility for sick freedmen whom they believed to be migrants from rural areas, strongly objected.[62]

The Richmond city council devoted more of its attention and funds to providing the capital with water and gaslights. The thirty-year-old city waterworks west of Richmond had proved unable to supply

Richmond's wartime population and people had became accustomed to drinking muddy James River water. Although the old pumps were repaired or replaced and the reservoir enlarged when peace came, in 1870 the waterworks could not meet the demands of Richmond's fifty-one thousand people. Its pumps could not fill the reservoir when the level of the James River fell during the periodic droughts. There was no filtering system. Eastern neighborhoods such as Church Hill suffered from low water pressure because of their high elevation.[63]

There was a serious water shortage during the summer of 1866, and again in March 1867. The council argued over the means to ensure an adequate supply of water, but it was unwilling to vote any funds. In the spring of 1869, the reservoir was completely drained when a flood stopped the pumps that supplied it. With no water to put out fires, the council was forced to admit that the system had been inadequate for years. It wasted money on an expensive consultant from Brooklyn who merely advised the construction of a new and much larger reservoir on slightly higher ground to the west. The council took no action until 1874. A new reservoir was completed in 1876.[64]

The city gasworks, located in Rocketts in the eastern part of Richmond, manufactured gas for public buildings, approximately one thousand streetlamps, and for several thousand customers in private homes. Much of its equipment had worn out during the war when new parts could not be obtained. In the first months after the war, Richmonders complained of the high cost and bad smell of the gas. The odor was later improved, but the gasworks achieved only marginal profits, as the costs of coal and lime increased. It became more and more difficult to collect bills from gas users, who complained that their meters malfunctioned. Many Richmonders turned to kerosene lamps out of preference or economic necessity.[65]

The bureau of police and the fire department protected persons and property in Richmond. Before the war the city had both a day police and a night watch in each ward. These officers had worked informally, had worn no uniforms, had not been required to carry weapons, and had possessed only limited authority. A modern police force had not been thought essential. Some people, including the aged mayor, Joseph Mayo, saw no need for police after the war either. Urged on by the *Richmond Dispatch* and pressured by Union authorities, the council finally established a department in December 1865 with a police chief and 120 patrolmen, all white, who were supervised by eight sergeants. The new patrolmen were paid by the city and were equipped with revolvers, clubs, and badges. They soon were wearing uniforms like those of the New York City police, which each man had to buy for himself.[66]

In 1865 Richmond's fire department consisted of a few men and some antiquated equipment. In February 1866 the council divided the city into four fire districts, but failed to support this improvement in the department's organization with additional equipment. After a series of damaging fires during the next three years, in 1869 property owners and businessmen petitioned the council to enlarge the fire department, to prohibit the erection of wooden buildings in the business district, and to enact a stiffer building code that would make new structures more fire resistant. The businessmen also asked the city to buy another fire engine to protect the residential section on Church Hill. The economy-minded council took no action on these proposals. Following an antebellum precedent, a group of insurance agents in Richmond later purchased a new steam fire engine and gave it to the city, as they despaired of any improvement of the fire department by the council, and thought that a new engine would be a wise investment.[67]

Richmond's food supply came from farms in the surrounding counties, particularly from the fertile valley of the Chickahominy River east of the city. Negro hucksters with canvas-covered two-wheel carts carried vegetables and fruit to the First Market, or Old Market, on Seventeenth Street in Shockoe Valley and to the Second Market at Sixth and Broad streets. Seafood came predominantly from the York River, with transportation delays until the railroad was rebuilt to West Point, but fish also were caught in the James River, especially during the spring, when schools of shad, perch, sturgeon, and herring came upriver to spawn. Cattle, sheep, and other animals were herded into the city and butchered for market on the northern outskirts of Richmond or in Butchertown in Shockoe Valley.[68]

The canal and the railroads brought fuel to the city. Canalboats carried coal from the Dover Pits on the James River above Richmond, and Richmond and Danville cars carried coal from mines in Chesterfield County south of the James. All of the railroads brought cordwood into the capital.[69]

Drainage in Richmond's hilly neighborhoods was good, and rains helped to carry waste products into the river. The system of culverts was enlarged after the war to provide more adequate sewage disposal throughout the city. The city scavengers were responsible for the removal of dead animals and other refuse from the streets and for emptying traps, sinks, and privies. Inmates from the penitentiary served on the chain gang that cleaned the streets. Most Richmonders still relied on indoor or outdoor privies, but wealthy inhabitants installed flush toilets after the war.[70]

In general, during the first year after the war, municipal taxation and spending was much reduced, although new taxes were levied upon professionals, merchants, and other self-employed businessmen, according to their yearly income. The waterworks and gasworks operated under federal supervision, and the Union army provided a police force until the end of 1865. A lack of circulating currency and the general impoverishment of the city's population forced a sharp cut in the council's spending on such items as street and sewer improvements, welfare, and charity.

• 5 •

While struggling to make a living during the first five years after the war, Richmonders also endured other hardships. One of the chief problems was the breakdown of law and order, which was accompanied by a general decline in the old standards of propriety. Richmond's social ills have been found in cities of all periods, but during the 1850s Richmond newspapers had mentioned such problems far less frequently. Undoubtedly the Civil War and Reconstruction contributed to some of the urban hazards encountered by the capital's inhabitants.

Richmond experienced an unprecedented crime wave in the postwar years. A police force was a necessity, but the police who began their duties in December 1865 were hindered at night by their long white overcoats, which made them highly visible to criminals. The reports of both the military and the city police indicate that blacks and whites were arrested in numbers roughly proportionate to the size of each group in Richmond. Many white Union soldiers as well as a goodly number of policemen were also arrested.[71]

A large number of criminals, both native- and foreign-born, were in Richmond at the end of the war or arrived shortly thereafter. Navy Hill, a black neighborhood on the north side of Richmond, became known as Robber's Retreat because it was inhabited by a large gang of escaped black penitentiary inmates. They roamed the streets at night, accosting unsuspecting freedmen, demanding to see the passes that had been required under slavery, and then beating and robbing them.[72]

Typically, Richmonders blamed much of the crime on outsiders, as they had during the war. Young white toughs from Baltimore, New York, and other northern cities were responsible for the crime wave, according to the *Richmond Whig*. Noisily patronizing the brothels and saloons during the day, they robbed and burglarized at night. The Burnt District was a dangerous place to be after dark because it was filled with "garroters, thieves, and . . . footpads," who robbed or even murdered those who mistakenly stumbled into the area. Both the *Whig* and the *Dispatch* ran daily accounts of burglaries, robberies, and assaults. Nights when there were no serious crimes were so unusual that they, too, were noted by the press. The visitors who came to Richmond on behalf of President Andrew Johnson and reported that it was perfectly safe to walk the streets at night must have toured the city on one of these rare evenings. River pirates plied the James in boats taken from the demolished pontoon bridge, and they infested both banks of the river. These well-armed whites and blacks lived together and stole chickens and produce from residents of the outer districts.[73]

Children also turned to crime, often because they were orphans or because their parents were unable or unwilling to work. White and black boys were caught in many petty crimes, acting together and separately. Swarms of dirty, ragged, skinny children filled the streets, begging from pedestrians and cursing those who refused them. A gang of small boys operated successfully as pickpockets in the Second Market, where they stole from women who were intent on selecting vegetables and meat.[74]

The city's judicial machinery changed little after the war. The mayor's court tried cases of public drunkeness, petty larceny, wife beating, and other misdemeanors; the hustings court heard felony cases, which could be appealed to higher courts, including the Virginia Court of Appeals, the state's highest tribunal. The hustings court was composed of the city's aldermen, who also possessed individual authority as magistrates. The aldermen, who had served originally as an upper house of the city council, had been elected from among the city councillors during most of the antebellum period, but after the war the five, and later three, aldermen were elected by popular vote in each ward. Although Richmond's mayor had relatively weak formal powers, a mayor with a strong personality and the ability to work with the common council had influence far beyond that defined in his legal responsibilites, especially if he held the office for many years. As the chief executive officer of the city, the mayor ran Richmond on a day-to-day basis, sharing some of this responsibility with the president of the council. In addition to presiding over the police court, the mayor also was the city's representative on official and ceremonial occasions.

Life in desolate postwar Richmond was unpleasant for reasons other than crime. In the winter, the unpaved streets were quagmires. In the summer their dust was pervasive. At night, Richmonders groped their ways home from work, often tumbling into deep holes in the streets, or falling over the stumps of signposts and telegraph poles that had burned during the fire. The smell of garbage rotting in the streets and in the vacant lots that served as unofficial city dumps made many a neighborhood's air almost unbearable. The stench of privies as well as flush toilets that had not yet been connected with the city sewer system, was disgusting in the summer.[75]

The city's hilly topography was a boon to those atop the hills, but drainage created health problems in other areas. City and Chamber of Commerce officials extolled the sanitary virtues of Richmond's hills, by which they meant that much of the city's filth drained into the James River. Reporters attributed at least two large fish kills in 1865 to the gasworks, which had poured coal tar and other wastes into the river. When several people died of cholera in the fall of 1866, the city council finally was persuaded to enforce the proposals made by the board of health: homeowners with the new flush toilets were required to connect them to the sewers and pay a culvert tax, assessed according to the footage of the fronts of their lots. The council initiated a system of garbage collection in June 1867. With such poor sanitation, it is not surprising that swarms of flies plagued Richmonders in late May 1865, or that the dogs that had fled the burning city returned in great numbers and, according to the *Whig*, devoured enough food daily to feed five hundred people. The paper called upon the Union army to destroy the animals since the city council refused to take action, but the canine population continued to trouble Richmonders throughout the years of Reconstruction.[76]

Yet there were amusements to divert the careworn inhabitants of Virginia's capital. A minstrel show opened three days after the evacuation. Richard D'Orsey Ogden, the Englishman who had managed the New Richmond Theater, presented *Don Caesar de Bazan*, on Tuesday, 4 April 1865, and invited President Lincoln and high-ranking Union officers to attend. *The Carpenter of Rouen; or, The Massacre of St. Bartholomew* played on Saturday. The following Monday Ogden took the role of Macbeth. He soon left for the North, where he sought to engage a new troupe of actors for his theater.[77]

In mid-May 1865, Stone and Rosston's Circus visited Richmond to the delight of children, black and white, in the city. The various performers received an enthusiastic reception, and war-weary citizens crowded the circus tent throughout the entertainers' engagement. Mrs. Andrew H. Christian, a proper Richmond lady of a prominent family, criticized her fellow townspeople's mania for any diversion regardless of cost. "There has been a circus . . . here attracting great crowds," she wrote to her son Richard when another circus came to Richmond in March 1866, attended by "even the elite of the city to their shame be it spoken, for I have always looked upon a circus entertainment as anything but genteel or suited to the tastes of the polished or refined." She said the circus "cleared $10,000 while here, so much to the discredit (I think), of our *poor impoverished* city." And there were musical events, such as concerts and operas. Mrs. Christian also reported to her son, a student at the University of Virginia:

> Tonight an opera begins . . . it is said $15,000 has already been paid for tickets. Everybody is going and even church members think it their duty to go and thereby encourage the fine arts. Indeed it is so unfashionable not to go to the opera that people don't like to acknowledge they have so little taste as to stay away and the Ladies are buying opera cloaks and opera hats who are not able to pay their debts, but so the world goes, and every day you hear of failures, and a general despondency among all classes but still these people must be excited in one way or another."

Operas continued to be popular in Richmond. In the fall of 1868 the Richings troupe presented six on successive nights: *Martha, Bohemian Girl, Crispino, Fra Diablo, Traviata,* and *Crown Diamonds.*[78]

All entertainment in postwar Richmond was not of this cultural level. Men liked to attend the illegal prizefights held, at the earliest morning hours, at remote locations outside the city or on one or another of the islands in the river. Others watched and wagered at cockfights. The most popular recreation among younger men was baseball. The *Dispatch* heartily endorsed baseball, and games were played even during the winter months. The city had more than a dozen baseball clubs, organized by neighborhoods, or among such groups as the Germans or the Union soldiers and veterans living in the city. By 1869 the men had also taken up the craze of bicycle riding, and eager learners attended two bicycle schools. Croquet engaged the time of young women. Fishing, which was better than it had been during the war because the underwater barriers to navigation had been removed and the fish could come up the river as far as the falls, was popular among Richmonders of both sexes, although in the first weeks after the war, hungry anglers suffered from a shortage of hooks and line.[79]

In their pursuit of comfort, some males strayed beyond the old norms of public behavior. The city's editors served as social censors. In May 1865 the *Whig* called attention to the men and boys who were bathing and swimming nude in full view of the steamer landing and the pontoon bridge. It was shameful that "ladies are daily obliged to have their modesty put to the blush of these exhibitions." A month later the *Whig* reported that the culprits were bathing next to Hollywood Cemetery and that they had been joined by many soldiers. That the practice continued, despite efforts by police to suppress it, is indicated by the *Dispatch's* call for public baths like those in Boston. In Hollywood Cemetery itself, during the summers, men offended ladies by removing their coats and rolling on the grass in an effort to cool themselves. And the newspaper editors scolded the groups of young white men who loitered outside fashionable churches on Sunday, disturbing the worship services with their talk, and ogling young women as they left church. The *Whig* attacked the increase in the use of profanity in public, and the *Dispatch* noted with approval the mayor's court decision to allow a landlord to forbid the "erection of indecent signs on the public streets" by his tenants.[80]

Richmonders of both races sought the comforts of religion after the war. Attending the sermons given by ministers of different denominations and comparing their eloquence was a popular pastime among many Protestants. A number of white ministers had been strong supporters of the Confederacy and resented the imposition of federal authority, which required them to pray for the president of the United States. Three who were particularly prominent were James A. Duncan, a Methodist; Moses Drury Hoge, a Presbyterian; and Episcopalian Charles Frederick Ernest Minnegerode, a German convert who was pastor of Saint Paul's, where Lee and Davis had worshipped. Duncan and Hoge had served the Confederacy so ardently, as publisher and foreign emissary respectively, that they had temporarily fled the city with Davis and his cabinet when it had fallen to the enemy. Among the important black leaders in Richmond were several well-known ministers: Jacob James, of the Second African Baptist Church; Scott Gwathney, of the Fourth African Baptist Church; Peter Randolph, of Ebenezer Church, a conservative leader; and William Troy, of the First African Church, a Republican. John Jasper, the evangelical pastor of the Sixth Mount Zion Baptist Church, became one of the most famous men in Richmond during the 1870s because of his spirited oratory. Richard Wells, originally of the Manchester African Baptist Church, was later called to a Richmond congregation. He was a more highly educated and intellectual minister, and an enemy and rival of Jasper.[81]

Richmond's inhabitants emerged from the Civil War with painful memories of slavery and of defeat. Both blacks and whites were sometimes embittered, and sometimes gladdened, by the events of Reconstruction. Their hope was still interlaced with doubt in 1870, but their city was no longer desolate. Recalling the recent past, they had no fear for Richmond's future. Their Babylon had fallen, but perhaps it could be rebuilt.

How doth the city sit solitary, that was full of people!
How is she become as a widow!
She that was great among the nations,
and princess among the provinces,
how is she become tributary!

She weepeth sore in the night,
and her tears are on her cheeks:
among all her lovers she hath none to comfort her:
all her friends have dealt treacherously with her,
they are become her enemies.

       . . .

The ways of Zion do mourn,
because none come to the solemn feasts:
all her gates are desolate:
her priests sigh,
her virgins are afflicted, and she is in bitterness.

Her adversaries are the chief, her enemies prosper;
for the Lord hath afflicted her for the multitude of her trangres-
sions:
her children are gone into captivity before the enemy.

And from the daughter of Zion all her beauty is departed:
her princes have become like harts that find no pasture,
and they are gone without strength before the pursuer.

Lamentations 1:1–2, 4–6

4

The City Reconstructed

1865–1870

WHITE Richmonders regarded the years after the Civil War as the nadir of the city's history. Most historians of Virginia have agreed with them: It was "a continuing nightmare," a time "diversified by humiliations ever more galling," as "military government was given absolute control."[1] From the fall of Richmond in 1865 until the readmission of Virginia to the Union in 1870, in this view, the city was occupied by United States troops and was ruled by despotic Federal commanders, greedy carpetbaggers, treacherous scalawags, and illiterate blacks. Then, the vandals finally were expelled from the Confederate shrine and Richmond's whites regained control of their city. Scholarly works on Reconstruction, including recent detailed studies, have challenged this view,[2] yet it remains the popularly accepted version of the first years of Richmond's postwar history. It is a myth. The true account of Richmond after the war is far more complex.

The second prevalent misconception is that the Reconstruction period marked a sharp break in the history of Richmond. There may be Richmond whites who still contend in jest that "history ended in April 1865," but it did not. There was much continuity between the periods of war and recovery. In some ways the later years repeated events of the earlier ones; many of the incidents of Reconstruction have apparent wartime parallels. In the postwar years Richmond experienced the same process of decay as it had during the war. As an American city, Richmond was less important in 1865 than it had been in 1860, and it became even less significant by 1870.

The third prevalent misconception about Reconstruction in both Richmond and Virginia is that it ended in January 1870 when the state was readmitted to the Union. It did not. Not until mid-March did conservative whites attempt to regain control of Richmond, and their return to power was contested by the Republicans in a series of bloody riots, bitter elections, and court battles that lasted through the fall. Although whites of the Conservative party regained substantial control of Richmond by the end of 1870, the Republicans managed to carry the city and state in the reelection of President Grant in 1872, largely with the aid of black voters. Republican influence continued during the 1870s and 1880s, partially as a result of the split between liberals and traditionalists among the ranks of Conservatives and Democrats. Although Republican strength slipped after 1888, with a sharp drop in the number of black voters, Reconstruction in Richmond did not end until a new state constitution in 1902 disfranchised Virginia blacks through the poll tax.

•   1   •

The first phase of Reconstruction in Richmond ran from the occupation of the city by Union troops on 3 April 1865 to the passage of the First Reconstruction Act by Congress on 2 March 1867. This two-year period is often called presidential Reconstruction. In fact, the president's leadership in the process of Reconstruction was short-lived. On 9 May 1865 Johnson recognized Francis H. Pierpont[3] as the legitimate governor of Virginia. During the war Pierpont, a pro-Union activist in the 1861 movement to separate the western part of the state from Virginia, had headed the Restored government of Virginia at Alexandria, a shadow state government recognized by President Lincoln that controlled only a small part of northern Virginia. By his proclamations of 9 and 29 May 1865, Johnson nullified Confederate authority in Virginia, threw his support behind Governor Pierpont as his agent for reasserting federal control in the state, and directed that elections be held in the fall for congressmen and state legislators. Much of Andrew Johnson's power in the Old Dominion ended in December 1865, when the Thirty-ninth Congress refused to seat the delegations from Virginia and the other southern states. For Richmond the next fourteen months were a transitional period between the presidential and congressional phases, as President Johnson impeded federal legislation with the veto, while the Republicans in Congress tried to agree on their own plan of Reconstruction. During these years Richmond was under military rule.

Control by soldiers was not something new to Richmonders. The Confederate army had had a forceful presence in the city during the Civil War, and the conquering Union army had taken its place. Both armies tried to govern the city under a mixture of martial and civil law. Both attempted to limit access to Richmond. Both assumed police powers, and both ran large hospitals. During the war, rebel soldiers had been ordered to leave their weapons in camp when visiting the city, and Union soldiers received the same orders during Reconstruction. In both cases soldiers often disobeyed them. Fast riding through the city's streets was forbidden, but it frequently took place. Soldiers were not supposed to steal civilian food or clothing, but they did—and the more numerous Confederates had stolen more often than their Yankee successors. Both Confederate and Union commanders limited the freedom of blacks and exploited their labor. Military authorities closed saloons and gambling halls, prohibited the sale of liquor, forebade the possession of firearms by civilians, and even tried to regulate hack rates; in all these attempts the Confederate and Union commanders achieved about the same degree of success. In fact the first nine months of the Union occupation offer evidence of the leniency of military rule. Dr. Brodie S. Herndon wrote that when the Union army entered Richmond "perfect order was preserved . . . and the bearing of the officers and men was as unexceptionable as possible. There was no exultation or offensive manifestations of triumph at the time nor has there been since." Richmond was under "a very mild government," and Herndon added that the "Federal Authorities have dispensed relief to a great many sufferers."[4]

In order to receive government rations, whites who could not prove their wartime loyalty had to take an oath to support the United States Constitution and its government and to accept the end of slavery. Most Richmonders in the late spring of 1865 accepted the reality of Confederate defeat and took the oath. Lawyers, other professionals, and businessmen, some of whom had been prominent supporters and even officials of the Confederacy, pledged their loyalty. James Thomas, Jr., a wealthy tobacco manufacturer, felt that God commanded him to obey established authority. In a less pious though more pragmatic vein, he argued that "the Confederate authority has no existence and our allegiance is rightly due to the U. States—there can be no question or hesitation about this. If you want to be a citizen of the U. States with equal rights of others—then the path is plain—I should say take the oath at once . . . everybody here nearly has taken the oath."[5]

The military took other reasonable steps to insure the overt loyalty of the city's whites. General Henry W. Halleck, commander of the Division of the James, forbade display of the Confederate flag. The gray uniform could not be worn unless the insignia were covered or removed. Ministers were required to pray for the president of the United States rather than for the president of the Confederate States. When, in the absence of their bishop, Richmond's Episcopal ministers refused to comply with this order, the military closed their churches for a brief period. In May army officials required white couples to take the loyalty oath before getting married, "to prevent so far as possible the propagation of legitimate rebels."[6]

Halleck's orders caused bitterness among most white Richmonders, who considered his actions unjust. Yet blacks and Unionists came to regard Halleck and his subordinates—Generals Edward O. C. Ord, commander of the Department of Virginia attached to the Division of the James, and Marsena R. Patrick, who was provost marshal general under Ord and, briefly, military commander of Richmond—as copperheads or worse. Ord was so friendly with Confederate supporters that he lent the army's calcium lights to a group of society ladies who were staging a play for the benefit of the white Confederate poor. Patrick sided so strongly with whites that Unionists and blacks protested. Grant suggested to Halleck that he be relieved, and eventually Patrick resigned voluntarily from the army.[7]

Initially the Union army was far harsher in its treatment of freedmen than of whites, and the whites recognized this, even while they complained about military tyranny. In May and June 1865 thousands of unemployed blacks, many of whom had come to the city from rural Virginia, were rounded up by the mounted provost guard, herded to the old slave pens, and shipped off to work on plantations. The newspapers skillfully exploited incidents between blacks and white soldiers and advised freedmen that their best friends were white Southerners. For instance, the papers fully reported the guard's arrest of Bernard H. Roberts, a black who ran a restaurant, and another black for their involvement in fights with whites. Soldiers strung the two men up by their thumbs in front of the Exchange Hotel. After William Ferguson, a black hotel barber who had witnessed the fighting, persuaded two white women to testify on behalf of the two blacks, soldiers assaulted him for contradicting their version of the incident.[8]

The army's treatment of blacks improved in June when General

Alfred H. Terry, a Connecticut Republican who had commanded black troops, replaced Ord as commander of the Department of Virginia. Terry insisted that the blacks were free men and subject only to the same restrictions that applied to whites. He struck down Richmond's vagrancy laws, which were used to harass blacks. Terry, who also quarreled with editors and suppressed several Richmond newspapers for brief periods, was the exception among the generals who commanded the city and state. The others enjoyed polite and even cordial relations with the city's conservative white leaders. The generals tended to be inherently conservative and their cautious temperaments together with their friendships with white leaders did much to modify the rigors of Reconstruction.[9]

With the exception of some officers of the Freedmen's Bureau, the United States Army never treated the blacks fairly. Both officers and enlisted men sided with the civilian police and conservative whites in every election disturbance and riot until 1870. Throughout Reconstruction, fights and racial incidents continued between white soldiers and black civilians. In June 1866, for example, after one such fracas, soldiers drowned Dick Roane, a black schooner hand who had not even been involved in the original fight. At the end of January 1867 a sentry fired into a black crowd around Libby Prison and killed Thomas Winston Hall. For all contentions of the myth of harsh military rule over Richmond whites, United States soldiers killed as many black Richmonders during the first five years of Reconstruction as were killed by police and white mobs.[10]

During its occupation, the military interfered in civil government only when provoked by stubborn whites or when it was pushed to act by Republicans. For two months after 3 April there was no civil government. Joseph Mayo, Richmond's mayor since 1853, left office along with other city officials when the capital fell. The city council did not meet, and the city markets and utilities were under military supervision. Within three weeks Governor Pierpont arrived in Richmond. He named the council president, David J. Saunders, as city manager. Later he restored all the old officials to office, including Mayor Mayo.[11]

Pierpont's course disappointed both Richmond's small band of Unionists and the many blacks in the city who had expected him to confiscate Confederate property and exclude rebels from office. Instead, when he summoned the Alexandria legislature to meet for a final session in Richmond, he urged it to pass several conciliatory measures, including the repeal of a provision in the wartime Restored government state constitution that disfranchised Confederates. The governor justified his actions on the ground that a republican form of government would be impossible if all but 5 percent of the voters were denied the ballot and kept out of office. As governor of the entire state, Pierpont had to appeal to a much broader constituency if he were to reconcile white Virginians to the Union and bolster the legitimacy of his own position.[12]

Richmond whites, however, like those elsewhere in the state, interpreted Pierpont's leniency as a sign of weakness. They returned to their old ways. Vigilantes aided the army in rounding up idle blacks. Joseph Mayo abused black vagrants and petty criminals in his mayor's court, which reopened in June. He required freedmen to carry passes, as if they were still slaves, and he threatened to return them to slavery. Prominent men in Richmond's well-organized black community protested to the district military commander with little success, but they had better luck with Orlando Brown, assistant commissioner of the Freedmen's Bureau for Virginia. The blacks also appealed to the president. Less than two weeks after Mayo's first return to office, General John Turner, who had succeeded Marsena Patrick as commander of Richmond and the District of Henrico, instructed his provost guard to ignore the directions of Mayo and other city officials, and Governor Pierpont removed the mayor from office. Soldiers replaced the city police.[13]

In July Governor Pierpont took his first step to restore civil government to Richmond. Instead of returning the obstructionist Mayo to office, he declared all positions vacant, whether filled by civil or military appointment, and announced a city election for 25 July 1865. Blacks could not yet vote. Few white Unionists participated, either because they were new to the city and poorly organized, or because the hostility of their neighbors made them fearful. Established parties did not yet exist. Personality, reputation, and a Confederate war record became the most important attributes of the candidates.[14]

For blacks, and for those whites whose devotion to the Union had been strong enough to earn them ostracism, prison terms, or expulsion from the city, the July election results seemed like a return to the old order. Richmonders elected Confederate colonel Nathaniel A. Sturdivant as mayor, defeating William Taylor, a northern-born merchant who had avoided the army and declared that his own qualification for office was his status as a Unionist. Only six other Confederate veterans were elected, most of them to minor positions. Three-quarters of the successful candidates, however, were wartime or antebellum incumbents. Twelve of the fifteen councilmen and all but one of the fifteen aldermen elected fell in this category. The few newcomers to office, all old Richmond residents, included a former slave trader and a banker.[15]

General Turner was shocked and angered by the results of the election. His reaction showed considerable naiveté. Like most of the generals who commanded the city, he had seriously underestimated the depth of conservative sentiment among the city's whites. He had mistaken outward compliance for inward loyalty and had expected Richmonders to renounce their old leaders. Their refusal to do so indicated a lack of contrition for supporting the rebellion. Three days after the election, Turner issued an order prohibiting the organization of the new city council and the swearing in of other officials. He nullified the election on the pretense that a handful of Union veterans had been denied the vote because during the war they had lost their status as residents. The same rule had not been applied to Confederates. Yet, the votes of the twelve to fifteen resident Union veterans would not have changed the election results.

An impasse followed. Turner asked Saunders to continue as provisional city manager, exercising all the powers of the council. Saunders then appointed to office most of the men who had been elected in July.[16]

The conflict that ensued between the general and Richmond's unofficial government was soon resolved. Turner allowed a majority of the city council to take office so that they could appoint officials to conduct the state election in October. Under heavy pressure from federal authorities, Sturdivant declined election to the office of mayor, and another prominent Confederate declined to serve as poorhouse superintendent. Turner then allowed the rest of the city officials elected in July to assume their posts.[17]

The general's action was prompted by the city's need for a government that would act to relieve the food shortage and end the reliance on army rations. Turner also wanted the city to assume the costs of the almshouse and of a civilian police force to replace his military patrols. For two months Turner entreated the city council to assume the police powers to which it was entitled. The councilmen, reluctant to bear the expense, delayed, and not until 28 December 1865 did the city police go on duty. Turner's actions were hardly those of a military dictator: he voluntarily surrendered police authority, something that the Confederate war department never had done.[18]

Although military rule continued in Richmond for four more years, the U.S. Army thereafter rarely interfered with the conservative whites' control of the city. When Joseph Mayo was elected mayor in

April 1866 the military did not intervene. Reconstruction legislation in 1867 and 1869 increased the powers of the district commander, but Generals John M. Schofield and George Stoneman seldom used this new authority to appoint radical Republicans to the city council and to other positions when the incumbents' terms expired, or when they were removed because of wartime disloyalty to the Union. Generally the military appointees were almost as conservative as the men they replaced. Although a few so-called radical Republicans gained office, they never had a majority on the council. They never ran the city. Richmonders did not vote under the bayonet. Troops were usually held on alert at discreet distances during the elections, although a lone sentry was often stationed at each polling place. There were few violent incidents between white soldiers and white civilians. And most of the Union commanders, who already shared in varying degree the conservative political and racial views of their Confederate hosts, were influenced by the white businessmen who continued to control the city.[19]

The Freedmen's Bureau was the major obstacle to smooth relations between Richmond's commanders and city officials. The most active subordinates of Colonel Orlando Brown, assistant commissioner of the bureau for Virginia, were Captain Benjamin C. Cook and Lieutenants Paul R. Hambrick and Halstead S. Merrell. Brown's integrity was above reproach, but that of his subordinates is more doubtful. A recent study concludes that these and other men formed "a cadre of competent, sincere and dedicated men" who were "loyal to the Bureau and its objectives," and that the few who "might have been guilty of peculations . . . were more the exception than the rule." Yet the conservative press's extravagant praise for Cook suggests that he might not have defended freedmen as actively as he could: he left the bureau in 1867 and was one of the few northerners who managed to stay in Richmond and prosper. Hambrick had to resign from the army to escape a court-martial for embezzlement. Merrell took advantage of the government's offer of free rations and transportation for freedmen looking for jobs. Without his superiors' knowledge, he shipped a dozen blacks to his father's New Jersey farm, and he may have sent others to one of his father's neighbors who wrote and asked for cheap laborers.[20]

Whatever their personal defects, this trio badgered the city council to provide adequate care for impoverished freedmen in Richmond. The four-year war between the bureau and the council began in November 1865, when Brown asked the council to care for two hundred pauper freedmen "belonging to your city." The council refused, arguing that the blacks were from all parts of Virginia and must be cared for by the towns and counties from which they had come. Until the fall of 1867 the council maintained its position that none of the freedmen were the city's responsibility. When John M. Schofield required localities throughout the state to take over the care of all indigent blacks being supported by the bureau, the Richmond city council committee on the poor asserted that "no length of time can make paupers residents . . . if they have not become residents before they became paupers." Finally, under military orders, the council drew up a plan that seemed generous and comprehensive, but in the council's administration of the plan the benefits derived by the freedmen were severely limited.[21]

As late as the fall of 1868 the city still had not provided general relief for black refugees. At Hambrick's urging, Generals Stoneman and Brown tried to persuade the council to spend the money that it earlier had voted for the care of the freedmen. Council president William H. Macfarland, a prominent banker, resisted this move, remarking that evil results were "often produced by undue haste or anxiety" in the granting of public charity. The generals forced the council to agree to feed about two thousand blacks daily and care for several hundred sick freedmen at the bureau's Howard's Grove hospital.[22]

After more than three years of evasion, the council began to provide general relief in January 1869. Free medical care was dispensed at the city's segregated wards in the Medical College. The bureau's soup house reopened under city management. The council's primary reason for being reluctant to distribute food is shown by the soup-house figures for March 1869: 2,877 rations were given to whites, and 28,854 to blacks. By May the soup-house manager, a former Confederate, was able to reduce the number of daily rations by two-thirds.[23]

After September 1869 there was little friction between the military and the council. Death, resignation, and removal by the military eliminated the conservative antebellum and wartime incumbents from the council. For the next six months, all the members were military appointees who had taken the ironclad oath, which required them to swear that they had never voluntarily fought against the Union or in any way aided the Confederacy. The city's blacks received better treatment during this brief period, and the army realized that its role in Richmond would soon end.

In June 1870, after the Conservatives regained control of the city government, the committee on the poor reported that for the year ending 1 March 1870 more than sixty-one thousand dollars had been spent on relief. While this was an enormous sum by antebellum standards, it represented a continuation of the wartime relief measures adopted by the council. The only change was that the city was giving blacks aid on a broad scale. The figure included care for 417 whites and 560 blacks at the separate almshouses, free rations for 21,506 whites and 251,068 blacks, and fuel for 876 white and 1,932 black families. The reason for the increase in costs was ascribed to the discontinuance of the Freedmen's Bureau; the chairman assured the councilmen that "your committee exercise great vigilance . . . to guard against fraud and imposition."[24]

Such vigilance was more easily maintained in the coming decades, when the military and the bureau were no longer in Richmond. Although most of the Freedmen's Bureau programs had failed, and although its officers had not been entirely successful in their efforts to protect black Richmonders and refugees, they helped many survive the initial years of freedom.

• 2 •

The second phase of Reconstruction in Richmond extended from the passage of the First Reconstruction Act in March 1867 until the adjournment of Virginia's constitutional convention in April 1868. Black Richmonders were more prominent during these months than any others. They were given the vote, and they became a political force for the first time. Encouraged by the passage of the Civil Rights Act of 1866 and the Fourteenth Amendment (ratified in 1868), blacks expected equal protection under the law. This status Richmond whites were unwilling to recognize.

Several riots, and much of the political activity commonly linked to Radical Reconstruction, occurred in 1867. This second phase of Reconstruction in Richmond is the period called Negro rule, a stereotype that has no more basis in fact than the myth of military despotism. Blacks comprised a majority of the registered voters between 1867 and 1869 and an overwhelming proportion of the city's Republicans, yet none served as councilman or alderman. The military did not appoint blacks to office, and white Republicans opposed nominating them. The only tentative move toward such an appointment came in May 1868, when the military commander removed Joseph Mayo as mayor and appointed twenty-eight-year-old George Chahoon, a radical Republican from New York. Chahoon suggested appointing black policemen but received no support from the military, and the idea was hooted down by the conservative press.[25]

More Richmond blacks held office in the state and federal governments than in the city government. In the constitutional convention, 24 of the 105 delegates, or about one-third of the Republican majority, were blacks, but only 2 were from Richmond. Blacks were elected to the legislature in 1869, but none represented Richmond. Several prominent blacks from the city belonged to the customhouse gang, their Republican loyalty having been rewarded with janitorial jobs at the United States Customs House. John Oliver, a native Virginian who came to Richmond from Boston in 1865 by way of Newport News, Norfolk, and the American Missionary Association, was the only black man to serve in the city government during Reconstruction. In 1868 he became the messenger of the city council, one of the lowest positions the city had to offer, but Oliver did replace a longtime white incumbent.[26]

Richmond's black community was split by faction. Those who had been free blacks before the war did not always cooperate with those who had been urban slaves; neither had much in common with freedmen from rural areas. Young blacks scorned the seeming subservience of their elders. Conservative leaders were attacked by liberals. Personal rivalries divided prominent men. All these factors were exploited by white Republicans. Blacks generally did not unite behind their own leaders, and when they did those leaders were often betrayed by white politicians. Blacks were excluded from jury duty in the city and state courts and denied other civil rights.[27]

Of the 135 blacks identified as leaders in Richmond, many were thought too conservative by their peers.[28] The conservative black leaders shunned politics or, at most, belonged to the conservative wing of the Republican party. Their natural constituents were their fellow church members, small businessmen, and those black laborers who held regular jobs. Those leaders deferred to whites and devoted their time to family, church, and business. Some of the prominent conservatives in the black community had been free before the war; they already held positions in the city that they might jeopardize if they became too radical. Some were businessmen—such as barbers, contractors, bartenders, caterers, restaurant owners, and band leaders—who were entirely dependent upon white patronage.[29]

Negro ministers usually were conservative, unless they were from the North and had no pastorship. Of the fourteen identified, most either were conservative Republicans or avoided politics entirely. They had immense prestige in the black community, and they were easy targets for white criticism. They feared for their churches and congregations, and with good reason: when, against the advice of conservative whites and the military, blacks in April 1866 planned a celebration to commemorate the Confederate evacuation of the city, arsonists destroyed the Second African Baptist Church, one of the largest in the city.[30]

At least thirty-two of Richmond's black leaders were more militant. They were members of the radical wing of the Republican party. They advocated disfranchisement of Confederates and confiscation of their property. They demanded a share of the political spoils and did not hesitate to compete with white Republicans. Many of these men came from outside Richmond, and some were northerners. They found supporters among those freedmen who had no jobs and seemingly no futures, many of whom had come to Richmond from rural Virginia. The leaders from the country, usually only recently emancipated, were not as well educated as the urban leaders. The black radical leaders had physical courage, oratorical power, and racial pride, qualities that appealed to the black masses. They did not avoid confrontation with whites, and as the boldest men of their race, they were most often involved in violent incidents with whites. As leaders, they were the ones most likely to be shot or arrested when they fought with the police, soldiers, or white civilians. To conservative whites, all such blacks were criminals and rioters, yet many of them only defended themselves against white attack. Others were involved in protests that became riots when the police arrested them for attempting to exercise their civil rights.[31]

Lewis Lindsay, for instance, who has long been regarded as the most radical of Richmond's black leaders, was a conservative until late 1867, and white editors praised his performance at the Convention of 1867–1868. But after the conservatives threatened to lay off black workers who had voted in the election, Lindsay made an incendiary speech. He was jailed briefly for his violent language, and the newspapers attacked him. Lindsay may have lost his temper, or he may have been trying to change his conservative stance to attract more black supporters, or perhaps he felt personally threatened. Whatever the reasons for his speech, his political career declined after this incident: he went from a clerical position in the United States Senate to a janitorial job at the customhouse, which he lost to Joseph Cox in 1872.[32]

Black moderates, like Cox, are harder to identify than conservatives or liberals. To most whites, any black who took part in politics, unless he affiliated himself with the Conservative party, was a radical. The moderates had to share their constituency with both ends of the black political spectrum, and as Reconstruction progressed events caused many moderate leaders to drift toward the conservative or liberal extremes. Moderates were not as vigorous in their demands as the liberals. They asked that blacks be allowed to vote and to enjoy their civil rights, but they did not support Confederate disfranchisement or property confiscation. They were more politically active and independent than the conservatives, but they did not seek direct conflict with whites.

Joseph Cox was typical of black politicians in Richmond. He remained a moderate throughout his brief political career. Cox, unlike Lindsay, had been free before the war. He had been a bartender and a day laborer, and had owned a small store. Cox served with Lindsay on the petit jury that was to have tried Jefferson Davis for treason in 1867 and was the other black delegate from the city to the constitutional convention. Like Lindsay, he was a fine speaker, but he remained on good terms with white Richmonders. But despite his moderation, Cox retired or was forced from office soon after he took Lindsay's job.[33]

Because Richmond's most prominent blacks assumed a moderate or conservative stance, many Richmond freedmen supported the more radical white Republicans and black leaders from rural areas. Until July 1869 more blacks than whites were registered to vote in the city, yet only about half of these were politically active. In the 1867 election for constitutional convention delegates, about the same proportion of registered blacks as of registered whites actually voted, but the military authorities had had to extend the balloting for two extra days to enable Republican politicians to usher this number of black voters to the polls. Widespread apathy is evident in the fact that of the eleven or twelve thousand adult black males in Richmond, only 6,125 registered to vote in 1867. White men were also apathetic; only 5,794 of the somewhat larger number registered.[34]

Few blacks were active on ward committees, in the Union League, or as participants in demonstrations and riots. Though many whites thought otherwise, the majority of blacks were peaceful, law-abiding citizens. Most Richmond blacks appear to have been more interested in making a living and raising a family than in politics. Black parents cared more for the education of their children than they did for the Republican party and its white leaders. There were more black church members than party members.

Despite the absence of lasting political victories, Richmond's black community grew stronger during Reconstruction because the status of blacks was changing. Black life revolved around antebellum institutions, such as the churches and various fraternal and benevolent groups. After emancipation these societies could operate openly, and new groups were formed, such as the Colored Barbers Association, a Masonic and an Odd Fellows lodge, and the Virginia Home Building and Loan Association. To these organizations were added the Republican party, and its adjunct, the Union League.[35]

Unlike the freedmen who came from rural Virginia to Richmond during and after the war, blacks who had lived in the antebellum city often had some education and property, especially if they had been free. One such independent black was Albert P. Brooks, who had bought his own freedom and that of his wife and three children. He had estimated the value of his hack and livery stable business at ten thousand dollars in 1860, but most of his horses and vehicles had been confiscated by the Confederate government. At first Brooks was moderately active in Republican politics, but white harassment forced him to withdraw from public life, and after 1867 he devoted his energies to rebuilding his business. Brooks sent one of his sons to Lincoln University and the law department of Howard University; another became a prominent Richmond minister.[36]

Successful blacks like Brooks did not always get along with the well-meaning northern whites who came to Richmond to help the freedmen. Such a man was Ralza M. Manly, chaplain of the First United States Colored Cavalry, a New Englander who was appointed in 1865 by Orlando Brown to coordinate the activities of the various northern organizations and to establish a uniform system of black education. The Freedmen's Bureau had neither the funds to pay teachers nor buildings to serve as schools. The American Missionary Association, the New England Freedmen's Aid Society, and other groups sent teachers for the school year of 1865–1866. Classes were held in black churches. When Congress passed the second Freedmen's Bureau Bill over President Johnson's veto in July 1866, Manly was able to expand the bureau's role in black education. He wanted to end the increasing sectarianism in the schools that pitted denominations and societies against each other in competition for black students. Manly persuaded some of the northern organizations to withdraw their teachers. Those who remained had to work under the school system that he inaugurated in the fall of 1866.

Well-to-do black parents continued to support private, independent schools run by the blacks themselves. Manly objected to these institutions because they charged tuition (although the bureau's schools eventually had to do this also), and he regarded them as elite competitors for the children of the wealthy blacks. The schools were not under his control, and they attracted the best students, but Manly also argued, contradictorily and without evidence, that the private-school teachers were not qualified. In his opinion blacks would require years of training before they could teach.

Like many of the sincere and idealistic northern whites, Manly's views of blacks were, at best, condescending and paternalistic. He thought that none were able to care for themselves, even though many had been free before the war, and some were educated and had successful businesses. Manly and his colleagues criticized the blacks' spending habits: they felt that any money not used for food, rent, or clothing should be spent on the Freedmen's Bureau schools. Of course, Richmond blacks continued to spend money on their churches, fraternal organizations, and recreational activities, and as a result Manly quarreled with ministers and other black leaders.[37]

The hostility of white Richmonders was another obstacle to the Freedmen's Bureau schools. Whites did not like northerners teaching the blacks. The city's gentlemen whipped male teachers who taught in the black schools. Boys jeered women instructors in the streets and pelted them with rocks. White Richmonders opposed even more vigorously any proposal for the integration of the bureau's schools and the free white schools. When Florence McCarthy, pastor of the Belvidere Baptist Church and a Republican member of an impoverished but prominent family, proposed integration, he was fired by his congregation and had to leave the city. Because the Republicans did not want to endanger their plan for a free public school system, they abandoned integration. Despite black protests, Republicans on the city council and in the constitutional convention quickly gave up the idea. Richmond took over the white and black schools in 1869 when a municipal school system, firmly segregated, finally was established by the city council. Education for blacks was the only one of the Freedmen's Bureau programs that survived Reconstruction—as part of the city school system.[38]

Segregation was not limited to the schools. Jim Crow's career in Richmond began on the day that slavery ended, if not before. The city almshouses and hospitals were nearly always segregated. In 1867 blacks and whites registering to vote came through separate doors. In some wards they even voted in different buildings, and white and black ballots were counted separately throughout the city. In 1870 the General Assembly, over the protests of black members, refused to integrate the state insane asylums and authorized the Central Lunatic Asylum for blacks in Richmond. The city cemeteries continued to be segregated. In July 1866, soldiers, blacks, and Freedmen's Bureau officers forced their way into Oakwood Cemetery and buried patients from Howard's Grove in shallow graves, on high ground near the Confederate dead. Promptly, a committee of the city council called on General Terry and secured his promise that in the future all blacks would be buried in an unoccupied section of pine barrens separated from the white cemetery by a creek.[39]

Segregation extended to public accommodations. It is not quite correct to say that "Negroes were nowhere admitted to public inns and hotels," since both races continued to patronize brothels, gambling halls, and groggeries in such areas as Screamersville. Yet, blacks clearly were not welcome in the city's better establishments. When the New Richmond Theater reopened in May 1865, it announced that antebellum rules were still in effect. Even the Monumental Hotel, which a northerner bought in 1865 and made second only to the Spotswood in prestige, was firmly segregated. In January 1868, when two whites and a mulatto friend entered its bar and asked to be served, the bartender ejected them. The whites attacked him and were charged with unprovoked assault. When a Republican convention met in the city in August 1867 white delegates stayed in various hotels, but Negro delegates had to stay in black-owned boarding houses. Because local blacks and black travelers encountered discrimination of this sort, Richmond blacks built hotels of their own in 1867 and 1869.[40]

Jim Crow in transportation caused Richmond the most trouble. The Richmond Railway Company refused to extend equal treatment to blacks on its six horsedrawn streetcars. Blacks could ride on the outside platforms of the cars. This rule did not apply to black mammies attending white children. These policies led to minor violence in 1866 after the passage of the Civil Rights Act and two major riots in 1867. In May 1867 three blacks of the Mounted Negro Guard paid their fares and sat down inside one of the cars. Police arrested them, and serious violence erupted as a black crowd made several attempts to rescue the prisoners. Company officials met with General Schofield and agreed to integrate four of the six cars. Two cars were to be reserved for white ladies and children and black nurses; anyone could ride on the others. The segregated cars were marked by a white ball on the roof. The assistant commissioner of the Freedmen's Bureau approved this arrangement, but it was a sham, as newspapers accounts clearly indicate that white men were allowed to ride on the ladies' cars, while black men were not. By November 1867, having secured the right to ride inside some of the city's streetcars, few blacks apparently did so. In 1870, ten of the twelve streetcars ran with white balls on their roofs.[41]

Although fights between black civilians and white soldiers and police were frequent, actual race riots between black and white civilians were rare, as the two seem to have avoided direct confrontations. White Richmonders did not have to fight to get what they wanted, and most blacks realized that they had nothing to gain by violence. With one exception, the Municipal War of 1870, the serious violent incidents occurred during the first two years of Reconstruction, before this tacit understanding had been reached, rather than in the later period when the blacks had far more power. Early in 1866 white newspapers reported that scalawags had organized into military companies several hundred blacks who lived in and around the former hospital on Chimborazo Hill. They were said to be holding nightly drills with rifles. In March some bachelors in a wedding party claimed that blacks in the area had shot at them, while the blacks claimed that the whites had stoned a Negro church during services. Blacks on the hill set up a defensive boundary and warned whites not to enter the area; they said that this was done to keep out nonresident white troublemakers. A few nights later a white man who claimed to be a resident was shot and wounded when he refused to halt for a black sentry. Police and soldiers fought with the blacks and arrested a dozen persons. Freedmen's Bureau agents had most of them released, as some had alibis and others could not be positively identified, but by the end of March the bureau also ordered nearly one thousand blacks out of the government quarters on Chimborazo Hill. A few days after the shooting, conservative papers retracted their earlier accounts of black violence when it became clear that white men and boys from Rocketts, a working-class section at the foot of Chimborazo Hill near the river that contained many Irish residents, had begun the series of incidents. The men of Rocketts attacked the blacks on Chimborazo again just before the Fourth of July. The battle left wounded on both sides. Taliaferro Fisher, a black, was charged with killing James Doyle, a white. He was convicted on the testimony of another black, whom Freedmen's Bureau officers believed had been bribed.[42].

Two other serious riots took place in May 1867. The first occurred during the visit of firemen from Wilmington, Delaware. Richmond's firemen and their guests held a public competition. A police captain shoved a black bystander. He hit the policeman, and a white civilian struck him. Police arrested the black man but claimed that they were unable to apprehend the white man. Black rioters twice rescued the man from his police captors, and they successfully prevented the police from taking him to jail. Reporters noted that while the blacks fought with the police, white civilians could walk undisturbed through their midst. The angry mob finally was dispersed by General Schofield and a company of infantry, and six companies were stationed in the city that night. Two days later another riot broke out when a policeman tried to arrest an intoxicated black. At least one black man was wounded, and possibly killed, although other blacks carried off his body. Soldiers from Libby Prison arrested twenty blacks.[43]

The final violence of 1867 came in October when the election was held for delegates to the constitutional convention. A group of blacks chased and assaulted several black voters who allegedly voted the conservative Republican ticket. Although conservative whites and police rescued the frightened blacks, there was no violence between the races. Soldiers arrested some of the blacks who had intimidated the black voters. Individual acts of violence between blacks and the soldiers and police continued, but there were no riots either in 1868 or in 1869.[44]

Black Richmonders had struggled for freedom and dignity during the antebellum and war years. They continued to seek these goals in Richmond after the war, but it seemed to many of them that they contended not only with local whites but also with the Yankee army and Republican politicians. What had appeared to be a final victory in 1865 became a stalemate by 1870. With the failure of Reconstruction, and with better economic opportunities in nearby northern cities, the relative size of Richmond's black population began to decline. "Best Negroes gone North—best keep going," city sheriff John Wright said, "those left not fair list of capabilities of the race."[45]

• 3 •

Military Reconstruction, the third phrase, extended from the spring of 1868 until the readmission of Virginia to the Union in 1870. The national commitment to military Reconstruction had begun in March 1867 when Congress passed the First Reconstruction Act over President Johnson's veto. In April the terms of Richmond's municipal officers had expired, and General Schofield had declared all offices vacant and suspended city elections until a new state government was organized under the terms of the act. Not until April 1868 did the military remove Governor Pierpont and replace him with Henry Horatio Wells, a native of New York, who had served in the Michigan legislature and as an infantry general in the war. In May, the military supplanted the aged mayor Joseph Mayo with George Chahoon. The new mayor finally dismissed Police Chief John Poe, Jr. (to the relief of blacks whom Poe had abused), but only after Poe's drunken assault upon a Republican politician in February 1869. Colonel George T. Egbert, of Pennsylvania, a more conservative Republican than Wells or Chahoon, replaced Poe. Despite deaths, voluntary resignations, and military removals, the last two wartime incumbents on the city council were not dismissed until August 1869.[46]

White Republicans played an important part in the public life of Richmond during these years. According to legend, these men were Radical Republicans, scalawags, and carpetbaggers who swooped down upon the helpless city, misled the ignorant freedmen, abused white citizens, usurped the city government, and robbed the city treasury. In fact, few Richmond Republicans deserve to be called radical.

In the political vacuum of the first year of peace, former Whigs seized the initiative because they were more willing to adjust to political reality than the embittered Democrats and because they had more northern allies. Governor Pierpont tried to unite Unionist and Confederate Whigs in a conservative party that he hoped would also attract pragmatic Democrats, if not unreconstructed ones like Jubal Early and Henry A. Wise. His effort failed.

When the Democrats began to show signs of political revival in the spring of 1866, the Unionists and conservative Republicans renewed their efforts to form a cooperative movement to moderate the policies of the Republican party in Virginia. The radical Republicans, led by the scalawag James W. Hunnicutt, competed with the conservatives for control of the party. Increasing his organizational efforts in Richmond early in 1867, Hunnicutt held the first big Republican meeting, attended mostly by freedmen, on 8 March. Hunnicutt criticized the General Assembly for refusing to implement the provisions of the First Reconstruction Act and planned a campaign to unseat Mayor Mayo. White conservatives countered Hunnicutt's appeal to the blacks with an address on 15 April, but the radicals held a larger and more successful rally that day to commemorate the death of Lincoln. Hunnicutt and the radical blacks dominated the first Richmond convention of the Union Republican party of Virginia, which met 17–18 April 1867. A few conservative Republicans attended this gathering, and, encouraged by Republicans like Horace Greeley, Thurlow Weed, and Senator Henry Wilson, of Massachusetts, they challenged the radical wing and called for a new convention in August. The conservative Republicans sought broader white support for the party, but when more conservative

Republicans came to Richmond for the second convention, the radicals controlling the meeting refused to admit them. Here the cooperation movement, which had been aimed at attracting Democrats to the party and thereby moderating the policies of the radicals, expired. The radicals also controlled a Republican nominating convention held on 15 October 1867.[47]

The Conservative party was created as a direct result of the radical victory in the election of 18–21 October, held to decide whether to call a constitutional convention and to choose convention delegates. Moderate and conservative whites, who had not organized for the contest, were disappointed at the outcome. Contrary to the whites' expectations, most of the registered blacks voted while only slightly more than half of the registered whites cast ballots. Most black votes and nearly one-fifth of the white voters supported a convention. White Richmonders who thought that the political stakes had become too high for them to remain inactive, but who could not stomach cooperation with even the conservative Republicans, decided to form a new party. With only three days' notice, the surviving members of the old state Whig and Democratic committees of 1860 answered a call to meet in Richmond as the "Executive Committee of the Conservative Party." On 11 November 1867 this body announced that a Conservative convention would be held in Richmond in December. Former Whigs dominated the meeting of the executive committee partly as an accident of geography; all the members of the Whig party's 1860 committee had lived in Richmond, while only two members of the 1860 Democratic committees (one each from the Breckinridge and Douglas committees) had been Richmonders. The Democrats were also underrepresented on the executive committee because many of their former leaders, particularly those of the states' rights variety, were discredited figures thought to be unacceptable to the northern politicians, and because others, such as Henry A. Wise, abstained from politics on principle. The founders of the Conservative party, whether they were former Whigs or Unionist Democrats, resented the men who had supported secession.

In mid-November white Richmonders packed ward meetings to elect delegates to the Conservative party's founding convention. Former Democrats would have preferred that the new party bear their old name, and former Whigs, desiring to avoid identification with their antebellum enemies, the party of secession and war, preferred to revive their old party. But many of the former Whig leaders, such as John Tyler, were dead, and others, such as John Minor Botts, supported the

Republican party. Then, too, as many of the former Whigs had become Know-Nothings in the mid-1850s, a new party might attract more support from the important bloc of immigrant voters if it avoided the Whig label. Consequently, Democrats and Whigs reluctantly accepted the name Conservative.[48]

The Conservative party gave most Richmond whites what they previously had lacked, a party organization. A central committee of nine Richmonders with overall control of party strategy directed affairs at the state level, while subcommittees were to handle politics in the congressional districts and counties. The Conservative organization's efforts soon raised the morale of whites and led to increased voter registration. In May 1868 the Conservatives held another convention in Richmond to nominate state candidates and choose delegates to the Conservative (Democratic) National Convention. Despite these activities, more than a year passed before the Conservatives could successfully challenge Republican rule in Richmond.[49]

Their opponents were men of varied background. Among the Republican leaders, scalawags (who were born in Richmond, or in Virginia or other southern states, or had lived in the city before and during the war[50]) were several times more numerous than carpetbaggers (who had come to Richmond after the Confederate evacuation). One hundred thirty men who were scalawags have been identified. Many were former Whigs, as was the case in the other Confederate states except Texas and South Carolina, where no regular Whig organization had existed for years before the war. Several of the most prominent Richmond scalawags had also been Know-Nothings, as had many of the city's Whigs during the mid and late 1850s. One-third were natives of the city or state. One-sixth had been born in Germany. Half of them resided in Jefferson Ward, a densely populated area in the center of the city, which had some of the poorest neighborhoods and many immigrant inhabitants. Few of the scalawags had been prominent in antebellum politics or business circles, and fewer had ever held public office. They were outsiders in antebellum Richmond; even the richest and most prominent (with a few exceptions) were not accepted by the city's elite because they had made their fortunes as distillers, butchers, or ice vendors. Several of the most respected scalawags had been avowed Unionists between 1860 and 1861, had remained loyal after secession, and had been imprisoned for various periods, or exiled from the city or state. In the minds of some Conservatives, these men were more worthy citizens than some lesser scalawags who had supported the Confederacy and had even held office in the Confederate, state, or city

government. Of the seventy-seven carpetbaggers, more than half were
officers or former officers, of the Union army. One-sixth were in the
Freedmen's Bureau, and one-tenth held other federal jobs as judges,
revenue agents, or post office workers. Of the half whose places of
origin are known, seventeen were from New York.

In the Republican party there were many factions, but three main
groups: conservatives, moderates, and radicals. Most black leaders were
conservative or moderate Republicans, as were the majority of blacks in
Richmond, many of whom abstained from politics entirely. Forty-nine
of the 130 scalawags (slightly more than one-third) can be identified
with reasonable certainty as members of one of the three main groups:
36 of these 49 men were radicals, 11 were moderates, and 2 were
conservatives; but the moderates included some of the most important
leaders, and thus had disproportionate influence in city politics. The
Richmond carpetbaggers, surprisingly, were less frequently radicals.
This was especially true after the early years of Reconstruction, when
they had won control of the city's Republican party from the scalawags,
and were modifying their policies in a last desperate attempt to secure
broader white support in Richmond and the state. Thirty-three of the
77 carpetbaggers (slightly more than four-tenths) can be identified as
members of one of the three main groups: 21 were radicals, 10 were
moderates, and 2 were conservatives. The army and the Republicans in
Congress tended to support the carpetbaggers against the scalawags,
since many carpetbaggers were army officers or veterans, or Freedmen's Bureau agents, or held other federal jobs. Secure in their
positions, they had less reason than the scalawags, most of whom had
neither offices nor financial backing, to make extreme appeals to the
black voters.

Of the three main groups, the conservative Republicans are hard to
distinguish from non-Republican white Richmonders. Conservative
Republicans did not support Negro suffrage or proscriptive measures
against former rebels, but they accepted the end of slavery and condemned secession and the war. They wanted a quick end to Reconstruction, the readmission of Virginia to the Union, and a return to
antebellum stability. Usually they had Whig backgrounds. Some were
ex-Confederates. They became Republicans for a variety of reasons.
Some did so because of northern upbringing, love of the Union, and
subsequent ill treatment by Confederate authorities. Others wanted to
protect their economic interests in Richmond after the war. And many
of these men hoped to win social acceptance and political influence in
Richmond by serving as intermediaries between the conservative white

elite and the president, Congress, and the army. Many were wealthy businessmen such as Franklin Stearns, who was said to be the richest man in Virginia. The Vermont-born Stearns, who had lived in Richmond for more than thirty years and had been jailed by the Confederacy as a Unionist, ran a large distillery. He avoided public office, but worked behind the scenes to gather like-minded Republicans, former Confederates, and Democrats into the Conservative party. Stearns helped to finance the election of Gilbert C. Walker as a coalition candidate for governor in 1869.[51]

The moderate center of the Republican party originally included many prominent whites, but in the last years of Reconstruction it was torn apart as some men went over to the conservative and some to the radical faction. Moderate Republicans accepted Negro suffrage and the blacks' claim to civil rights without endorsing social equality. They did not feel that blacks were qualified to hold office. The moderate group included many more northerners than the conservative faction, and among the moderates were a number of Union officers. Two of these were General John E. Mulford and Colonel Albert Ordway, military appointees to the city council who were prominent in Richmond politics for several years. They usually sided with the conservatives against the few radical Republicans, and they helped to ease Reconstruction for former Confederates. Horace L. Kent was another Republican moderate. A native of Connecticut, he came to Richmond in 1821 and founded a large dry goods firm. A former Whig and Know-Nothing who had strongly opposed secession, Kent had thrown all his wealth behind the Confederacy when war came and had refused to pay his debts in the North. But the unreconstructed *Richmond Examiner* charged that Kent was a member of the Ferrets, a secret group of Unionists and scalawags whose aim was to ferret out any supporters of the Confederacy who might be considered for office, and by informing on these men thereby advance their standing with Republicans in Congress and their own chances of being appointed to office. Kent was appointed to the city council in 1868 and was elected president a year later, when most of the remaining old members were removed. Although he seldom was associated with the radical Republicans, in 1870 he ran on their ticket (perhaps because he was not among the conservative Republicans reappointed to the council by Governor Walker) in an unsuccessful bid for a council seat. Except for that lapse, he might well be called a conservative. When he died, in 1872, conservative papers published tributes.[52]

The radical Republicans comprised the third and best-known group of the party. They advocated Negro suffrage as early as 1866, and they claimed to support the right of blacks to hold office, although in practice many of them opposed black candidates. They demanded Confederate disfranchisement and property confiscation, free schools, fair taxation, and racial equality. They allied themselves with the Republican majority in Congress in opposition to President Johnson. Sometimes they argued with army officers and Freedmen's Bureau agents. Black radicals, such as Lewis Lindsay, often threatened to split the radical wing over such issues as school integration. Individual radicals competed bitterly for office and the support of black voters, and the radical leadership changed much more frequently than it did in the other groups within the party, or among white conservatives.

In Richmond the radicals originally were led by scalawags like James W. Hunnicutt, a Baptist minister from South Carolina who had moved to Fredericksburg before the war, where he had denounced blacks and Republicans from his pulpit and in a religious paper that he edited, the *Christian Banner*. Although Hunnicutt owned slaves, voted for secession, and was alleged to have served in the Confederate army, after secession he had gone to Alexandria where he became prominent in Pierpont's Restored government. In 1865 Hunnicutt moved to Richmond and began to publish the radical *New Nation* in 1866. He and his son advocated extreme radical measures. Because he supported Negro suffrage well before it was a generally accepted part of the Republican platform, Hunnicutt became the foremost white leader of Richmond blacks for several years. Feared by most white Republicans, Hunnicutt was rejected as a candidate to succeed Governor Pierpont in 1868, despite his strength among the black voters. He then deserted the radicals and became a moderate. For this heresy Hunnicutt was virtually expelled from the Republican party. Blacks came to regard him as a traitor, and by the summer of 1869 he had altered his stance so much that the conservative *Richmond Dispatch* endorsed him for Congress in a race against the radical Republican Charles H. Porter. He lost the election because blacks voted against him and because conservative whites could not bear to vote for him. Hunnicutt later fled Virginia.[53]

Next to Hunnicutt, the most conspicuous radical Republican was Burnham ("Born Ham") Wardwell, a native of Maine. An ice merchant in antebellum Richmond, Burnham Wardwell was alleged to have spied for General Benjamin Butler and had been forced to flee the city for his Unionist activities. After the fall of Richmond he returned, joined the Ferrets, and became a friend of the blacks and Hunnicutt's "right bower." In 1867, when Hunnicutt refused to support his candidacy for the constitutional convention, Wardwell broke with his "friend and hero." Hunnicutt was elected as a delegate, but Wardwell lost. Orlando Brown recommended that General Schofield appoint him to some office so that he would "keep still," and after Governor Wells made him superintendent of the Virginia penitentiary in April 1868, Wardwell stopped making radical speeches, became a moderate, and instituted prison reforms for the inmates, most of whom were black. Conservatives removed Wardwell from office in 1870, and he fled to New Jersey, leaving behind debts and unanswered charges of bribery and corruption within the prison.[54]

In 1868 the carpetbaggers led by Wells, Chahoon, and others began to displace the scalawags like Hunnicutt and Wardwell as leaders of Richmond's black and radical white Republicans. They rose to power because they had more influence with Congress and the army, partly because many of them were former army officers.

Most of the Republicans who served on the city council and in the municipal government were moderates and conservatives. Only a few were radicals. In 1868 the *Dispatch* described a bloc of four "extreme radicals" who tried to delay council business by boycotting meetings. Their desperate course was to hope for the lack of a quorum, but these men had little influence with other members. When one of them tried to have "Confederate" members removed from the council he was voted down twelve to three.[55]

The other Republicans proposed and instituted reforms during their terms on the council. General Mulford headed a committee on economy that reduced expenses by eliminating offices created during the war as havens from the Confederate conscription acts (including four of the six scavenger posts) and proposing an ordinance to prevent conflicts of interest among council members in the granting of city contracts. Colonel Ordway suggested the adoption of standard weights and measures in the city markets. The council granted police chief Egbert's request for a police and fire telegraph alarm system like that used in New York and other major cities. Mayor Chahoon asked the council to require saloon keepers to post their licenses. Chahoon also wanted a force of city lamplighters so that police patrols would not have to perform this arduous duty at the beginning and end of the night shift, but the economy-minded council rejected his idea. The council also refused to adopt the mayor's plans to control the growing dog population.[56]

The Republicans, who achieved a clear majority on the council in mid-1868, guarded the city's finances as carefully as the conservative

Whigs and Democrats who preceded and followed them. They refused to honor small notes issued by the council during wartime because, having been approved by the Confederacy, they were illegal tender. The city's lawyers argued the case in the United States circuit court and won a decision that supported the council's action. Republican councilmen tried to get the army and the secretary of war to return the house occupied by Jefferson Davis. Although the Confederacy had only rented it from the city, to northerners it symbolized the very seat of the rebellion. Yet, the council audaciously claimed back rent from the army, as well as reimbursement for furniture that had been removed and for damages to the mansion.[57]

For five years after the war a group of liquor merchants pressed the city to reimburse them for alcohol destroyed on the night of the Confederate evacuation. Both Conservatives and Republicans refused to pay the forty thousand dollars in claims, even after the merchants won court decisions. The council persuaded General E. R. S. Canby to stay execution of the judgments, arguing that the city could not afford to pay the damages. In March 1870 the merchants had the Henrico County sheriff seize all of Richmond's fire engines. Before a fire could threaten the city, six Republican councilmen signed personal bonds as security for the merchants' claims and recovered the fire equipment. Richmonders were grateful, but the Conservatives removed four of the six from office shortly thereafter.[58]

Between Gilbert C. Walker's election as governor in July 1869 and his appointment of a new council in March 1870, many of the Republicans on the council and elsewhere in city government resigned voluntarily. Some left the city and others stayed. Those who stepped down were often praised in the conservative press. Those who did not were quickly removed when the Conservatives came to power. In 1870 the General Assembly passed a bill of questionable legality known as the Enabling Act, but known to Republicans as the disabling act. It allowed Governor Walker not only to fill vacant offices, but also to appoint new officials in place of incumbents, both military appointees and elected officers. In Richmond, each ward sent nominations for the council to Walker. He selected the new councilmen and appointed them to serve until regular elections could be held. Only three of the Republicans, Mulford, Ordway, and William C. Dunham, were retained.[59]

The most serious violence of Reconstruction erupted when Conservative forces tried to oust the Republicans in the city government. The new Conservative council met on 16 March 1870 and elected Henry K.

Ellyson as mayor. Ellyson, a former Whig, was publisher of the *Richmond Dispatch*, former city sheriff, and one of the founders of the Conservative party. When John Poe, Jr., was returned to the office of police chief, Mayor Chahoon and his Republican supporters, black and white, refused to surrender the city government. The power struggle between the Chahoon and Ellyson forces started the Municipal War, a series of violent incidents similar to those that marked the return of conservative white rule in other southern cities. For several weeks Richmond had two municipal governments: two mayors, two court systems, two police forces, and two sets of city officials. The gasworks and waterworks superintendents sided with the Conservatives, but many of Chahoon's police remained loyal to him and refused to give up their guns and badges. The Conservatives deputized some white civilians and all the city's firemen as special police.

Although each side occupied and controlled several major city buildings, the Conservatives managed to surround Mayor Chahoon and many of his men in their headquarters at the police station above the Old Market. On 18 March 1870 the Ellyson forces cut off the Republicans' food, water, and gaslights, and let no one enter the building. The siege lasted for several days and inspired bits of verse adapted from an English music hall tune:

> Up in a balloon, boys, up in a balloon,
> All around the station house a-peeping at Chahoon.

Comedy turned to tragedy when a crowd of black Republicans tried to rescue the besieged Republican mayor and was fired upon by Mayor Ellyson's police. One black Republican was killed. General Canby sent troops into the city to prevent further violence, and Ellyson's policemen retired from the scene under protest. The black crowd perceived this as a retreat, followed the police, and stoned them. The police fired again and several blacks were wounded. A few nights later black Republicans ambushed Ellyson's police and killed a German-Catholic baker who was on duty as a special deputy. Neither the Conservative policeman who killed the black Republican, nor the man who killed the deputy, ever was identified.[60]

Traditional accounts depict Richmond in a chaotic state during the Municipal War, but for ordinary Richmonders life went on as before. George H. Clarke, a student at Richmond College who clerked in the family store on Main Street, coolly noted in his diary that "today we had a fight in front of the store. About a hundred shots were fired and the Negroes ran. Quite an exciting time." The evening of the market house

riot, young Clarke followed his usual social routine, meeting friends at
the First Baptist Church to hear a sermon. Tragic as they were, only
two deaths occurred when the Conservative "Redeemers" wrested
Richmond from Republican control. This is a marked contrast to the
much greater bloodshed in cities such as New Orleans and Memphis.[61]

The end of the Municipal War left the Conservatives with de facto
control of the city. Governor Walker charged General Canby with
exceeding his authority, and the general withdrew his troops from the
city. The Republicans did not give up the struggle. They appealed to
Judge John C. Underwood's circuit court and to Chief Justice Salmon
P. Chase. Their case was referred back to the Virginia Court of
Appeals, and Conservatives and Republicans packed the Capitol on 27
April 1870 when a decision was to be handed down. When the
courtroom gallery gave way under the weight, the second-story court
chamber collapsed into the hall of the House of Delegates below. Sixty
persons were killed and several hundred were injured. The tragedy
eased tensions and united both sides in mourning. Two days later the
court announced its decision in favor of Ellyson, and he was installed as
temporary mayor.

The campaign that followed was marked by renewed violence. In an
election held late in May 1870 to choose regular city officials, early
ward returns showed that the Republicans had won. Men carrying the
ballot box from the Jefferson Ward precinct that had recorded the
largest majority for Chahoon were attacked in broad daylight, and the
ballots were stolen. A count of the remaining ballots gave the victory to
Ellyson, who refused to serve as mayor unless he was elected honora-
bly. A second election was held, with different mayoral candidates.
Anthony M. Keiley, a Roman Catholic native of New Jersey, an editor,
and a Confederate veteran, was elected amid Republican charges of
widespread fraud. Keiley's victory ended Republican rule.[62]

The year that saw the triumph of the Conservative party came to be
known in Richmond as a year of "horrible disasters."[63] The city
residents who were gladdened by the ultimate victory of the Conservatives saw their joy turn to sorrow in October 1870. A flood did
extensive damage in the city. Then came news from Lexington of
Robert E. Lee's death. And on Christmas Day, the Spotswood Hotel,
which had played host to Presidents John Tyler and Jefferson Davis,
burned. Eight persons died in the fire.

During Reconstruction, Republicans, black and white, Yankee and
Virginian, tried to control the city. Their ideas were hardly radical
when compared to emancipation and Confederate defeat, and the

Table 5
Populations of Fifteen American Cities, 1840–1900

	1840	1850	1860	1870	1880	1890	1900
St. Louis	16,469	77,860	160,773	310,864	350,518	451,770	575,328
Baltimore	102,313	169,054	212,418	267,354	332,313	434,439	508,957
Cincinnati	46,338	115,435	161,044	216,239	255,139	296,908	325,902
New Orleans	102,193	116,375	168,675	191,418	216,090	242,039	287,104
Louisville	21,210	43,194	68,033	100,753	123,758	161,129	204,731
Memphis	. . . . . .	8,841	22,623	40,226	33,592	64,495	102,320
Atlanta	. . . . . .	2,572	9,554	21,789	37,409	65,533	89,872
Richmond	**20,153**	**27,570**	**37,910**	**51,038**	**63,600**	**81,388**	**85,050**
Nashville	6,929	10,165	16,988	25,865	43,350	76,168	80,865
Charleston	29,261	42,985	40,522	48,956	49,984	54,955	55,807
Savannah	11,214	15,312	22,292	28,235	30,709	43,189	54,244
Norfolk	10,920	14,326	14,620	19,229	21,966	34,871	46,624
Wheeling	. . . . . .	. . . . . .	14,083	20,000	30,737	34,522	38,878
Mobile	12,672	20,515	29,258	32,034	29,132	31,076	38,469
Knoxville	. . . . . .	. . . . . .	5,300	8,680	9,693	22,535	32,637

SOURCE: U.S. census data.

retention of some of their reforms after 1870 shows the merit of their innovations: Richmonders decided that they needed a modern police force and a free public school system. In other areas conservative whites, often aided by Union commanders, blocked the Republican programs: Confederates were not disfranchised, their property was not confiscated, few were even excluded from office. Despite the partial loss of power by white Richmonders, racial segregation probably was more extensive than it had been in the antebellum era. And blacks held no important offices in the city government.

Despite these facts, Reconstruction in Virginia's capital has been depicted as five years of unbroken tyranny, and for generations the city's whites have been viewed as victims of the horrors of Reconstruction. The horrors were largely of their own making. Only the Lost Cause has been more successfully merchandised. This achievement, this successful manipulation of the memory, is both a tribute to the strength of Richmond's traditions, and an indictment of a society that would not adjust to changes sweeping over the United States in the second half of the nineteenth century.

Richmond is a lovely miniature metropolis. Few northern towns have so many natural advantages, and there is nowhere a more desirable locality for persons of refined and cultivated tastes. The legislative halls and the grounds adjacent, including the residence of Governor Wells with the Washington monument, surrounded by statues of distinguished sons of this mother of commonwealths, have always been regarded as more attractive than those of any other of the State capitals. The business streets and those occupied by the wealthy inhabitants are laid out with great taste, and the private houses, like the buildings of the merchants, are handsome and substantial.

John W. Forney

5

A Miniature Metropolis

1865–1870

THE spirit of restoration obscured the fact of Richmond's decline in the first five years after the war. The Civil War had weakened Richmond, even though the city's white inhabitants rebuilt it, enlarged it, and to some extent modernized it. In some ways the attempt to regain the city's antebellum status succeeded, but the effort needed for complete recovery was too great, and perhaps beyond the city's resources. Not all Richmonders desired the kind of material progress that excited later exponents of the New South creed. The city was unable to adjust to rapid change in the decades after 1870, for its leaders were hampered by the weight of history and tradition.

• 1 •

Despite the loss of temporary wartime residents, Richmond's population was considerably larger in 1870 than in 1860. Ranked before the war as the twenty-fifth largest American city, Richmond had overtaken Charleston, South Carolina, and was twenty-fourth in 1870, with a population of 51,038. Richmond remained the second largest city in the former Confederate states, behind New Orleans, until the end of the century (see table 5).

Richmond's population changed in three important ways between 1860 and 1870. First, there was a quick expansion of the population during the war years from thirty-eight thousand in 1860 to a total that has been estimated between ninety and one hundred fifty thousand. At the end of the war, there was an equally abrupt contraction, as the

117

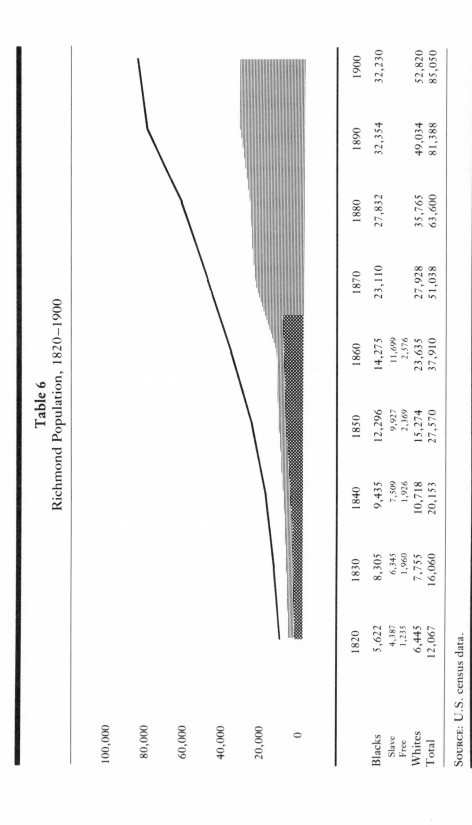

Table 6

Richmond Population, 1820–1900

	1820	1830	1840	1850	1860	1870	1880	1890	1900
Blacks	5,622	8,305	9,435	12,296	14,275	23,110	27,832	32,354	32,230
Slave	4,387	6,345	7,509	9,927	11,699				
Free	1,235	1,960	1,926	2,369	2,576				
Whites	6,445	7,755	10,718	15,274	23,635	27,928	35,765	49,034	52,820
Total	12,067	16,060	20,153	27,570	37,910	51,038	63,600	81,388	85,050

SOURCE: U.S. census data.

Table 7

Black Population in Twelve American Cities, 1870

Total Population		Black Population		Percentage	
New York	942,292	New Orleans	50,456	Charleston	53
Philadelphia	674,022	Baltimore	39,558	Savannah	46
St. Louis	310,864	Washington	35,455	**Richmond**	**45**
Baltimore	267,354	Charleston	26,173	Mobile	43
New Orleans	191,418	**Richmond**	**23,110**	Memphis	38
Washington	109,199	Philadelphia	22,147	Washington	32
Louisville	100,753	St. Louis	22,088	New Orleans	26
Richmond	**51,038**	Memphis	15,471	Louisville	15
Charleston	48,956	Louisville	14,956	Baltimore	15
Memphis	40,226	Mobile	13,919	St. Louis	7
Mobile	32,034	New York	13,072	Philadelphia	3
Savannah	28,235	Savannah	13,068	New York	1

SOURCE: U.S. census data.

Confederate forces dissolved. Secondly, most of the city's net increase in population during the 1860s came from the migration to Virginia's capital of rural blacks who knew that they could receive food, shelter, and medical care from the Freedmen's Bureau. Despite the Union army's vigorous attempt to restrict movement into Richmond and the United States government's removal of large numbers of both races to their rural homes, 45 percent of Richmond's residents in 1870 were Negroes, compared to 38 percent in 1860. The 1870 census shows that the city's population had increased by 4,293 whites and 8,835 blacks since 1860 (see tables 6 and 7).[1]

The third change in Richmond's population was the decline in the number of foreign residents. Richmond was becoming less cosmopolitan, less like the northern cities that it had faintly resembled in 1860 when more than one-fifth of the white inhabitants were foreign-born. It was becoming more insular, more like most southern cities. Despite antebellum obstacles to immigration, in 1860 Richmond's 4,956 immigrants had comprised better than 13 percent of the total population. By 1870 there were only 3,702 foreigners, only 7 percent of the total population. Some of the immigrants died during the war, while others fled to the North. Industrialists like Joseph R. Anderson, president of the Tredegar Iron Works, complained of the loss of skilled workers. Few new immigrants came to postwar Richmond to replace those who left. They were unwilling to compete with black workers, and they disliked the southern food and climate.[2]

Table 8
Foreign-born Residents of Richmond, 1860–1870

Place of Birth	1860		1870	
Germany	1,623	(33%)	1,621	(43%)
Ireland	2,244	(45%)	1,239	(33%)
England	357	(7%)	289	(8%)
Scotland	199	(4%)	146	(4%)
Canada	74	(2%)	42	(1%)
France	144	(3%)	144	(4%)
Other	315	(6%)	263	(7%)
Total	4,956	(100%)	3,744	(100%)

SOURCE: U.S., Bureau of the Census, *Eighth Census of the United States, 1860, I, Population Statistics* (Washington, D.C., 1860), xxxi; and *Ninth Census of the United States, 1870, I, Population and Social Statistics* (Washington, D.C., 1872), 388.

Apart from blacks, the largest ethnic groups in Richmond were the Germans and the Irish (see table 8). There were 1,623 Germans in Richmond in 1860 and about the same number in 1870. Most worked as manufacturers, or as traders and dealers, and many members of the German community were Roman Catholics or Jews. The number of Irish in Richmond dropped by nearly half between 1860 and 1870. The Irish did not form as many societies as the Germans, and as a group they were poorer. Almost half of the Irish worked in service occupations; 30 percent of the total Irish workers were laborers, and 6 percent were domestic servants. Despite the significant loss of Irish strength, names such as Cowardin, Keiley, and many others were prominent in postwar Richmond.[3]

The experiences of war and reconstruction seemed to unite the diverse groups of whites. Ecumenism and tolerance of religious and ethnic differences were more prevalent in the decades after the war than at any time before or since. This may seem strange. Native white Richmonders were conservative in temperament and politics, and were predominantly Protestant. Nativism had been strong in Richmond during the 1850s, when the Know-Nothings attacked Roman Catholicism and made the German and Irish immigrants of that faith objects of scorn and ridicule. Jews had been accused of profiteering during the Civil War, and anti-Semitism had appeared in newspapers as well as in private diaries.[4]

After the war, anti-Semitism apparently abated. During Reconstruction Jews were elected both to city offices and to one of

Richmond's seats in the House of Delegates. Hebrew religious holidays received extensive coverage in the newspapers. Rabbis were respected. Jews belonged to the elite Richmond Blues; they were prominent members of the business community; Jewish boys were listed on the rosters of several of the neighborhood gangs.[5]

Both German and Irish Roman Catholics, who were more numerous than Jews, still felt some hostility. Their behavior was frequently criticized, and they were alleged to be heavy drinkers. The Richmond papers published reports of Irishmen fighting in the streets, often with blacks. Yet the Roman Catholic bishop of Richmond was widely respected, and there are many references in the newspapers of the day, and in local histories and memoirs, to the friendly regard in which the parish priests and nuns were held. Catholics were not as prominent in business as Jews, although they played an important role in Richmond publishing. For instance, the *Richmond Daily Dispatch*—its circulation equal to that of the six other dailies combined—was published and edited by James A. Cowardin, an Irish Catholic, and Henry K. Ellyson, a Baptist. Some Roman Catholics achieved high political office. Anthony M. Keiley came from his native New Jersey to Richmond by way of Petersburg and the Confederate army. He was elected mayor during Reconstruction and later served for years as the city commonwealth's attorney. John M. Higgins, who came to Richmond from Petersburg in 1860, was a liquor dealer and Unionist who ran several times, without success, for a seat on the common council during the war. In 1870 he was elected from Jefferson Ward and served on the council for the next eighteen years as a conservative Democrat.[6]

Doubtless there were religious bigots and nativists among the white Protestants of postwar Richmond, but most of them neither expressed their sentiments publicly nor left a private record of such feelings. The predominant social tensions in postwar Richmond were racial. Seeking solidarity against the blacks, who constituted 45 percent of the total population, and their handful of mostly northern-born allies, members of the conservative white majority worried less than before the war about religious and ethnic differences among themselves.[7]

• 2 •

Antebellum Richmond had been characterized by many isolated neighborhoods, separated from each other and from the city in the valley by topography. Residents identified strongly with their neighborhoods and subconsciously thought of themselves as "hill cats," a term that the boy gangs used proudly and deliberately. A neighborhood usually bore the name of a topographical feature, such as a hill, or of an activity that was carried on in the area. On the hills east of Shockoe Valley, such as Libby, Church, and Union, and on those to the west, such as Council Chamber, Shockoe, and French Garden, lived the successful realtors, tradesmen, manufacturers, and shopkeepers of Richmond. Pediments and small porches with Doric columns often adorned their frame or brick houses. One of the city's largest middle-class neighborhoods was Church Hill. According to the *Dispatch* its location combined the advantages of town and country, and its inhabitants included "very many refined, intelligent, truly moral, and excellent people, affording the best society." By 1867 the neighborhood had five times as many stores as before the war, including new meat and vegetable markets that relieved Church Hill residents of the arduous journey to the First Market far below in Shockoe Valley on Seventeenth Street. Church Hill and its neighbors were physically close to the center of the city, before that center began to move west with great speed in the postwar era, but hill residents probably felt increasingly isolated from Richmond as they looked down on it from their lofty height.[8]

Richmond was beginning to change its older pattern of settlement, in which upper-class residents lived close to the center, surrounded by concentric rings of middle- and lower-class inhabitants. With the extension of a transit system to the west end, the wealthy began their move to western developments, and they were followed by the middle class. Many of the lower class stayed where they were.

Although the people in Richmond's neighborhoods attempted to return to the stable, ordered life that they had enjoyed before the war, this was not always possible. Municipal improvements repaired some of the damage and neglect that the neighborhoods had suffered, but the eastern sections began to decline in vitality. The movement of the white middle class to the west beyond Shockoe Valley hurt the eastern neighborhoods and lessened the variety of Richmond's neighborhoods, because the new ones in the west could not recreate the unique qualities of those in the east.

As sewage culverts were built and as streets were extended, the new west end became more attractive as a residential neighborhood. Gullies had to be filled and a few elevations leveled, but these were minor obstacles compared to the imposing hills and deep ravines to the east. Many Richmonders had reasons to move west. There were families on Church Hill, for example, that either could not afford to maintain their beautiful old houses or did not need the extra space after younger family members moved away. The workingman, the homemaker going to market, and the child walking to school had to get up and down the eastern hills in all kinds of weather; in the west they might live just as far from the bustle of the city, but the streetcars gave them ready access to the downtown area. Increasing numbers of Richmonders moved not to streetcar suburbs but to the city's only streetcar suburb. The extension of population into "the far west end," which continues in Richmond to this day, had already begun by 1870.[9]

The wealthiest, if not always the most distinguished, Richmonders lived west of Shockoe Creek. Of the forty-eight men and women with annual incomes higher than five thousand dollars in 1868, all but three lived in the western half of the city. Most had moved from the east during the previous decade. Twenty of the forty-eight resided in a neighborhood three blocks wide and nine blocks long, just two blocks west of Capitol Square. A smaller group of wealthy people lived north of Broad Street in an area known as Court End. Here were the homes of John Marshall and, more recently, Jefferson Davis, Alexander Stephens, and former governor Henry A. Wise. After 1870 a growing concentration of blacks in the areas north of Broad Street made the Court End less attractive to wealthy whites, who gradually moved south and west. The houses of the very rich might be three-story Federal-style townhouses, palatial Greek Revival mansions, or imposing gothic Victorian structures.[10]

Most of the laboring class, including many Irish and Germans and the majority of blacks, worked at semiskilled or unskilled jobs in Richmond's factories, warehouses, and docks. These workers crowded into the lower parts of the city along Shockoe Creek and the river, and onto the flat land that extended east to Rocketts. But there was limited room in central Richmond, and many of the laborers lived in distant suburbs such as Fulton, which was laid out in 1852 at the foot of Fulton Hill beyond Rocketts and Gillies Creek. Fulton by 1867 had fifty or sixty frame tenements of three to five rooms, with porches and tiny front yards. The inhabitants, as in many other suburbs, were mostly mechanics who had long daily walks to and from their jobs in the central city.[11]

Western suburbs included Sydney and Oregon Hill, which were populated chiefly by ironworkers and stonecutters. A valley separated Oregon Hill from Gamble's Hill, a better neighborhood to the east that encompassed the homes of the owners and superintendents of the ironworks. At the head of this valley stood the state penitentiary and execution grounds, immediately surrounded by a poor black neighbor-

Table 9
Whites, Slaves, and Free Blacks in Richmond's Wards, 1860

	Jefferson Ward		Madison Ward		Monroe Ward		Total
White	7,266	(59%)	8,788	(63%)	7,581	(66%)	23,635
Black	5,148	(41%)	5,235	(37%)	3,892	(34%)	14,275
Slave	4,170		4,686		2,843		11,699
Free	978		549		1,049		2,576
Total	12,414		14,023		11,473		37,910

SOURCE: U.S., Bureau of the Census, *Eighth Census of the United States, 1860, I, Population Statistics* (Washington, D.C., 1872), 519.

hood known as Penitentiary Bottom, where convicts on the chain gang dumped their street sweepings. Several prosperous church congregations supported missionary chapels in this area. The fact that boy gangs of the day called the general vicinity "Gully Nation" indicates that its terrain was still unfilled after the war.[12]

To the north were such suburbs as Harvietown, Scuffletown, the fairgrounds that later became Monroe Park, and the campus of Richmond College. Just beyond the city line was a black and immigrant neighborhood called Screamersville for its crime and raucous nightlife. The neighborhoods of 'Postletown and Navy Hill housed many blacks and Germans, the latter principally in the area around Saint Mary's Roman Catholic Church.[13]

Between 1866 and 1870 the number of houses in Richmond increased by 62 percent, to 8,033 dwellings. The city's annexation of parts of surrounding Henrico County accounted for much of this increase. According to the 1870 census an average of 6.35 persons lived in a house, while the average family had 5.21 members. These figures indicate that many families had a boarder or live-in servant. The average number of persons living in a dwelling increased as one approached the central wards of Richmond.[14]

Blacks and immigrants were almost evenly distributed among Richmond's three wards in 1860 and throughout the city's five wards after the 1867 annexation (see tables 9, 10, and 11). Since the wards were fairly large geographical units, however, members of the two races did not necessarily live in integrated neighborhoods after the war. There were predominantly black and white sections within each ward, but there were also some mixed neighborhoods, such as Union Hill,

Table 10
Race and Ethnicity in Richmond, 1870

	Jefferson Ward		Madison Ward		Monroe Ward		Clay Ward		Marshall Ward		City-wide Totals	
White	7,406	(55%)	6,741	(57%)	7,455	(52%)	3,469	(57%)	2,857	(54%)	27,928	(55%)
Black	6,159	(45%)	5,061	(43%)	6,839	(48%)	2,632	(43%)	2,419	(46%)	23,110	(45%)
Total	13,565		11,802		14,294		6,101		5,276		51,038	
Foreign-born	1,089	(8%)	1,042	(9%)	900	(6%)	447	(7%)	300	(6%)	3,778	(7%)
Native-born	12,476	(92%)	10,760	(91%)	13,394	(94%)	5,654	(93%)	4,976	(94%)	47,260	(93%)
Total	13,565		11,802		14,294		6,101		5,276		51,038	

SOURCE: U.S., Bureau of the Census, *Compendium of the Ninth Census of the United States 1870* (Washington, D.C., 1872), 472–473.

Table 11
Registered Voters in Richmond Wards and Precincts, 1870

	White Voters	Black Voters
Jefferson Ward total	1,996	1,795
First precinct	727	518
Second precinct	432	410
Third precinct	413	629
Fourth precinct	424	238
Madison Ward total	1,701	1,330
First precinct	241	314
Second precinct	531	408
Third precinct	494	271
Fourth precinct	435	337
Monroe Ward total	1,664	1,791
First precinct	423	293
Second precinct	335	399
Third precinct	603	505
Fourth precinct	303	594
Clay Ward total	807	653
First precinct	408	180
Second precinct	399	473
Marshall Ward total	700	651
First precinct	318	278
Second precinct	382	373
Total registered voters	6,868	6,220

SOURCE: *Richmond Daily Dispatch*, 18 May 1870.

where free blacks and white mechanics had lived before the war. Richmond voting figures that are broken down by precincts show roughly equal numbers of white and black voters living in almost every precinct of every ward in 1870. Richmond's whites occupied 62 percent of the 5,039 houses in Richmond in 1866, and owned 93 percent of them. None of the 368 houses owned by blacks had been bought since the arrival of the Freedmen's Bureau, according to the *Dispatch*. As rural freedmen came to the city and as urban blacks left the slave quarters in the yards behind the houses of their former masters, slums began to develop. Although there was still no de jure residential segregation, more and more blacks located themselves in sections where cheap housing was available. Black houses were twice as crowded as those occupied by whites.[15]

The fairly even distribution of blacks throughout the city would change radically after 1870 when many of them were gerrymandered into a single ward. If there was any benefit to the blacks in this concentration, it was in the possibility that increased racial and community consciousness might emerge. Political awareness came at a high price, however, for the concentration of black voting strength in one ward cost black Richmonders much of the political power that they had held for a brief period during Reconstruction.

•   3   •

Richmond's political subdivisions, the wards and precincts, bore little relationship to topography or neighborhoods. Until 1867 Richmond had three wards, Jefferson, Madison, and Monroe, divided by boundaries that ran perpendicular from the river or canal to the corporation line on the north. In February 1867 the Virginia General Assembly authorized the city's annexation of two and one-half square miles of surrounding Henrico County. About eight thousand people lived in the annexed area. Much of the annexed area, which included the islands in the James River, was thinly settled, but it also included heavily populated neighborhoods on Union and Chimborazo hills, as well as the part of Church Hill that lay north of Broad Street. The western suburbs, the city waterworks, and the reservoir became part of Richmond, as did the black neighborhood along Bacons Quarter. Because of the 1867 annexation, a new ward was added at each end of Richmond: Marshall on the east and Clay on the west.[16]

The 1867 annexation—the only legal and geographical expansion of the city between 1810 and 1892—more than doubled Richmond's size, from 2.4 to 4.9 square miles. Richmonders had taken fifty-seven years to occupy the land annexed early in the century. Postwar expansion would require another annexation toward the west within a generation. While the quickened pace of the city's expansion may have been a sign of urban strength, it is well to remember the three principal reasons for the 1867 annexation. The city hoped to derive more revenue from real estate and personal property taxes. City officials also hoped that people would move to these suburbs, thus reducing the demand for housing in the old wards and lowering the rents. A third motive for the annexation, which had to be approved by the Republican-controlled General Assembly, may have been the potential increase in black voters, since several annexed neighborhoods were predominantly black.[17]

Many of the inhabitants of the annexed area were trusting countryfolk unfamiliar with the ways of the city. They somewhat naively expected that since they had become city taxpayers they would share in such city services as gas and water, street improvements, sewage culverts, bridge repairs, and police and fire protection. Once the city had taken the land, however, its officials resisted demands for improvements in the annexed areas, just as they had neglected to improve many old neighborhoods. Municipal services continued to be hampered after the war by the same conservative and inept leadership that restricted badly needed social services.[18]

The residents of Rocketts, a part of Richmond since 1780, had experienced such neglect. They complained that although they paid city taxes, their streets and bridges were in disrepair and that city culverts inadequately drained their low-lying neighborhood and fostered cholera in the summers. A local poet lauded,

> Ye mariners of Rocketts!
> That guard our ancient river,
> Whose flag has braved for many a year,
> The ague and the fever.[19]

John Newton Van Lew, a hardware merchant and the brother of the famous Union spy Elizabeth Van Lew, did his best as a new member of the common council to represent his Marshall Ward constituents. His efforts and those of the other councilmen from the new wards were easily defeated by the members from the old wards, who were in the majority. During the winters after a hard rain, Broad Street, as yet unpaved, was impassable from the bottom of Shockoe Valley to the top of Church Hill. In November 1868, Van Lew asked that $1,200 be appropriated to be used for street improvements at the discretion of his ward's street committee, provided that the ward's residents paid an equal amount in taxes. Van Lew's motion was tabled until the council could compare receipts and expenditures in each ward. On 13 January 1869 the council finally authorized the road repairs, still with the provision that no work be done until Marshall Ward had paid an equal amount of tax to the city.[20]

Conditions in other suburbs, new or old, were no better. In October 1868 Oregon Hill residents complained that their houses were accessible by wagon only from the west through Sydney. Early in 1869, two years after the annexation, Sydney's people met to protest the poor street conditions and the lack of improvements in their neighborhood. An anonymous humorist expressed their feelings in a letter to the editor of the *Richmond Dispatch*, in which he described Sydney as "a considdible town lately atatched to Richmond, altho' the Sidneyyuns didn't

Table 12
Richmond Work Force in 1870 Census Categories

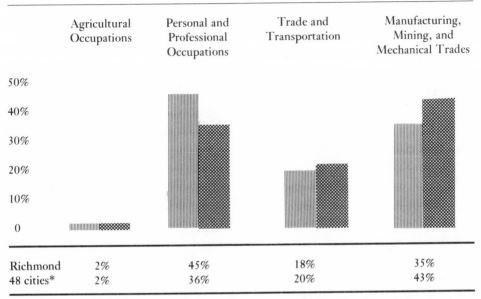

	Agricultural Occupations	Personal and Professional Occupations	Trade and Transportation	Manufacturing, Mining, and Mechanical Trades
Richmond	2%	45%	18%	35%
48 cities*	2%	36%	20%	43%

*This statistic represents the average percentage of the work force in 48 of the 50 largest American cities engaged in each occupational category. Springfield, Massachusetts, the 50th largest city in American in 1870, was not listed in the census occupational table.

SOURCE: U.S., Bureau of the Census, *Compendium of the Ninth Census of the United States, 1870* (Washington, D.C., 1872), 618–619.

want it to be attached." The writer complained that "there is no gas works out here, . . . there aint no hydrunts . . . an then a man can't walk here on a muddy day except he has stiltz." He asked the *Dispatch* to publicize his complaints, and promised to "rite again, which will bee upon more powerful abeuses than these." The "Sidneyyuns" sent a committee to ask the city council for the improvement and extension of streets, for the installation of fire plugs, and for the draining of some ponds, the erection of a market house, and doubled police protection.[21]

The representatives of the old wards of the city who served on Richmond's common council were no more inclined to allocate a fair portion of the city's resources for improvements in the heavily taxed annexed area than they were ready to provide for the relief of the poor and the sick among the city's population. In their defense, it is true that there was not as much wealth to tax in the new wards as in the old, for there were fewer people; but the annexed area needed municipal improvements even more than the older part of Richmond.

• 4 •

Of the city's total 1870 population, 36 percent, or 18,545 workers, formed the regular labor force of Richmond. Only 311 Richmonders, less than 2 percent of the regular labor force, farmed. The report of their product fills only two pages in the 1870 agricultural schedule, although the 1867 annexation brought land that was still farm acreage into the city.[22]

A very large proportion of the Richmond work force—far higher than the average for the nation's forty-eight other large cities—engaged in professional and personal services. But Richmond's pattern may have been rather typical of southern cities, seven of which (including Washington, D.C.) also had 40 percent or more of their workers in service occupations (see table 12).

Richmond was only a little below the national average in the percentage of its work force engaged in trade and transportation, a category that seems to reveal a crucial factor in urban growth during the last half of the nineteenth century. Eight of the ten largest cities had 25 percent or more of their workers in this category; Richmond had 18 percent. Atlanta and Memphis, two of the fastest-growing southern cities, both of which passed the Virginia capital in total population between 1890 and 1900, had more workers in trade and transportation than in manufacturing and mechanical industries.[23]

Richmond shared some characteristics with, but did not closely resemble, the nine other American cities of about the same size: Richmond was a state capital—like Providence, Rhode Island, New Haven, Connecticut, and Indianapolis, Indiana—and it was a port of entry—like Charleston, South Carolina, Providence, and New Haven. But Richmond had 11 percent more workers engaged in service occupations than the average of the other nine cities—a higher percentage than any single city except Charleston with 53 percent—and fewer workers in trade and transport than all but two of the cities of its size. The number of Richmond workers employed in manufacturing, mining, and mechanical industries was a full 8 percent below the national average for larger cities, and 10 percent below the average for other cities of its size, but Richmond's 35 percent in this category exceeded the percentages of other southern cities such as Charleston, Memphis, New Orleans, Washington, Savannah, and Mobile (see table 13).[24]

Richmond had twice as many manufacturers in 1870 (531) as in 1860 (262), but the total value of their manufactured product had fallen by $1,786,307. This 15 percent drop reflected the fact that the city's

Table 13
Work Force of Forty-nine Largest American Cities, 1870

Population Size		Personal and Professional Occupations		Trade and Transportation		Manufacturing, Mining, and Mechanical Trades	
New York	1st	Detroit	68%	Memphis	30%	Lawrence, Mass.	78%
Philadelphia	2d	Washington	63	Portland, Me.	30	Fall River	74
Brooklyn	3d	Savannah	62	Brooklyn	28	Lowell	74
St. Louis	4th	Mobile	58	Cleveland	27	Lynn	69
Chicago	5th	Charleston	53	Jersey City	27	Paterson	64
Baltimore	6th	New Orleans	47	New Orleans	27	Newark	61
Boston	7th			Chicago	26	Scranton	55
Cincinnati	8th	**Richmond**	**45**	Indianapolis	26	Worcester	55
New Orleans	9th			San Francisco	26	Dayton	51
San Francisco	10th	Toledo	44	St. Louis	26	Reading	50
Buffalo	11th	Kansas City, Mo.	44	Baltimore	25	Utica	50
Washington	12th	Louisville	43	Boston	25	Philadelphia	49
Newark	13th	Memphis	43	New York	25	Rochester	49
Louisville	14th	San Francisco	41	Mobile	24	Cambridge	48
Cleveland	15th	Buffalo	40	Milwaukee	23	New Haven	48
Pittsburgh	16th	Allegheny, Pa.	38	Rochester	23	Allegheny, Pa.	47
Jersey City	17th	St. Louis	38	Cincinnati	22	Providence	47
Detroit	18th	Baltimore	37	Kansas City, Mo.	22	Cleveland	46
Milwaukee	19th	Chicago	37	Toledo	22	Syracuse	46
Albany	20th	Pittsburgh	37	Columbus, Ohio	21	Troy	46
Providence	21st	Wilmington, Del.	37	Louisville	21	Albany	44
Rochester	22d	Boston	36	New Haven	21	Cincinnati	44
Allegheny, Pa.	23d	Hartford	36	Providence	21	Columbus, Ohio	44
		Indianapolis	36	Syracuse	21	Hartford	42
Richmond	**24th**	Jersey City	36	Albany	20	Brooklyn	41
		Milwaukee	36	Dayton	20	New York	41
New Haven	25th	Reading	36	Hartford	20	Pittsburgh	41
Charleston	26th	Albany	35	Philadelphia	20	Wilmington, Del.	41
Indianapolis	27th	Columbus, Ohio	34	Pittsburgh	20	Buffalo	40
Troy	28th	Troy	34	Cambridge	19	Milwaukee	40
Syracuse	29th	Cincinnati	33	Charleston	19	Boston	38
Worcester	30th	New York	33	Troy	19	Baltimore	37
Lowell	31st	Cambridge	32	Utica	19	Indianapolis	37
Memphis	32d	Portland, Me.	32	Buffalo	18	Portland, Me.	37
Cambridge	33d	Providence	32			Chicago	36
Hartford	34th	Brooklyn	31	**Richmond**	**18**	Jersey City	36
Scranton	35th	Syracuse	31			Louisville	35
Reading	36th	New Haven	30	Savannah	17		
Paterson	37th	Scranton	30	Newark	16	**Richmond**	**35**
Kansas City, Mo.	38th	Utica	30	Allegheny, Pa.	15		
Mobile	39th	Philadelphia	29	Reading	14	St. Louis	35
Toledo	40th	Dayton	28	Scranton	14	Toledo	33
Portland, Me.	41st	Worcester	28	Worcester	14	Kansas City, Mo.	32
Columbus, Ohio	42d	Rochester	27	Lynn	13	San Francisco	32
Wilmington, Del.	43d	Cleveland	26	Paterson	13	Charleston	26
Dayton	44th	Newark	22	Washington	13	Memphis	24
Lawrence, Mass.	45th	Paterson	22	Detroit	12	New Orleans	24
Utica	46th	Lynn	17	Wilmington, Del.	12	Washington	23
Savannah	47th	Lowell	16	Fall River	10	Savannah	20
Lynn	48th	Fall River	13	Lowell	9	Mobile	17
Fall River	49th	Lawrence, Mass.	13	Lawrence, Mass.	8	Detroit	15

SOURCE: U.S., Bureau of the Census, *Compendium of the Ninth Census of the United States, 1870* (Washington, D.C., 1872), 618-619.

Table 14
Richmond's Capital Investment and Industrial Product, 1860–1870

	1860	1870	Change In Amount Of Capital Invested (Real and Personal)	Change In Value Of Product
Per capita	$ 108.15	$ 80.15	−26%	−37%
Per worker	600.00	587.22	−2%	−16%
Per manufacturer	15,648.02	7,703.49	−51%	−58%

	Aggregate Total 1860	Aggregate Total 1870	Change
Total capital	$ 4,099,780	$ 4,090,555	−0.2%
Total product value	12,038,345	10,252,038	−15%
Total population	37,910	51,038	35%
Total workers	6,833	6,966	2%
Total manufacturers	262	531	103%

SOURCE: U.S., Bureau of the Census, Eighth and Ninth Census, 1860 and 1870, Industrial Schedule MSS, Archives Branch, Virginia State Library, Richmond.

factories and shops were smaller than they had been before the war. In 1870 the average number of workers per manufacturing establishment was half what it had been in 1860. The number of workers (as opposed to manufacturers) employed in manufacturing increased by only 2 percent, from 6,833 to 6,966, while Richmond's population increased by 35 percent during the decade.[25]

These facts show the impact that the Civil War had on Richmond. Although the total amount of capital investment, real and personal, in Richmond business dropped by less than 1 percent between 1860 and 1870 (see table 14), that figure is deceptive. It does not take inflation into account, and it obscures the fact that much of the 1870 investment capital had been used to replace stores and factories destroyed during the war.

The shoemaking industry illustrates why the number of postwar Richmond manufacturers increased and why their productivity declined. In 1860, fifteen boot and shoe manufacturers employing 149 workers had a combined capital of $49,150 and a total product valued at $166,100. During that year the average manufacturer, with a work force of 10 and capital investment of $3,277, produced boots and shoes valued at $11,077. Ten years later the same number of manufacturers employed a total of only 27 workers, fewer than 2 per firm. The combined capital of the postwar companies was $15,720 (an average of $1,048 for each firm) and their total product was valued at $37,118 (an average of $2,475 for each manufacturer).

Part of the decline in Richmond shoe manufacturing was attributable to the emergence of smaller-scale shoemakers. Only 5 were listed in 1860, with only 10 workers, $590 in total capital, and a product valued at $7,250. But by 1870 the number of smaller-scale shoemakers had increased to 121. With 128 workers and a total capital of $13,365 ($110 for each) these small concerns produced goods valued at $105,425 ($871 for each shoemaker). Many of these men had probably worked for one of the large manufacturers in 1860 and since gone into business for themselves. Some were undoubtedly veterans, perhaps leg amputees. A man who had lost a leg could work at a cobbler's bench all day; he needed little money to buy a supply of leather and a few tools, and not much skill to make crude shoes, particularly if he had learned to mend his own in the army. Similar developments in other industries, although less striking, may help to explain why the number of manufacturers in 1870 had doubled while the average size of the work force in each shop was half what it had been in 1860.[26]

The labor force in Richmond changed significantly after the war. Social restrictions on female labor had relaxed as women worked in war industries and government offices. Postwar manufacturers found that women and children would work for less than adult males. By 1870 the number of working women had trebled, from 158 in 1860 to 687. No white child laborers were listed on the census returns for 1860, but Richmond manufacturers employed 862 white children in 1870. (Slave children, listed separately on the manuscript slave census, had worked in industry along with slave women, so the increase in the total number of female and child laborers is less stark than suggested from the industrial schedule of the 1870 census alone.) By 1870, women and children already had begun to work in the tobacco factories in sizeable numbers. Photographs and pictures of the workrooms show that often these women were white; they may have been Confederate widows, or married women who had to work to support their impoverished families.[27]

As the 1860 and 1870 censuses do not show what porportions of the work force were black, however, it is hard to tell whether the percentage of black workers increased. Other evidence, including travelers' observations and comments in the Richmond press, is contradictory. It was often reported, for example, that most of the men working in the

tobacco factories after the war were black, but this had been true before
the war. Newspaper articles described the laying off of black workers in
the tobacco industry during seasonal lulls in the business, but the
significance of this is uncertain, for slaves were either owned by the
tobacco manufacturers or hired from their owners for a year at a time,
and could not have been laid off. Emancipation worked both ways,
however, for there were also postwar complaints that a lack of available
workers during busy periods was causing the decline in the tobacco
industry. One traveler who visited a postwar factory noted that all the
men rolling and pressing tobacco were blacks, but that they did not
earn as much working all week as they had earned for overtime while
slaves. Black men as a rule would work for lower pay than white men,
but some of Richmond's blacks were exceptions to the rule: often
among skilled workers in the tobacco, iron, and milling industries there
was no discrepancy in the wages paid. Wages for a day laborer were
$.75 with board, $1.00 without. A carpenter worked for $2.25 a day
without board, and a female domestic could be hired for $2.50 a week if
she boarded out. The average cost of a week's board for a laborer was
$3.50.[28]

Most of Richmond's manufacturing, and all of the heavy industry,
were conducted either in Shockoe Valley or along the river and canal.
Most of the tobacco factories and warehouses stood east of Shockoe
Creek, close to the docks and railroad depots. The flour mills, which
needed access to water power, were located in the center of Richmond
along the river and on the canal basin. The large ironworks and rolling
mills generally were situated in the western part of Richmond along the
river, although the Old Dominion Iron and Nail Works, one of the
largest, occupied Belle Isle in the James River. Smaller manufacturers—
blacksmiths and wheelwrights, carpenters, shoemakers, tailors, milli-
ners, and dressmakers—could be found throughout the city. Certain
objectionable industries were located on the outskirts of Richmond
because they generated noxious odors or waste or were potential fire
hazards. Lewis Gimmi's tannery and Joseph Schook's soap and candle
factory stood on the northern edge of Richmond. Breweries were
nearby, or in Rocketts along the river near the city gasworks. Following
a series of fires, lumberyards were banned from the downtown area
after the war.[29]

• 5 •

Three great industries dominated Richmond's economy throughout
the nineteenth century: tobacco manufacturing, wheat and corn milling, and metalworking. In the colonial and antebellum periods these

major industries had moved from what economist Wilbur R. Thompson describes as the stage of export specialization—"in which the local economy is the lengthened shadow of a single dominant industry or even a single firm"—to the more advanced stage of the export complex—in which local production expands to other products, extends to include more of the various aspects of production, and benefits from the appearance of local suppliers and of local consumers for its intermediate products. Although in 1860 and in 1870 alike the three major industries were responsible for about 85 percent of the city's total manufactured product, the war weakened them and crippled Richmond's movement toward the next level of development. Richmond never fully reached the stage that Thompson calls the "stage of economic maturation . . . in which the principal expansion of local activity is in the direction of replacing imports with new 'own use' production; the local economy fills out in range and quality of both its business and consumer services."[30]

Richmonders bought more and more consumer goods from the North, while the city's major industries became increasingly dependent on raw materials from sources outside Virginia. Defects that before the war had been nonexistent in tobacco manufacturing, and that had seemed to be minor or only potential problems in the iron and milling industries, became critical weaknesses in all three. Richmond's postwar industrialists were unable, or unwilling, to deal with these problems, and were thus increasingly unable to compete with the nation's new centers of industry.

Although Richmond had ranked only twenty-fifth in population among American cities in 1860, its industrial production had ranked thirteenth—a significant achievement for a city of thirty-eight thousand people. The regression of its economy in the postwar years weakened Richmond's potential capacity for industrial greatness, and caused an actual drop in industrial production during the depression of the mid-1870s.

Richmond had fifty tobacco factories in 1860, but only thirty-eight in 1870; their product was worth about $5 million in 1860, but only a little more than $4 million in 1870. A heavy internal revenue tax, which was not lowered until 1871, was one reason for the drop in production, for revenue inspectors were scrupulously active in Richmond after the war. Slavery had ensured a high level of productivity in the tobacco industry, as it had always provided an adequate supply of skilled laborers. Workers could not always be found in sufficient numbers after the war, nor were they always skilled, or tractable, or willing to work for low wages.[31]

Other war-related factors slowed the recovery of Richmond's tobacco industry as well. Much of the piedmont tobacco belt of Virginia and North Carolina had been scarred by the conflict. Emancipation had forced planters to enter contracts with laborers. Although the war had prevented Virginia and North Carolina tobacco products from reaching their antebellum markets, foreign and domestic consumer demand had continued. Farmers in Ohio, Missouri, and, especially, Kentucky excelled in tobacco production during and after the war. Kentucky became the leading producer of white burley tobacco, which gained widespread popularity while Virginia's dark leaf was unavailable. Flue-cured bright tobacco, which also began to appear on the market, soon was found to grow best in the piedmont counties of the Virginia southside and of North Carolina. The geographical—and manufacturing—center of the tobacco industry began to shift toward the southwest: first, from Richmond to Danville, and then, in the 1870s, to the North Carolina towns of Raleigh and Durham.[32]

The milling of flour and meal, Richmond's oldest industry, recovered slowly during Reconstruction. Little flour was milled in 1865 because many of the city's mills were inoperable. In 1866, with more mills functioning and a good crop of Virginia wheat, it was reported that many of the state's western farmers were sending their wheat to Baltimore, both because they got better prices than in Richmond and because the Baltimore and Ohio Railroad and its subsidiary lines provided cheaper transport from the Valley of Virginia. In 1868 the total daily capacity of Richmond's flour mills was about thirty-five hundred barrels a day. The Gallego and Haxall mills turned out two hundred thousand barrels in some years, but antebellum production levels had been much higher; the city flour inspector had examined as many as half a million barrels annually in the years before the war (see table 15).[33]

Several things prevented Richmond from recovering its antebellum share of the export flour market. Before the war Richmonders had owned thirteen fast brigs that carried flour to South America and twenty-three large schooners for the coastal trade. After the war the city's flour was exported in foreign- or northern-owned vessels. Richmond's millers claimed that prices on the local flour exchange were five to seven cents higher than in Baltimore, one or two cents above New York's, and comparable to those of Boston. Yet the frequently heard complaint that farmers were sending their grain to rival cities indicated that Richmond millers could not offer the highest prices. Limited storage facilities and the local millers' failure to pick up their

Table 15
Flour Trade in Richmond, 1836–1868
(In Number of Barrels Inspected)

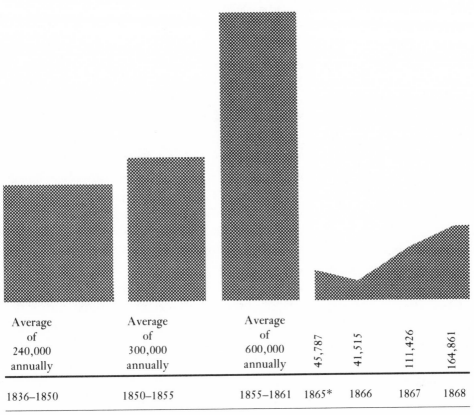

Average of 240,000 annually	Average of 300,000 annually	Average of 600,000 annually	45,787	41,515	111,426	164,861
1836–1850	1850–1855	1855–1861	1865*	1866	1867	1868

SOURCE: Report of flour inspector, *Richmond Daily Dispatch*, 17 Sept. 1868, 1 Jan. 1869.

*Statistic for 1865 reflects only June through December.

consignments of wheat promptly also retarded postwar growth in the flour industry.[34]

Competition presented Richmond's millers with another problem after the war. Despite the great distance involved, California flour often was shipped to the East Coast and sold more cheaply than Richmond's product, and technological developments gave the Richmond flour industry a closer and more serious competitor after 1870. Until then, despite the destruction of its mills and the loss of its flour fleet, Richmond's mills produced more flour than those of Minneapolis. But in 1870 Edmund N. La Croix, a Minneapolis miller, invented his middlings purifier. When used in his city's new roller mills, La Croix's purifier made Red River Valley spring wheat from Minnesota and North Dakota—which had always yielded a dark, mediocre product—into a superior grade of flour. These inventions transformed the American milling industry and enabled the Pillsbury empire to surpass Richmond's millers. In 1870 the city's mills produced less than two hundred thousand barrels of flour, only one-third of which was exported.[35]

Of the city's three big industries, Richmond's ironworks was the only one that increased the value of its product from 1860 to 1870. War needs had spurred the growth of the city's foundries, especially Joseph R. Anderson's massive Tredegar Iron Works, the forge of the Confederate arsenal. Unlike some of its competitors, the Tredegar plant had not burned in the evacuation fire of 2–3 April 1865. Anderson had promptly made his peace with the Yankees (too promptly, thought some bitter Richmonders), and by 1870 the Tredegar's eight hundred workers produced goods valued at $1 million. Other foundries and rolling mills, as well as tin, brass, and copper works, were rebuilt or reestablished soon after the war to help reconstruct Richmond's and Virginia's railroads.[36]

Although in 1870 the iron industry seemed to compare more favorably with its 1860 status than either the tobacco or flour industries, already it, too, exhibited signs of weakness. The slight increase in the number of workers directly employed in the industry was misleading. According to the *Richmond Dispatch*, about thirty-five hundred mechanics had worked in the iron industry before the war, and, if their families are considered, fourteen thousand persons had depended upon it for a living. Another six thousand mechanics, miners, and laborers had worked in allied industries. In 1866 only a third as many men had jobs in the industry. The growth of the industry was clearly hindered by the destruction suffered as a result of the war. Expressing dismay that orders for ironwork were being placed outside Richmond, the *Dispatch* argued that the work could be done as well and as cheaply in the city as elsewhere, and that local orders would help the city's foundries and unemployed.[37]

In addition, Richmond's foundries experienced shortages of raw materials such as high-quality iron ore and anthracite coal, and were forced to depend on supplies from outside Virginia. Such had not been the case before the war. Until the 1840s, the mines along the James River west of the city produced more coal than any others in the United States. Richmond's proximity to these coal deposits, as well as to sources of low-grade iron ore, gave its iron industry an advantage over northern rivals. But after the Pennsylvania anthracite fields were developed in the 1830s, hard coal became widely available and its price fell. By the 1840s Richmond's northern rivals had found anthracite superior for general industrial purposes, particularly ironmaking. Technological advances in the industry also began to require a higher-grade iron ore than was generally available in Virginia, putting postwar Richmond manufacturers at a disadvantage. As early as the end of 1866 the *Dispatch* reported that the Old Dominion Iron and Nail Works—a firm with a capital investment of two hundred thousand dollars, a two-hundred-fifty-man work force, and a capacity to produce 325 kegs of nails daily—was using each day eight hundred pounds of iron ore brought fifteen hundred miles from the shores of Lake Champlain.[38]

Richmond's big tobacco, flour, and iron industries survived the Civil War and, to a degree, even recovered from damages suffered as a result of the conflict. Yet each industry had serious problems that eventually weakened its relative position in the national economy. The inadequate supply of raw materials, the lack of a cheap and efficient rail system, the reluctance to modernize production facilities, and the failure to provide a channel and harbor adequate for large ships, impaired Richmond's ability to compete with out-of-state rivals.[39]

• 6 •

Richmond remained a city of pedestrians long after northern urban centers developed transit systems. Street maintenance, common in many other cities of the day, was a particularly significant deficiency in hilly Richmond. Efficiency and morale were diminished in a labor force that had to walk, sometimes considerable distances, to work. Both Richmond's business and government leaders were to blame for their failure to unite more closely the sections of the city.

The majority of Richmond's working men and women walked to work after the war. The cost of keeping a horse or mule was prohibitive, and any kind of horsedrawn vehicle would have been a hopeless extravagance for laborers. Some workers were able to live within a few hundred yards of their jobs. Many "sons of Vulcan," as the ironworkers were popularly known, lived in cottages in Sydney and on Oregon Hill overlooking the foundries along the river. Some tobacco factory workers lived close to their jobs in the crowded neighborhoods of Shockoe Valley. Limited housing prevented most laborers from living in central Richmond, however. Rents were often too high for poor white families, although it was reported that groups of black workers split the expense by sharing dwellings. The many workers who could not find living quarters in the central district had to live in suburbs on Richmond's perimeter, such as Fulton, Shedtown, 'Postletown, Duval's Addition, Graham's Addition, Scuffletown, or Harvietown. Men who lived in these outer neighborhoods might have to walk two or more miles to work each day.[40]

The arduous routes available to pedestrians compounded the problem. Richmond's unpaved streets were in poor condition. Sidewalks were rare. Pedestrians faced many steep hills and encountered numerous ravines and creeks without bridges or guardrails. The common council made sporadic efforts to improve conditions, experimenting with concrete sidewalks, granite paving blocks, macadamized streets, and cobblestones. The city built bridges over some of the gullies and creeks, and began the process of channeling streams through culverts.[41]

Workers had no significant alternative to the streets, however, for few could afford the early forms of public transportation. Richmond's many hacks were too expensive for laborers. An omnibus line started in June 1865, similar to one that had operated for a short time before the war, ran hourly from Rocketts to Brook Avenue from 6:00 A.M. to 7:00 P.M. Most of its passengers were northern tourists and reporters; the fare was too high and the service too infrequent for working men. The line soon failed.[42]

A horsedrawn street railway, like the one that ran briefly before the war, began operating in December 1866. The new line followed a short and inefficient route between Eighth and Twenty-eighth streets, but to Richmonders it represented progress. The ten-cent fare was high although packages of tickets were sold at a discount. Recognizing that the high fare and short route limited the line's success, the *Dispatch* called for a cut in the fare and urged that tracks be extended west to where the Richmond, Fredericksburg and Potomac Railroad met Broad Street—a connection that would carry travelers between the various rail and steamship depots and allow people to reach downtown from the west end.[43]

This long-awaited extension was completed late in the summer of 1869. Service began on 29 September to Hollywood Cemetery, the waterworks, Richmond College, and the western suburbs. The tracks connected the west end with both the central city and the steamer depots at Rocketts, and the ticket price was reduced by 30 percent. It then became possible for many laborers, clerks, women, and children to visit green spaces on the weekends or on summer evenings. The railway did little for the residents of Union Hill, Shedtown, and other neighborhoods along Shockoe Valley to the north, and it did not directly serve people who lived north of Broad Street. Its horsecars were often slow, sometimes crowded, and always noisy, and the poorest of the working class still could not afford to ride them daily. But for all their defects, the horsecars were better than walking, and they provided Richmond's only regularly scheduled public transportation until 1888.[44]

Along with topography and existing transportation terminals, the location of the western suburbs that had existed before 1866 determined the route of the city railway extension. Before 1890 Richmond was long and narrow. West of Shockoe Valley the city lay between the curve of the river on the south and the curve of the deep valley of Bacons Quarter Branch on the north. Broad Street ran west of Shockoe Creek along the spine of the highest ground in that part of Richmond, and the horsecar tracks were laid running east and west along Broad and Grace streets. Consequently there was only one route, rather than a number of routes radiating from a central hub as in post–Civil War Boston, but most Richmonders thought that their system was the epitome of modernization. Some, who wished to keep the noise and smells of horsecar traffic out of their neighborhoods and the rails off their streets, opposed both this connection of the city's sections by streetcars and later innovations like the free bridge over the James River. Residents of Grace Street, for instance, objected to the extension of the tracks on their fashionable avenue, but the other inhabitants of the wealthy neighborhood west of Capitol Square had more influence with the common council and their views prevailed.[45]

For generations the James River had been a barrier to Richmond's growth, as well as to its pedestrian and vehicular traffic. City leaders had failed to provide free access between Richmond and the town of Manchester, with its flour and cotton mills, rail depots, and rich farm lands on the south bank. Union engineers erected a pontoon bridge in April 1865, but conservatives destroyed it as soon as they could. The stated reasons for removing the bridge were that it was ugly and that it kept fishermen's boats from moving upstream; the real reasons were that it had been built by Yankees and that the Mayo family wanted to keep its old monopoly. Instead of keeping the free pontoon bridge to facilitate increased traffic between Richmond and the southside, it was removed and the Mayo family's new toll bridge was built there by Union engineers.[46]

Removal of the pontoon bridge was an obvious mistake. Despite its political conservatism and its racist views, the *Richmond Dispatch* was a superb civic booster, and its editors usually knew what was good for progress. About three years later they called for two free, lighted bridges to Manchester. Free bridges would increase the volume of business between the two sides of the river. An outsider, A. D. Fowler, formerly of New Jersey, came to the same conclusion:

> The greatest drawback to our present prosperity [in Manchester] is that we are saddled with a monopoly. . . . Manchester is connected with Richmond by three bridges—two of them devoted to railroad purposes, while the third is the only causeway by which the city may be reached from this direction by foot or carriage. This is a toll-bridge, which has been in the possession of the Mayo family for—the Lord knows how many generations. The family have a complete monopoly, and, I believe, a perpetual lease; and every man, woman, child, darky, or quadruped, crossing is obliged to contribute his, her, or its, mite to the already plethoric purse of the Mayo's. The tax on foot passengers is comparatively light, being one cent *per capita*, but on vehicles it is decidely onerous, amounting to 30¢ (15¢ each way) for a single horse and carriage, and in proportion for teams.

Fowler added that Manchester's manufacturers paid huge sums for cartage in and out of Richmond, as they had to cross the bridge each time that business took them to the city. An old resident told Fowler that the annual tolls of an antebellum Manchester cotton factory had amounted to more than five thousand dollars. Fowler concluded that "a free bridge is a palpable and public necessity, and must one day be built," but the free Ninth Street Bridge was not completed until 7 June 1873. Once built, the city failed to provide for its regular maintenance, and the bridge was often closed for long periods because it was unsafe and needed repairs.[47]

The early signs of Richmond's postwar decline were intermingled with the omens of its seeming restoration. To casual observers, during the five years following Appomattox, Richmonders seemed to keep step with the forces of recovery, expansion and growth. Most contemporaries failed to recognize evidence that the city was losing its antebellum momentum during these same years. Richmond's whites, who led the effort to redeem Virginia from the hands of the Republicans, regarded the end of Reconstruction as a triumph. Local historians, sympathetic to their cause, have seen only progress in the city's escape from the grip of Reconstruction. The city's white leaders achieved their immediate political goals, but at the same time they relinquished crucial advantages to rival cities and northern economic interests. The conservatives kept Richmond at a traditional, rather than a modern, stage of urban development. Their reluctance to part with the past would cause Richmond's decline. Virginia's capital city was destined to remain a miniature metropolis.

Resolved that such guards and guarantees be and are hereby demanded from the Chesapeake and Ohio Railroad Company, that the City of Richmond shall be and forever remain the Eastern terminus of said . . . Railroad.

Richmond Common Council, 8 July 1867

No question can be considered by this council that is of more vital importance to the prosperity of our city than the improvement of the navigation of James River. . . . The future of Richmond is undetermined. . . . Vast railroad interests are growing up and encircling us on every side, and still we sit with folded hands, allowing them to give or deprive us of whatever chance may determine. It is a conceded law of trade that all freights from the interior seek the water at the nearest available point. If we intelligently avail ourselves of our opportunity we have everything in our grasp.

Colonel Albert Ordway, U.S.A. (ret.)

Once the Commonwealth owned all the highways by water and by land. . . . Now the highways are the property of great corporations. . . . Each of these roads points virtually to New York. . . . ; to one corner of Wall Street in that city, centre all their debts, their loans, their revenue, their chief management.

Robert L. Dabney

6

The Decline of the Entrepôt

1871–1881

IN the decade after Virginia's readmission to the Union, Richmond lost its status as an entrepôt. The city's transportation network had been rebuilt by the end of 1870, but the larger system of which Richmond had been a part was being transformed in the swirl of change set in motion by the Civil War. Politics, economics, geography, and new technology, each contributed to the city's diminished role as an intermediary center of trade and commerce. The leaders of the Conservative-Democratic regime in postwar Virginia allied themselves with northern businessmen, whose interests were not always friendly to Richmond. An economic resurgence that began in Richmond in 1870 fell with the Panic of 1873, which forced railroads, factories, and banks throughout the state into receivership. Recovery took five more years, and by the end of the decade the question of funding the antebellum state debt had split the Democratic party. The decline of Richmond as an entrepôt affected society, politics, trade, and industry in Richmond and Virginia throughout the last part of the century. In 1871, as in 1860, Richmond was the state's busiest rail center and port. But despite continued improvement of the city's transportation system in the early 1870s, Richmond already was starting to lose its place as an intermediary commercial center. New, larger steamships, with screw propulsion and iron hulls, revolutionized international trade. Coastal ports grew while fall-line river cities stagnated. By 1881 the rival city of Norfolk had surpassed Virginia's capital as a transport center, and the upstart towns of Newport News and West Point had taken much of the trade that formerly came to Richmond. The creation of national railroad systems, directed from offices in New York City, put control of the state's railroads into the hands of outsiders. Richmond's failure to survive as a major port was inextricably linked to its demotion from a major rail terminus to a provincial junction at which three trunk lines converged. Richmond's ebbing port was at once cause and consequence of the city's sidetracked railroads—and vice versa. Both weakened the entrepôt.

• 1 •

In 1865, with the help of Union engineers, Richmonders had found it easier to reopen the blockaded James River than to rebuild war-damaged railroads and turnpikes. The wartime loss of river-borne passenger and freight traffic to Norfolk and City Point (now Hopewell) proved temporary, and by 1872 more tonnage entered or left Richmond on the river than by all other means combined. Sailing vessels, towed up and down the river by steam tugs, comprised most of this traffic as they carried Richmond's flour, tobacco, and other goods to Europe, South America, and Australia, as well as northern cities.[1]

Steamboat companies competed on the James in the early postwar years, too. Side- and stern-wheel vessels carried passengers and some freight between Richmond, Baltimore, Philadelphia, and New York. The fastest ships, such as the *John Sylvester*, traveled the hundred miles to Norfolk in six or seven hours, even with several stops along the way. Baltimore was an overnight journey. As long as competition existed, the companies kept fast ships on the river.[2]

As railroads were rebuilt, service on them improved and left less traffic for the steamship companies. Richmonders could reach Norfolk by rail via Petersburg before 1870, and in that year the Richmond and York River Railroad was completed. Travelers en route to northern cities could save several hours by taking the train to West Point and catching a York River steamer. Increased competition from the rail-roads drove some steamship companies out of business. Those that remained divvied up the routes to end the price wars of the early years and ensure each company enough business to survive.[3]

The end of competition on the James River brought the demise of fast steamers. The steamboat races had been dangerous and expensive. Boiler explosions and collisions with sandbars, rocks, and other vessels had been frequent. But with no other line to beat, companies found it safer and more profitable to steam their vessels at moderate speeds, making as many local stops as possible to take on rural passengers, freight, and mail. A passenger aboard the once speedy *John Sylvester* complained in 1873 that the voyage to Norfolk took more than eleven hours, while by train the trip took only six. Baltimore had become a full twenty-four hours away by water.[4]

Other impediments hindered navigation and delayed improvement of the river channel. The tides at Richmond, which generally ranged between three and four feet, as well as high winds, floods, and droughts affected the channel's depth. Floods might help to deepen the channel, but in doing so they damaged docks, warehouses, and goods, and tore vessels from their moorings. For at least a day after each flood, high water and strong currents made navigation almost impossible between Richmond and City Point.[5]

Richmonders have traditionally blamed the decline of their port on the federal government, which failed to deepen the James River. In fact, Congress appropriated considerable funds to improve Richmond's harbor and channel in the postwar years. In 1869 a committee appointed by the common council to ask Congress for aid visited Congressman Philetus Sawyer, the powerful Republican from Wisconsin who was then chairman of the House subcommittee on rivers and harbors. Sawyer authorized the initial survey of the river that was necessary before any appropriation could be made. The next year Congress voted to deepen the James River to fourteen and one-half feet at low tide, and between 1870 and 1881 Congress voted $665,000 for this project. (The federal government directed another million dollars in aid toward improving the James River during the last two decades of the century.)[6]

Working jointly, the United States Army Corps of Engineers and city employees deepened the James River channel from about nine feet at low tide to eleven feet by 1874. By 1876 the depth was fourteen feet at high tide, but solid granite ledges in the riverbed prevented significant improvement beyond this depth, despite the use of dredges, divers, diamond drills, and high explosives. Every freshet washed sediment downriver into the new channel, and almost constant dredging was necessary to maintain the depth of the improved channel.[7]

As the world's trade moved into bigger ships, an even deeper channel became necessary. New docks were built further downriver, more than a mile beyond the city limits, but ships with drafts over fourteen and one-half feet—which were increasingly common by 1880—could not reach these wharves. The *Gaston*, for instance, a small screw freighter built in 1881 for the Old Bay Line, which served Richmond, drew nineteen feet of water and could not reach the Richmond docks. The larger ships that carried flour, tobacco, and coal from newly discovered West Virginia deposits could not load to their full capacity. Such vessels had to complete their cargoes at City Point or Norfolk, an inconvenience that caused higher freight rates for Richmond shippers. Even passenger steamers with more shallow drafts had difficulty navigating the river's narrowly winding channel with its tricky currents. This problem was compounded as ships became longer.[8]

In the last third of the nineteenth century Richmond found it increasingly difficult to compete with Norfolk. During the colonial and antebellum eras, Norfolk's spacious, twenty-six-foot-deep harbor had been a disadvantage because it had been unnecessarily costly to drive long piles for piers and docks when most ships had shallower drafts. After the Civil War, however, Norfolk's deep water attracted shipping, and as its rail connections with the interior improved, captains could load their freighters to capacity without a difficult journey up the James.[9]

Both in the annual value of direct imports and exports and in the total tonnage of domestic and foreign vessels, Richmond fell behind Norfolk in the mid-1870s. In 1875 direct imports to the capital reached their peak value of five hundred seventy thousand dollars. By 1880 Richmond's direct imports, as opposed to goods brought to the city in bond by common carriers, were valued at only forty thousand dollars—a figure surpassed by the much smaller city of Norfolk. Norfolk's direct imports exceeded Richmond's in all but four of the next twenty years, and the value of its direct exports surpassed Richmond in 1875 and increased rapidly. By 1881 Norfolk exported almost $18 million, compared to Richmond's less than $2 million.[10]

Although the James River and Kanawha Canal paralleled the river to the west for more than two hundred miles, it was a route to nowhere, and the canal failed the city during the 1870s. Lynchburg was the only upriver city on the canal. The planned connection of the James and Kanawha rivers, whose Appalachian headwaters were only thirty-three miles apart, was never made. Despite the investment of millions of dollars in the project, the canal company never achieved its goal of a water link with the Ohio River and the Midwest. Serving only the James River valley, and competing with railroads that flanked the river and tapped this market at Richmond and Lynchburg, the canal suffered. Its carrying capacity was limited and it was frozen during much of the winter. When rail transportation became faster and safer in the 1870s, the canal was unable to compete with the railroads for passengers or fast freight.[11]

The James River itself contributed to the canal's failure. Despite a system of locks that helped preserve the flow, summer droughts lowered the water level and made the canal useless. Yet, floods frequently damaged the locks, dams, and towpath, adding to the cost of maintenance and closing the canal periodically. In 1870, after all the wartime damage to the canal had been repaired and the entire antebellum route of the canal put in operation, a terrible flood undid much of the repair work. After great additional expense, the canal was again repaired and reopened, but in November 1877 a bigger flood damaged the canal again and effectively ended its life.[12]

Joseph R. Anderson, head of the Tredegar Iron Works and the president of the common council in 1877, was the first city leader publicly to back a seven-year-old proposal to replace the canal with a railroad built along the towpath from Richmond to Clifton Forge—the so-called straight shoot to the west. Anderson publicly agreed with skeptics who had been saying privately for years that the canal would never reach the Ohio and that it could not prosper unfinished.[13] Anderson's plan stirred up controversy. Many Richmonders supported a towpath railroad because they hoped to control the straight shoot, or because other railroads in which they were interested would benefit if the canal were closed. Others objected to the plan. Some owned stock in the canal company; some wanted the canal company to repay its debt to the city and state; some simply refused to surrender George Washington's dream of a water link with the Ohio. Outside Richmond, area farmers liked the canal and feared railroads.

Virginia's Board of Public Works proposed to restore the canal completely and link it with the Ohio, but a majority of the city council opted for the railroad. The canal company's debt was $1.3 million, and, second only to the commonwealth of Virginia, the city was the largest stockholder and creditor. Richmond had invariably paid the largest part of the cost of repairing the canal after floods. In January 1878 the council resolved that the canal was "inadequate, unreliable, and undesirable, as a permanent means of transportation totally unselfsustaining, and should be abandoned as soon as a railroad can be substituted." Motions to spend $25,000 to repair the canal were voted down.[14]

The demise of the canal brought Richmond more problems. The council thought that it had an understanding with the canal company, whereby the company's debt to the city would be canceled in return for the use of the canal as a viaduct to increase Richmond's water supply. But the stockholders of the James River and Kanawha Company decided to sell the entire property in March 1880. The buyers, a group of ill-advised northern investors, including James G. Blaine and native Virginian Cyrus H. McCormick, had organized the Richmond and Allegheny Railroad and sustained unrealistic hopes for the traffic their new line would attract. After spending large sums of money for railroad construction, the company went into receivership in 1882. (The Chesapeake and Ohio Railway leased the line and later bought it.) The Richmond and Allegheny Company had sold its water rights to various city mills and factories, however. This severed the water supply to the municipal reservoir and caused a city-wide panic in the summer of 1881.[15]

• 2 •

Richmond's immediate postwar recovery as a rail terminal had occurred rapidly. Four of the five antebellum railroads—the Richmond, Fredericksburg and Potomac to the north, the Virginia Central to the west, the Richmond and Danville to the southwest, and the Richmond and Petersburg to the south—had been quickly rebuilt. Work on the extensively war damaged York River line to the east was impeded by marshy terrain and labor and financial troubles, and not completed until 1869. In 1868 and 1869 more freight entered Richmond by rail than entered Baltimore, Philadelphia, and Norfolk combined. In 1869 the tonnage of incoming freight was second only to New York's. These high tonnage figures derive, in part, from construction material imported to rebuild the Burnt District; nevertheless, the transportation figures suggest the extent to which Richmond's rail network had recovered within a few years of Appomattox. Richmond's decline as a rail terminal in the 1870s was a result of political and economic events, including the simultaneous decline of the city's port, rather than geological or technological causes.[16]

Two laws, passed in March 1871 by "Virginia's worst Legislature,"[17] hastened this decline. The first measure was a funding bill designed to pay off the large debt Virginia had incurred for the construction of railroads, canals, and internal improvements during the 1850s. The state had been devastated by war, it was short of money, and it had lost the revenues arising from the counties that had seceded to form West Virginia. Yet, unlike Georgia, Alabama, and the Carolinas, where white redeemers repudiated their state's antebellum debt, Virginia's Conservative leaders, known as Funders, committed the state to repaying the entire debt at high interest rates. The Readjusters, who represented the less traditional wing of Virginia's Democratic party, opposed this plan, but the Funders, who were especially strong in Richmond, generally prevailed until 1881. To guarantee the state's debt the Funders neglected social programs that met the needs of Virginians. Passage of their Funding Bill, which historian James T. Moore calls "the most disastrous piece of economic legislation in Virginia history," was the work of "an unholy combination of the forces of the bankers, brokers, speculators and railroads."[18]

The second measure was pushed through the legislature in the spring of 1871. It provided for the sale of the commonwealth's stock in all but one of Virginia's railroads. Subsequently, the Panic of 1873 forced several railroads into receivership and weakened others. Outside investors bought up this stock, and all of the state's large railroads fell into the hands of northern investors, who did not have Richmond's interests at heart. As river and canal competition receded, the railroads were free to set higher rates. Allegations of rate discrimination were made in many bitter editorials in the *Richmond Dispatch* and in angry letters from salesmen and merchants. And, as the city lost its deep-water port, rail traffic sought another outlet to the Atlantic.[19]

William Mahone's Atlantic, Mississippi and Ohio Railroad played the most important role of the railroads involved in Richmond's decline. Mahone—a civil engineer, a former Confederate general, and a power in Virginia politics for a generation after the war, both behind the scenes and as the head of the Readjuster party—had been instrumental in securing lenient terms for Virginia's readmission to the Union and the election of the state's first Conservative governor, Gilbert C. Walker. During Reconstruction Mahone had assumed the presidencies of three small railroads serving Norfolk, Petersburg, Lynchburg, and Bristol. He wanted to forge his local lines into a railroad that would stretch from Norfolk across the entire state and through Tennessee to Memphis. Despite opposition from Richmond politicians who feared a diversion of their city's trade, Mahone pushed his consolidation bill through the legislature in June 1870.[20]

As the Richmonders feared, Mahone's A. M. & O. diverted trade from Richmond to Norfolk and built up Virginia's southside, at the expense of those interests north of the James. But Mahone did not savor triumph for long, for his road, like the other main Virginia lines, fell under the control of northern investors. Buffeted by the Panic of 1873, it was sold in 1881 to a group of Philadelphia entrepreneurs who reorganized it as the Norfolk and Western Railway. The N. & W. carried millions of tons of coal, cotton, and produce and hundreds of thousands of passengers annually to Norfolk, ensuring the future prosperity of Richmond's rival and contributing heavily to the growth of that port in the 1880s and 1890s.[21]

Of the other Richmond-based railroads that sought a deep-water port to compete with the A. M. & O., the first was the Chesapeake and Ohio. Formed in 1867, the C. & O. extended the old Virginia Central line, which connected Richmond, Charlottesville, and Staunton, toward a projected Covington and Ohio River road. Northern investors bought into the railroad, and in 1869 railroad magnate Collis P. Huntington secured control. Initially Huntington's drive to extend the C. & O. to the Ohio River benefited Richmond by providing a link to the west for which Richmonders were grateful. By 1873 the city council and individual Richmonders had invested more than $3 million in the C. & O., for which they had the company's solemn promise that Richmond would always be its East Coast terminus. Richmonders raised three hundred thousand dollars to tunnel beneath Church Hill so that C. & O. freight could be loaded directly aboard ships at the railroad's docks below Rocketts. In October 1873, after several cave-ins and fatalities caused by shoddy construction, the Church Hill tunnel was completed.[22]

Running directly through the huge coal fields of West Virginia, the C. & O. by 1876 was carrying more than a quarter million tons of coal to Richmond for local use or export each year. As new coal fields were discovered along the railroad, the price of coal in Richmond fell by half, and the quality of city gas manufactured from it improved even while its cost went down. Because shipowners knew that they could always load outbound coal at the railroad's piers, freight rates for shipping Richmond goods to northern cities decreased, too.[23]

Unfortunately, Richmond's newfound importance as the terminal for an east-west trunk line lasted only eight years. The council and Chamber of Commerce had promised the C. & O. eighteen feet of water to accommodate coal ships. When blasting and dredging produced a channel less than fifteen feet deep, the C. & O. management felt released from its obligation to keep its eastern terminal in Richmond. After surveying possible sites, Huntington chose the fishing village of Newport News at the tip of the peninsula on Hampton Roads, a vast natural deep-water harbor. The C. & O. extended its tracks to Newport News and in 1882 began carrying all its coal and grain to its new piers and elevators there. Much of its other freight, as well as many C. & O. passengers, also rode through Richmond to the new terminal. The Richmond and Danville Railroad found a deep-water terminal by obtaining permission to run its rolling stock on the Richmond and York River line to West Point, at the head of the York River, the deepest natural channel on the Chesapeake Bay.[24]

In 1871 the Richmond and Danville and the Richmond and York River railroads, both originally owned by Virginia and Richmond interests, fell under the control of the Southern Railway Security Company, a holding company headed by Tom Scott, president of the Pennsylvania Railroad. Two years later William Clyde, of a powerful Philadelphia shipping family, bought controlling interest in the York River line, and eight years later he gained control of the Richmond and Danville. When Clyde reorganized the railroad as the Richmond and West Point Terminal Company, Richmond was reduced to a stop along a trunk line between the Deep South and Chesapeake Bay. Cotton, dried fruit, grain, tobacco, and passengers went directly to the new terminal at West Point, where Clyde's steamers carried freight and travelers to northern cities.[25]

Both of the smaller railroads that served Richmond also fell under northern control. The Richmond, Fredericksburg and Potomac—the only railroad in which the state of Virginia had not sold its stock—was owned and managed by the Robinson family chiefly as a passenger link between North and South. During the 1870s President John M. Robinson refused to allow the Pennsylvania Railroad to run as many trains on R. F. & P. tracks as it wished, and he persistently maintained the contract with the Potomac Steamboat Company, which for decades carried the railroad's passengers between the line's Aquia Creek terminal and its B. & O. connection in Washington, D.C.[26]

The Pennsylvania Railroad acquired the other short line to Richmond, the Richmond and Petersburg, in 1871. Using this line to the South, Tom Scott retaliated against the R. F. & P. by running all Pennsylvania Railroad through traffic between Washington and Richmond over other companies' rails. Squeezed by satellites of the powerful Pennsylvania and weakened by the depression of the mid-1870s, the R. F. & P. management finally yielded to the Pennsylvania Railroad's pressure for unlimited through traffic and severance of the connection with Potomac shipping. Despite a stockholders' revolt over these concessions between 1878 and 1880, Virginia interests finally lost. The Virginian who served as interim president in this period, forced to resign in 1881, was replaced by a Philadelphian. Scott's victory was complete. The Pennsylvania now had, on its own terms, a southern trunk line through Richmond.[27]

Richmond's city council had done little to make the city a railroad hub. After a struggle lasting several decades the R. F. & P. had been driven off Broad Street, and the railroad had moved its depot west to the city limits, far beyond the settled business and residential neighborhoods. The council refused it permission to connect with the Richmond and Petersburg even after the company constructed its own tunnel beneath Gamble's Hill. The council also frustrated connections between the Richmond and Danville and the York River lines, and although it finally allowed this rail link, the council placed so many limitations on its operation that the route had little value. On the other hand, the council permitted the C. & O., which represented the city's lifelong dream of a transportation link to the West, to run trains through the heart of the city.[28]

The Richmonders' stubborn resistance to northbound through traffic and naive attempts to secure their city as the eastern terminus for traffic from the West failed in the long run. As in the antebellum era, some rail shippers continued to avoid the city because of the lack of through connections, and the consequent delays, damages, and drayage costs. Some shippers used alternative routes through Danville and Charlottesville. The Pennsylvania Railroad bypassed Richmond entirely, building a bridge over the James River several miles west of the city. During the 1870s Richmond lost its chance to become a major southern rail center. The failures of its port and of its railroads were closely related. After 1881, railroads carried little to Richmond that was not directly consumed by its factories or its people.[29]

• 3 •

Richmond's decline as an entrepôt was partly the fault of businessmen and politicians who failed to organize and sustain a concerted effort to improve the transport routes to Richmond. Few in 1870 were farsighted enough to see the obsolescence of the canal, the city's increasing dependence on the railroads, or the technical difficulties in deepening the river. Most businessmen concentrated on building new stores and enlarging their stocks. Many were struggling to survive after the Panic of 1873. Although the newly organized Chamber of Commerce and the *Richmond Dispatch* were active civic boosters, few of the city's prominent men heeded the calls to improve rail and water transportation routes.

This shortsightedness among postwar Richmond leaders was coincidental with a change in the social status and economic position of the men who controlled the city government. During the war most council members had distinguished, multiple careers: David J. Burr, founder of the postwar Chamber of Commerce, was also a lawyer, manufacturer

Table 16
Occupations of Members of Richmond Common Council
July 1871 to July 1882

Manufacturers (24.5% of total)	29	White Collar (16.8% of total)	20	Professionals (13.4% of total)	16
Tobacco	8	Clerks	5	Lawyers	6
Metal	8	Public		Doctors	3
Food	4	officials	5	Druggists	2
Grain	2	Company officers	5	Bankers	2
Wood	2	Teachers	2	Brokers	2
Paper	2	Bookkeeper	1	Insurance agent	1
Leather	1	"Agent"	1		
Brick	1	Journalist	1		
Drugs	1				
Skilled Trades (14.2% of total)	17	Unskilled (2.5% of total)	3	Merchants (28.6% of total)	34
Carpenters	6	Laborer	1	Commission	
Machinists	3	Teamster	1	merchant	11
Plasterers	2	Huckster	1	Grocers	9
Plumbers and				Coal and wood	
gas fitters	2			dealers	6
Cooper	1			Restaurateurs and	
Shoemaker	1			caterers	2
Barber	1			Paper and books	2
Painter	1			Ice dealer	1
				Dairyman	1
				Dry goods	1
				Boots and shoes	1

SOURCES: *Richmond Daily Dispatch;* Records of the Richmond Common Council, City Clerk's Office, Richmond City Hall, Richmond; [B. W. Gillis, comp.], *Richmond City Directory . . . , 1871–2* (Richmond, 1871); J. H. Chataigne, comp., *Directory of Richmond, Virginia . . .* (Richmond, 1881).

NOTE: A few of the 115 councilmen had more than one occupation, and the occupation of one council member could not be determined; the total is 119.

of steam engines, and investor; Larkin W. Glazebrook was a commission merchant, miller, bank director, and turnpike company founder; George Wythe Randolph, scion of a prominent Virginia family, was a naval officer and lawyer before serving as a Confederate secretary of war; and the remaining councilmen were either attorneys, manufacturers, or prominent merchants. Only three of the wartime incumbents were skilled laborers—a painter, a blacksmith, and a carpenter.[30]

During the years of Reconstruction, from 1865 through 1870, a more diverse group of men served on the council. Five of the ninety-eight men who served during this period were retired army officers. Eight held other, usually federal, public offices. The two largest groups were merchants and manufacturers: eight liquor, seven commission, and five clothing merchants; and five tobacco and five iron manufacturers. The Reconstruction-era council had four lawyers, three druggists, and a doctor, and among the skilled workers four machinists, three carpenters, and a painter. Some of the city's most important residents continued to seek council seats: six bank presidents and two of the city's forty-eight richest men served on the council during Reconstruction. The presence of fourteen of the wartime councilmen supplied a measure of continuity.

With the redemption of Richmond by white conservatives in 1870, the diversity of occupations represented on the council increased. Black voting and the increased political participation of white workingmen made postwar politics in Richmond a less genteel calling. Many gentlemen declined to serve in municipal office. Only three of the nineteen wartime members of the council served after 1870. From the election of 1871 through that of 1881, 114 men were elected to the council (see table 16). Of this number, more than half were merchants and manufacturers. White-collar and skilled workers were more numerous than professional men. Three councilmen were unskilled workers. Almost one-fifth of the members had served during the Reconstruction years.

Service on the city council seems no longer to have been important to Richmond's most influential men, the largest manufacturers and businessmen and the representatives of prominent families. Twenty-four men who won council seats resigned: seven gave no specific reason; three members said they lacked time because of business concerns; seven moved from central city wards to better neighborhoods in the west end (five of whom then were reelected to the council from their new wards); four used council membership as a stepping-stone and were elected to the General Assembly; two moved out of Richmond; and one resigned when President Grant prohibited dual officeholding. His federal job was more important to him than city office. The total number of men who chose not to remain on the council is probably greater than the resignations suggest, for many councilmen simply did not seek another term. Those who did want to remain on the council usually were secure in their positions. In all but one of the five biennial elections between 1872 and 1880 fifteen incumbents were returned to the thirty-man council. Voters in the old, central wards of Jefferson, Madison, and Monroe were far wealthier, according to real and personal property tax returns, than those in the newer, outlying wards of Marshall, Clay, and Jackson. Two-thirds of the manufacturers and professional men on the council came from the wealthier wards. The poorer wards tended to elect men of lower status: three-fifths of the merchants, three-fourths of the white-collar workers, and four-fifths of the laborers.

Ten blacks—the first of their race to hold high office in the city government—served on the common council between 1871 and 1881. All were elected from Jackson Ward, which was created in April 1871 soon after the Conservatives regained full control of the city. The Conservatives had resorted to fraud and violence in a series of mayoral elections in 1870 in order to install their candidate. To lessen the chance of contested elections and reduce the need for violence to control the black vote, Richmond's Conservative leaders pushed their plan to create a sixth ward through the council, over the opposition of the Republican members. The Conservatives skillfully gerrymandered the boundaries of the new ward, which probably was named for President Andrew Jackson,[31] to include most of the city's black population and few whites. It came to be known as the "shoestring ward." The formation of Jackson Ward ensured white control of the five other wards and of the council. City council elections in five of the six wards tended to be noncompetitive, as Democratic majorities were certain and the nominees were chosen in party primaries. Former Democratic leaders, their talents no longer needed to win city elections, may have withdrawn from city politics for this reason. In closely fought state or national elections, the Conservative-Democrats had only to concentrate their efforts on reducing the black Republican vote in Jackson Ward.[32]

As in other southern cities in the 1870s, Richmond used the white primary and, in consequence, had low turnouts in the regular election. The few independent candidates who bolted the Democratic party to run for the council against its regular nominees were scorned. Republicans offered regular and significant opposition, but put up complete tickets only in Jackson Ward, which voted Republican in every presidential election from 1872 through 1892. Only in the 1872 reelection of President Grant, however, did the Republicans carry the city.[33]

Jackson Ward witnessed Richmond's most vigorous political contests, for the ward was congenial to the independents, to an occasional Readjuster, and, later, to labor candidates. Democrats did not concede control of the shoestring black ward. Registrars, policemen, and party officials challenged each black voter at length, in order to delay the balloting as long as possible. Bullies intimidated blacks, sometimes with violence. Thousands of blacks were disfranchised in the 1870s for petty larceny convictions or failure to pay the poll tax.

The Democrats' rough tactics in Jackson Ward backfired in the 1876 election. On election night a black crowd celebrated the victory of Rutherford B. Hayes over Samuel J. Tilden—a ward victory won despite intimidation by the Democratic ward heelers and precinct captains—by smashing windows in houses where lights could be seen and threatening Democratic party workers when they were found. After making its way through much of the city, the crowd finally was dispersed by a determined body of policemen, backed by ironworkers and stonecutters from the white working-class neighborhood of Oregon Hill.[34]

The men who served on the council during Richmond's decline as an entrepôt were skilled ward and precinct politicians, as their continued presence on the council indicates. They dispensed jobs, liquor, food, and cash to their followers, but they did not advance the city's larger interests as effectively as their wartime and antebellum predecessors. They failed to maintain the free Ninth Street Bridge to Manchester properly, they made dangerous cuts in the fire department, and they were unable to provide the city with adequate supplies of gas and water. Charges of corruption usually have been leveled at the carpet-baggers and scalawags during Reconstruction, but the 1870s offered more evidence of crooked municipal politics. A ring uncovered in the municipal gasworks stole thousands of dollars from the city, and Richmonders heard frequent charges of corruption in the James River improvement projects and in the construction of the new reservoir.[35]

• 4 •

Richmond's black community lost much of the political power it had gained during Reconstruction after it was gerrymandered into Jackson Ward. If black Richmonders got any benefit from the new ward system, it was the increased opportunity for the development of racial pride and community spirit. The growth, after 1870, of organizations free from white control and led by blacks is one indication of the increasing independence of Richmond's black community. For instance, some of the black militia units formed during Reconstruction survived into the 1870s. The Attucks Guards—named for Crispus

Attucks, who was killed in 1770 in the Boston Massacre—went by special train to Washington, D.C., in the fall of 1873 and by chartered steamer to Fort Monroe in 1876 for competitions with other black militia units. Also present at the contest were the Virginia Grays, headed by Captain Ben Scott, one of the black leaders Richmond whites most feared during Reconstruction. Many black leaders in Jackson Ward headed similar military clubs. Scott liked to drill his troops at night in white neighborhoods; perhaps it was during one of these exercises that three white men assaulted Scott and abused his men. A police justice fined each of the whites five dollars.[36]

Black unions had been established by the end of the 1870s, but, like white unions, most were for skilled or semiskilled laborers, and they represented only a small number of workers. In 1880 Richmond had at least ten black unions (for waiters, shoemakers, printers, undertakers, stevedores, clerks, grocers, other merchants, barbers, and mechanics), and their total members numbered more than four hundred. The ranks of black chapters of the Odd Fellows, Good Templars, Knights of Pythias, Independent Order of Saint Luke, and other secret, fraternal, and mutual benefit associations swelled in the 1870s, at least partly because blacks were excluded from similar white groups. The first black insurance companies grew out of such organizations. The Grand Fountain of the United Order of True Reformers, founded in Richmond in 1881, grew to become a joint-stock company with one hundred thousand members, a bank, department stores, a newspaper, and an insurance firm. Richmond blacks also took part in the city's booming construction industry through the Richmond Land and Financial Association, chartered by the legislature in the 1870s. In 1875 John Mercer Langston, who later became the only black Virginian ever elected to the House of Representatives, accepted the presidency of the association, whose purpose was to purchase land parcels to be resold to black individuals in small lots.[37]

White Richmonders esteemed neither the black independent businessman nor the black militia leader. They praised blacks such as John Dabney, who had become famous before the war for his juleps and catering, and the younger Miles C. Debress, a noted barber in the 1870s and later. But among Richmond whites John Jasper, a tobacco worker who was born a slave, was most highly regarded. He was probably the single most famous black Richmonder. He first became widely known in Richmond in 1878 for his popular sermon, "The Sun Do Move." Basing his argument on Joshua 10:12, Jasper refuted the Copernican theory to the delight of white audiences that included members of the General Assembly and the most fashionable Richmonders. His thousand-member Sixth Mount Zion Baptist Church was among the city's largest. More highly educated black ministers such as Richard Wells, William Jones, and Robert C. Hobson criticized Jasper for being unscientific and for making blacks look foolish. Perhaps in part they were jealous of Jasper's following, or of his popularity among white Richmonders, who contributed to his church. Whites liked Jasper for several reasons. Many were fundamentalists who took the Bible as literally as Jasper. Jasper made other whites feel superior to blacks, because they knew his theory was scientifically wrong. Jasper's fame led him to the northern lecture circuit and to England, and white Richmonders felt he brought Richmond favorable publicity. But especially, as a politically inactive black leader who entertained listeners of both races with his sermons, Jasper was a man with whom Richmond whites were comfortable.[38]

Segregation in most areas of city life was the rule in Richmond during the 1870s. William Saunders, an Englishman who visited the capital in the latter years of the decade, found "no social intercourse between the two [races]. I never saw white and coloured men in friendly conversation, and so great is the separation that not in a single instance did I find white and coloured children playing together. . . . There seems to be an impassable barrier between them." Saunders noted that the schools were completely segregated, and the churches nearly so, except for some white preachers before black congregations. In March 1875 there was a near riot at the Richmond Theater when two blacks tested the new federal civil rights act by seating themselves in the white audience for a performance of *Davy Crockett*. The theater manager avoided trouble on subsequent nights by barring blacks from the white sections.[39]

Yet, isolated incidents show that some blacks were able to get around Jim Crow and win admission to public facilities and the professions. In January 1876 the *Richmond Dispatch* reported that a fashionably dressed black couple had attended a performance at the Richmond Theater, where they occupied a box and were seen walking in the parquet. That same month the first black lawyer allowed to practice in Virginia was accepted by the judges of the Henrico County court and the Richmond hustings court. He was Robert P. Brooks, a graduate of Lincoln University and of Howard University's law school and the son of Albert P. Brooks, one of Richmond's most successful black businessmen.[40]

In other areas segregation was more strictly enforced. White Richmonders liked to tell visitors that the Virginia Central Lunatic Asylum in the city was the only such institution for blacks in the world. It was often overcrowded, but blacks who needed treatment were refused admission to the white asylum in Williamsburg, which had vacancies, and were held in the city jail. Richmond had no public library until the 1890s, but the Virginia State Library was available and the YMCA had a reading room. Because the blacks were not admitted to either facility, black pastors petitioned the YMCA's International Congress, which met in Richmond in 1875, for a separate YMCA building for blacks. The plight of blacks, few of whom had enough money to buy their own books, led postmistress Elizabeth Van Lew and a committee of black leaders to call for donations so that a library could be established for Negroes.[41]

There were more flagrant types of discrimination. In the early 1870s the police abridged the rights of blacks through wholesale arrests and the confiscation of their money. This practice was outlawed by Mayor Keiley, but Richmond was reputed to have the highest arrest rate of any city in the country. The theft of bodies of hundreds of blacks from the segregated cemeteries by grave robbers in the employ of medical schools was the subject of bitter editorials in the *Virginia Star*, a black newspaper published in Richmond during the 1870s. Few whites served time in the state penitentiary, and even fewer served on the chain gang, which cleaned Richmond's streets as late as 1878. Listening to a debate on the whipping post in the Virginia Senate, diarist Robert Skipwith commented with evident satisfaction that the Senate was "in favor of preserving this useful and venerable institution," which seems to have been used primarily, if not exclusively, for the punishment of blacks.[42]

• 5 •

Richmond's economy was as turbulent in the 1870s as its social and political life had been in the 1860s. A business revival that began after Virginia's readmission to the Union was cut short by the Panic of 1873, which broke in September when the New York financial house of Jay Cooke and Company failed. Runs on the Richmond banks occurred, and one small bank and one brokerage firm went under. During the next two years, however, a depression took its toll on the Richmond economy. The C. & O. railroad went into receivership in the autumn of 1875. The Tredegar company followed in January 1876 when Joseph

Anderson announced that his ironworks had been unable to collect its bills due from railroads and other customers. Smaller firms also went into bankruptcy. After 1875, jobbing sales had declined almost to the 1874 level, but by 1878 there was a phenomenal increase in sales.[43]

After five years, a general business recovery began in 1878, and became an economic boom in the 1880s. In 1880 Richmond was the second largest manufacturing city in the South, behind New Orleans. It had ranked first in 1860. Richmond's economy had become more diversified and less dependent on the traditional big three industries—tobacco manufacturing, flour milling, and ironmaking— but signs of weakness in these major industries were even more evident than in 1870.[44]

Tobacco still dominated the city's economy. Ninety-five tobacco companies employed half of the laboring force and produced $8 million worth of tobacco products, more than a third of the total value of Richmond's manufactures. These figures represent a marked increase over those of 1870, but the percentage of city workers employed in tobacco factories was the same as it had been in 1860 and the value of tobacco manufactured in 1880 had dropped by $5 million from the postwar peak of $13 million in 1876. The census showed that the Richmond manufacturers still led the tobacco industry, their factories consuming more than 17 million pounds annually. Lynchburg, Petersburg, and Danville were ranked fourth, fifth, and sixth, and Durham, the closest North Carolina town, ranked ninth. Still, Richmond had manufactured 52 percent of the tobacco in the Virginia–North Carolina area in 1869, but only 30 percent in 1879. Durham, Winston, and Reidsville, North Carolina, were now ahead in the aggregate.[45]

Several things reduced postwar Richmond's role in the tobacco industry. The first was the rising popularity of new types of tobacco, such as Kentucky's white burley and southside Virginia and North Carolina's flue-cured bright. A change in the system of grading, sorting, and marketing leaf tobacco also contributed to Richmond's decline. For decades state inspectors in Richmond had been a guarantee of quality to foreign buyers. In the late 1870s the state Grange secured an alternate arrangement, which allowed public auctions in privately owned warehouses, and the appointment of inspectors by the tobacco companies. While Richmond clung to its old way, other centers adopted the new system. By 1880 nearly 31 million pounds of tobacco were sold at auction annually in rising North Carolina towns, while one-tenth of that amount was sold under the old system in Richmond and Petersburg. The 1879 crop of tobacco, reflected in the 1880 census, showed that North Carolina raised 27 million pounds to Virginia's 23 million.[46]

The third contribution to the decline of the city's tobacco industry was the large manufacturers' resistance to machines for processing tobacco. In the 1870s the leading Richmond firms still used procedures that involved handwork at most stages of production. Allen and Ginter, the city's largest firm, continued to do so until 1889, when it was absorbed by the American Tobacco Company. A Richmonder had invented a leaf-cutting machine in 1866. By 1873 tobacconist David D. Mayo had developed a mechanical bag packer to keep pace with the cutting machine. Lumpers, who shaped the tobacco used for fillers, and stemmers, who separated the tobacco leaf from its stem, were still needed for handwork in the 1870s. A lumping machine first was manufactured in Richmond in 1877 and with improvements was employed in six plants by year's end, but the limited use of machines such as these did not foster large-scale production of tobacco because hand labor was still necessary for various operations.[47]

Cigarette manufacture began in Richmond in 1875. City manufacturers exhibited samples at the Philadelphia exposition in 1876, but New York and other northern cities then dominated this part of the industry. Although cigarette production did not become the most important part of the Richmond tobacco business until the 1880s, manufacture of the "poor man's smoke" gradually increased from 3 million cigarettes in 1875 to 65 million in 1881. Most of these cigarettes were made by Allen and Ginter, which employed hundreds of women workers—blacks for stemmers and whites for rollers.[48]

Richmond's milling industry had stagnated by the 1870s. A series of disastrous fires and unreliable local waterpower, together with the westward shift of the American grain belt and the diversion of grain supplies not only to Baltimore but also to the rising milling centers of the upper Mississippi Valley, contributed to the decline of the city's large flour mills. Richmond's five mills produced flour and corn meal valued at $2,443,732 in 1880—a substantial increase over their 1870 production but only 12 percent of the city's total product (as compared with 17 percent in 1870 and 25 percent in 1860).[49]

Richmond mills continued to export flour to South America, Spain, and Australia, but it was no longer carried in a fleet of locally owned brigs and schooners, nor were the returning vessels importing as much coffee as they had. The value of Richmond's flour production hovered between $2 and $3 million during the 1870s and peaked at $3.25 million in 1881. Then both the industry and the export trade entered a decline from which neither recovered. The Richmond milling trade had suffered a blow in 1875 when three of the four major mill owners died, and inventions such as the La Croix middling process and steam-powered roller mills also hurt the Richmond flour industry, but when the Chesapeake and Ohio Railroad moved its terminal to Newport News in 1881 Richmond ceased to be a major grain export center.[50]

Ironmaking, the first of Richmond's major industries to recover after the war, continued to flourish in the 1870s, although it was seriously affected by the Panic of 1873. From a high of $5.5 million in 1872, iron production dropped to $1 million in 1878, then increased sharply and peaked at $5.25 million in 1881. The fortunes of the Tredegar company, the city's largest single employer, rose and fell with the industry. In January 1873 almost two thousand men worked in buildings that occupied fifteen acres. The company had $1 million in capital and used tens of thousands of tons of iron ore each year. Railroad cars, its postwar speciality, were shipped all over the country. Permanently weakened by the Panic of 1873, Tredegar declared insolvency in 1876. It lacked capital to make the change from iron to steel manufacture, and by 1880 Anderson's firm had capital valued at only $.5 million and only six hundred fifty workers.[51]

As the tobacco, milling, and iron industries declined, others did expand. The manufacture of leather goods, such as boots, shoes, saddles, and harness; of clothing and textiles; and of vehicles continued to be profitable. Printing, publishing, and papermaking showed modest gains, as did the building and wooden products trades. The food, drug, and chemical industries showed the greatest increases. The Southern Fertilizing Company, perhaps the largest of Richmond's new drug and chemical firms with a capital investment of two hundred thousand dollars, produced fertilizer worth $225,000 in 1880. The Valentine Meat Juice Company, founded in 1871 by Mann S. Valentine, a member of one of the city's most prominent families, grew so quickly that a new plant was necessary in 1877. By the summer of 1881, when dying President James A. Garfield was sustained by toast soaked in Valentine Meat Juice, the company was world renowned.[52]

• 6 •

Richmond in the 1870s was a city at war with itself, uncertain in its direction and divided in its loyalties. Many of its leaders fancied that they could erect a modern northern-style city on the ruins of the old Richmond. Others doubted that Richmond was changing for the better. "The rapid growth of Richmond," Edward King wrote in *The Great South*,

> doubtless carries sadness to the heart of the Virginian of the old school. For in the steady progress of the capital toward promi-nence as a manufacturing centre he sees the symbol of decay of the society which produced him and his. He hates large cities, with their democratic tendencies, their corruption, and their ambitious populations. He looks upon the rich manufacturer as a *parvenu;* the lordly agriculturist is still, in his mind, the only fitting type of the real aristocrat.[53]

Travelers who visited Richmond during these years were equally uncertain about the city's progress. A New Englander praised the city's beauty, but he felt that "more enterprise might make the city livelier." William Wells Brown, who had escaped from slavery forty years earlier, saw a lack of physical and intellectual progress in 1878, when he wrote that "the effect of the late Rebellion is still visible everywhere, and especially amongst those who were leaders in society thirty years ago." George A. H. Sala, an Englishman with prosouthern sympathies, agreed with the more critical black visitor, when in 1879 he found Richmond "still . . . a town gradually rising from her ashes," and a "seemingly thriving but really struggling place." Blaming the city's condition on the Civil War, Sala praised the signs of its recovery but concluded that "many more years must pass away before the stage of struggling is passed and that of permanent prosperity sets in." Thomas R. Wilkinson, another Englishman, saw Richmond in 1880 and re-ported that "one fact impressed me strongly—except in the main lines of thoroughfares where the tramcars run, I did not see one street that was not grass grown."[54]

Captain Willard Glazier, who visited in late 1880 or early 1881, was more optimistic. Richmond, he thought, had "rapidly recuperated since the war." Unlike Charleston, South Carolina, Richmond was surrounded by a well-inhabited rural region whose residents marketed their goods in the city and bought their supplies there. "It will never attain the commercial importance of Savannah or of Norfolk," Glazier predicted, "but as the centre of the tobacco region, and the seat of large manufacturing interests, it will always possess a certain importance and prosperity."[55]

The slowing tempo of life in Richmond can be seen in the gradual lessening of business, government, and social activity during the hot, humid summers. The common council and board of aldermen usually overruled the mayor and suspended operations for several months. Many firms kept reduced hours. Social activity shifted to the springs of Virginia. If a businessman could not leave the city, he sent his wife and children without him to the mountains for healthy recreation. Each spring and summer the *Richmond Dispatch* printed long lists of resorts, describing their proprietors and the transportation facilities serving them.[56]

During the fall and winter months upper-class white youth met at dances held by the various German clubs, exclusive affairs at which marriages were planned and family alliances made, and at which young women made their debuts into polite society. For relaxation, white males repaired to their clubs—the Commonwealth, the Westmoreland, and the Richmond—and Jews to the Commercial. Military organizations continued to be popular, as did scull racing on the James River. Clubs were organized not only by athletic enthusiasts but also by religious, ethnic, neighborhood, and hobby groups.[57]

The cult of love and beauty arose in the seventies. Belles, such as Mary Triplett and Mattie Ould, competed with each other for beaux and fame before admiring male eyes in Richmond and at the mountain and beach resorts. Mary Triplett's affection was the object of a tragic duel between two friends, John B. Mordecai and Page McCarty. Both men loved her, but she chose Mordecai. She broke her engagement with McCarty, who lamented her faithlessness in bitter lines of verse in the *Richmond Enquirer*. In the duel that followed, Mordecai suffered a fatal wound. McCarty sustained a serious wound from which he never completely recovered. Mary Triplett's name "was never mentioned in contemporaneous newspaper accounts," a columnist reported in 1908, "and, of course, will not be mentioned here, though it is known to hundreds."[58]

Richmond society was reflected in its educational system. Although white enrollments in the public schools increased steadily for twenty years after their founding in 1869, with black enrollments lagging behind, probably less than one-half of the city's school-age children were ever enrolled in the public schools at any time during the postwar decades. An increasing number went to the factory rather than the school: in 1870 child laborers numbered 858; in 1880, 2,113. Many white Richmonders, particularly those who could afford private schools for their own children, did not approve of public education. "Hewers of wood or drawers of water" were "as necessary . . . as the scientists, the statesmen, the jurists, the philosophers," an 1881 letter to the *Richmond Dispatch* advised: "What cook will bake a potato root after analyzing a Greek Root?"[59]

Leading men felt that they could neglect the public schools when the city had so many fine private schools. The 1870s were the golden age of these exclusive institutions, perhaps because the well-to-do had more children to educate, or perhaps because they felt that a private school was more important than parents did in the 1880s and later decades. One-third more of these schools were operating in the decade before 1881 than in the decade after. Almost a third of them had been founded before 1871—five had originated before the war. The Panic of 1873 closed five private schools, and fewer schools were founded after 1881 than in the preceding decade. Eight of the schools were special institutions: a kindergarten, two German-English schools, a school of modern languages, a military academy, a stenography school, and two business colleges.[60]

During the 1870s Richmonders still felt ambivalent about their place in the Union. The city could not yet afford to erect a monument to J. E. B. Stuart, as it had promised after his death in 1864, but it sent ten thousand dollars to the victims of the Chicago fire in 1871. When a group of English gentlemen paid for the statue of Stonewall Jackson that was erected in Capitol Square, more than ten thousand people turned out for its dedication in 1875. Richmonders fretted when the House of Delegates refused to approve a request from Governor James Lawson Kemper and the Senate for ten thousand dollars for a Virginia exhibit at the Philadelphia Centennial Exposition of 1876. Henry Ward Beecher lectured in the city in 1877 and 1881, and received an enthusiastic welcome after paying the obligatory tribute to General Lee. Despite his contested election, Richmonders greeted President Rutherford B. Hayes warmly in the fall of 1877 when he came to the state fair.[61]

Organizations of Confederate veterans were beginning to hold conventions in Richmond, but the cult of the Lost Cause was not yet in full flower. Enduring Confederate sentiment showed in the city's failure, well into the 1870s, to observe the Fourth of July. Although they celebrated Queen Victoria's birthday in May, the birthday of the United States evidently had little meaning for Richmonders. In 1870 Confederate veteran and novelist John Esten Cooke had bitterly attacked the holiday. And for diarist Robert Skipwith, who lived in Richmond for years, Independence Day 1872 was "A day once glorious—a day sanctified by the deeds of Great Virginians—but not dear to us as once. Richmond very quiet, stores generally closed." The gradual return of national patriotic feeling was helped by the centennial celebration in 1876, and possibly by the prospect that the Democrats would elect the next president. In 1876 Governor Kemper, who had been seriously wounded and captured while leading his brigade in Pickett's charge at Gettysburg, authorized thirteen and thirty-eight gun salutes at midnight and dawn of the Fourth. The railroad depots and most businesses closed, and the steamer did not make its run to Baltimore. A letter to the *Richmond Dispatch* stated that "since the war there has not been a . . . national holiday celebrated in the old-fashioned style," and urged an all-day celebration.[62]

The resurgence of American, if not Union, sentiment in Richmond may have begun in January when the council accepted an invitation from Boston to petition Congress for the erection of a monument at Yorktown to commemorate George Washington's victory over Cornwallis. From then on, preparations continued for the city's part in the 1881 centennial celebration of the battle of Yorktown. In the summer of 1881 the council and board of aldermen finally agreed to spend fifteen thousand dollars for the event, as well as the costs of entertaining the president, distinguished French visitors, and other guests.[63]

Crowds flocking to Yorktown for the celebration traveled past Richmond and down the peninsula on the newly completed extension of the C. & O. They bypassed the Confederate capital, just as the nation and the trends of commerce and industry were beginning to bypass Richmond. The decline of the entrepôt, with its far-reaching effects upon Richmond trade and manufacturing, was a prelude to the city's increasing importance as a shrine of the Lost Cause. Imperceptibly, Richmond was becoming the old city of the New South.

The immense Southern night would descend on us all and then the talk would start . . . ; our grandfather would tell us about the Civil War.

On and on. The Seven Days' Battle, the Wilderness . . . General Lee. The sound of the Yankees' pickaxes, digging under Petersburg. And Richmond, always Richmond. To save Richmond. It became a holy place to us, a place to be loved forever like Plymouth Rock and Valley Forge and the Mississippi River. On and on. . . . Whenever our grandfather had finished talking, we would sit on for a while, alone . . . in the great motionless night, and our hearts would nearly break within us. We had lost, we had lost.

Ben Robertson

7

Old City of the New South

1882–1890

THE 1880s in Richmond were frenetic. The city was "roaring with progress" and visitors were likely to be dusted with mortar from its new construction. Richmonders seemed about to embrace the New South promoters' hope that industrial growth and scientific agriculture would bring prosperity, sectional reconciliation, and racial harmony. Tobacco eased the city through a brief depression that momentarily slowed the economic recovery begun in 1878. Flour milling made modest advances after 1885, and new ironworks—including a large locomotive factory—were built. Richmond's wholesale market expanded through the South into the Midwest, and local retail and real estate sales reached unprecedented levels. "The new order has taken its place," *Harper's Weekly* reported in 1887, "and foremost among its promoters and supporters stands Richmond, a leader of the industrial South, as twenty-five years ago she was of the Confederate South."[1] Amid a swell of national patriotism, white Richmonders poised as though they might be ready to rejoin the Union and to accept political practices such as a two-party system and black voting. Temperance advocates and organized laborers challenged the city's Funder Democrat establishment, and a continued split within the Democratic party in Richmond gave black voters increased political power.

Despite these signs that the 1880s might break with the past, however, by 1890 Richmond had turned back. A passion for the Lost Cause became the vogue for white residents, who divided their allegiance between a dead nation and a living one and convinced themselves that they were both loyal Americans and steadfast rebels as they worshiped at Confederate shrines. By the 1890s, tradition, sentimen-

171

tality, racism, and the collective weight of the past had eclipsed the progressive vision and the decline was complete. As the city's war with itself finally ended, Richmond became what it remained for decades: the old city of the New South.

• 1 •

"The most noted death of the year of 1884," the *Richmond Dispatch* proclaimed, "was . . . sectionalism." Although the comment was premature, journalistic diatribes against the North did appear less frequently, for nationalist sentiment had begun to blossom in Richmond after the Yorktown victory centennial observance of 1881. Newspaper writers remained touchy about the bloody shirt tactics of some northern politicians, or about what white Richmonders saw as northern interference with their handling of race relations, but the 1884 election of Grover Cleveland—the first Democratic president in a generation—further reduced animosities that lingered from the war and from the disputed 1876 presidential contest. While Union veterans flocked to the Confederate capital for tearful reunions with their former enemies, and while northern lecturers and conventioneers enjoyed the city's southern hospitality, Richmond's theater managers, hotel keepers, and restaurant owners tallied the profits from Yankee visitors. In 1885 the common council proclaimed an official day of mourning to mark Ulysses S. Grant's funeral, to which elite militia units accompanied the governor of Virginia. By the early 1890s Richmonders were far along the road to reunion; they rushed to serve in the Spanish-American War.[2]

And there were other, tentative signs that the city might be breaking with its past. To a reporter of the *New York Times* Richmond in 1887 was both "pregnant . . . with a new epoch" and "born again." Here was "a new Richmond, with snap and go, with push and enterprise, with commercial ambition, with industrial purpose, upon development intent." By 1890 hotels, banks, and office buildings began to hover over Jefferson's state Capitol and obscure it from view. The classical white structure, symbol of the statecraft of old Virginia, was being overshadowed by the symbols of the new Richmond. Emily Clark later claimed that Richmond's "political rulers were restrained by force from painting the statues of the great Virginians on the Washington Monument in the Square . . . a nice, new shiny black, to prove how truly progressive this new South has become."

The city government acted to keep up with progress. In 1884 the common council modified an ordinance that had allowed residents to tie off the streets so that traffic could not pass along a block in which someone was sick. The new law allowed a street to be roped off only for three days in cases of extreme illness certified by a doctor. This quaint custom was repealed entirely in 1887, to the relief of city merchants and manufacturers; at the end of 1890 the council voted to provide all-night ambulance service. Conscious of the image-making power of street names, the council changed those that seemed inappropriate or colloquial. The council passed laws to regulate horses, to keep farm animals from wandering in the city, and to prohibit hogs entirely. In 1885 the council moved a stone marker from Main Street to a less frequently traveled sidestreet: the stone had marked the level reached by flood waters in 1877.[3]

The fashion of making New Year's calls, originally copied from the North but long out of vogue there, was still followed in Richmond in the mid-1880s. The custom died out by 1891, and was replaced by another northern practice, the consumption of elaborate dinners at the city's leading hotels on New Year's Day. And, the 1880s saw the death of the duel when, in 1882, the Readjusters passed a strong law against duelling and made it stick. Two years later John S. Wise, a Confederate veteran, noted athlete, duelist, and prominent Readjuster Republican, publicly refused a challenge from Page McCarty, who in 1873 had killed his former friend John B. Mordecai in a duel over Mary Triplett. Wise's action effectively ended the resort to the field of honor, and newspaper publisher Joseph Bryan, a veteran of Mosby's Rangers, administered the coup de grace in 1893 when he refused a challenge from an irate Democratic politician and turned him over to the police.[4]

• 2 •

The general prosperity of 1880s Richmond showed in the real estate and construction boom of the city's ten building and loan associations. Only one had been established before 1880 and seven had been formed after 1886. Several of these enterprises had been organized by blacks, and together the building and loan associations boasted a total of $4.3 million in authorized capital. Hundreds of houses and stores were built each year. An 1883 police census found 5,297 brick and 4,917 frame houses in the city. The new houses were often constructed of more expensive materials, such as James River granite and West Virginia brownstone, but brick continued to be popular. Four hundred brick and eight hundred frame houses were erected in 1884, at a cost of $1 million. Four hundred houses were built in 1886, five hundred in 1887, and six hundred in 1889, including those in the town of Manchester across the James River.[5]

As new houses began to fill the outlying neighborhoods, the council authorized massive street improvements. West end streets were being paved by the end of 1884. In the spring of 1885 the council appropriated funds for cobblestones on major streets and terra-cotta pipes and sewers. Streets scheduled for improvement as much as six years earlier were completed. After 1885, the notations of street improvements alone filled six to ten pages annually in the records of the common council. The council also improved the city parks, and voted funds to purchase land for new parks in the outer wards. Despite this improvement program, urban boosters called for still more funds. Lewis D. Crenshaw, a rich and socially prominent miller, scoffed at the $40,000 approved by the council for streets in 1890. Agreeing with the *Richmond Dispatch* that the city needed more and better streets to sustain its economic boom, he called for the expenditure of $545,762. The council eventually appropriated $100,000.[6]

Richmond's population increased from 63,600 in 1880 to 81,388 by 1890. The movement of residents from the old central wards to the new outer wards was both a cause and a result of the expansion of the suburbs. By 1890 Clay and Jackson wards, created in 1867 and 1871 on the west and north sides of the city, were Richmond's largest. The adjacent old ward, Monroe, had between three and four thousand fewer residents. Marshall, another new ward created as a result of the 1867 annexation, had more inhabitants than either Jefferson or Madison, the central wards. Both the east and west ends benefited from shifting population and new house construction. Richmond also expanded northward beyond Bacons Quarter Branch into Laburnum, a real estate development financed by tobacco magnate Lewis Ginter, and Barton Heights. Suburban real estate prices rose throughout the 1880s.[7]

Wealth left the central city more slowly during the 1880s than did population. Real and personal property values were highest in Madison Ward. Jefferson Ward had less than half the wealth of its neighbor to the west, and Monroe, Clay, and Marshall wards followed. Jackson Ward, where 42 percent of the black population lived, trailed far behind.[8]

The growing west end population repeatedly demanded more city services. Both west and east end parents complained of inadequate school facilities. An 1881 letter to the *Richmond Dispatch* complained that the west end lacked a market house, and suggested that one would soon be built if only the councilmen from the three western wards united. Three years later residents organized as the Elba Market Association petitioned the council, and finally in 1888 the council voted funds for a market. Various delays occurred, however, and the new market was not completed until after 1890.[9]

Improved transportation aided suburban growth, but change came slowly because councilmen from the central city resisted innovation. Early in the decade the council restricted the speed of the horsecars that ran through central Richmond from the east to the west end. It also rejected a plan approved by the board of aldermen for the extension of the street railway and for terminal depots. By 1885 council sentiment had been brought to favor urban transportation systems, and the city of Manchester's streetcar network was allowed to connect with the Richmond City Railway via the free Ninth Street Bridge across the James River. The Richmond Union Passenger Railway began operation early in 1887 and, although it primarily served the area east of Shockoe Valley, the company competed successfully with the older City Railway. In the summer of 1887 the Manchester line was allowed to enter the city, and by September there was a brisk competition and exchange of passengers among all three lines.[10]

When electric streetcars replaced horsecars on the Union line in the spring of 1888, Richmond became the first city in the country with an electric transit system successfully operating over a route of more than a few blocks. While the electric streetcar system suggests that Richmond's postwar character was modern and progressive rather than essentially conservative, this was not the case. The directors of the Richmond Union Passenger Railway, many of them Republicans, were not representative of the Richmond establishment; the old elite operated rival lines, tried to stop the Union plan, and ridiculed the electric railway when it first began operation.[11]

Within a few months of its inception in 1886, the Union Passenger Railway secured permission to use electricity to power its streetcars and hired New York engineer Frank Julian Sprague to lay out a route and install the necessary equipment. The councilmen approved the Union Passenger Railway proposal not because they believed in the unusual motive power but because they themselves were caught up in the expansive optimism of the 1880s. A wave of unregulated and unplanned development swept the city until it broke in the Panic of 1893. The council approved virtually every proposal, no matter how farfetched, submitted during this period; if a scheme represented something new and seemed likely to encourage the city's growth, it was approved. Not surprisingly, many never came to fruition. Just as wartime councilmen had taken unprecedented steps to meet critical needs in social welfare, so their sucessors felt that they were confronting vastly changed circumstances to which they had to respond.

The electric streetcar was only a part of the expansion process during the booming 1880s: pedestrian viaducts were built, bridges improved, interurban lines constructed, existing routes connected, and sewers and streets extended. Fortunes were made in real estate. Conservatives eventually recognized that there was money to be made in the development of new residential neighborhoods, and this was a powerful inducement for them to accept change. Yet, the more progressive, Republican businessmen often took the lead, secured outside capital, and risked bringing new technology to the city. Once it was shown to be practical, as with Sprague's successful electric streetcar, the conservatives followed. Later in 1888 both the Manchester system and the Richmond City Railway won approval to electrify their streetcar lines, and by 1889 the council had authorized the formation of several other electric streetcar companies. One was an interurban line that ran east to the hamlet of Seven Pines, where the city locomotive works maintained a recreation area for its workers.

The increasing number of streetcar companies caused problems. By the end of 1890 there were eight streetcar lines in Richmond, and another was being built. More than thirty-two miles of track had been laid, all of it double except in the black neighborhoods of Jackson Ward, where passengers had to wait from two to four times as long for a streetcar as white customers elsewhere. With many firms competing for a limited number of passengers, some companies failed to meet schedules, and there were many complaints about poor service. A consolidation bill was discussed in the General Assembly, but did not pass.[12]

The North Side Viaduct Company received permission in 1890 to run streetcars across a viaduct over Bacons Quarter Branch and to connect with one of the city lines south of the branch, and its viaduct opened in the spring of 1891. City council considered an even more daring plan, a bridge spanning the whole width of Shockoe Valley to carry Broad Street from the top of Shockoe Hill to the top of Church Hill, but the project was not carried out, at least partly because of the Panic of 1893.[13]

A majority of councilmen continued to oppose attempts to expand the city's boundaries. Manchester residents sought annexation in 1886, and an annexation plan approved by the Board of Public Interests found much support. But like similar proposals in 1871 and 1879, it was voted down by the council and the board of aldermen. Some councilmen felt that the city could not afford to expand its services into Manchester; others feared the potential impact that Manchester's largely working-class population might have on city politics. (In 1910, after streetcar service across the James improved sufficiently to allow Manchester residents to commute to jobs in Richmond and after the council decided that Manchester residents who worked in Richmond were escaping city taxes, annexation finally occurred.)

Some councilmen also resisted the efforts of west end residents to have their neighborhoods annexed. These members argued that much of the area annexed in 1867—Clay and Jackson as well as Jefferson and Marshall wards—lacked street improvements and city gas, water, and sewage service. The council majority was not rigidly opposed to annexation. An 1887 resolution to instruct the city's representatives in the legislature to oppose a bill extending the city limits was voted down because a majority feared that if the council took a firm stand against annexation, suburban developers might lay out new streets that would conflict with the city's own street plan. Other members of the council, like their friends in the Chamber of Commerce, hoped by annexation to raise Richmond's population to a higher rank among American cities in the upcoming census of 1890.[14]

• 2 •

In Richmond as in many other postwar southern cities, the 1880s witnessed conflict between the principles of laissez-faire and of municipal regulation—especially between existing city utilities and newer privately owned firms. The most important instance of this conflict involved electrical power. Private enterprise took the initiative in this new field in 1881 when the Virginia Electric Lighting Company was organized with an old-line Virginian, John H. Montague, as president. Two former councilmen, Charles E. Whitlock and Charles U. Williams; tobacconist Lewis Ginter; and the Vermont-born vice-president of the Richmond and Allegheny Railroad, Henry C. Parsons, were on the board of directors. The council, hoping that competition would bring lower rates and better service, chartered two more power companies in 1883, one of which was headed by a prominent confectioner, Andrew Pizzini, who was serving on the council. Then, in the mid-1880s, the city itself entered the electric business, substituting electric streetlights for gas lamps in 1884, and beginning work on a city power plant in 1885. No local firms submitted bids to build a city light system, and the council gave its contract to a Hartford, Connecticut, firm. In 1886 the city's major streets and some city parks were illuminated by electricity generated in the city's plant and, despite a council decision to keep some streetlights lit all night, after 1887 the private power companies' principal customers were the streetcar lines. As the demand for electricity increased, the city became a maze of wires: some companies used overhead lines, other buried cables beneath the streets. An electricity monopoly promised safer and more convenient power, although the council's decision to allow a simple private monopoly also was influenced by the inability of competing local firms to supply adequate electrical services. Chartered in 1890, the Richmond Railway and Electric Company promptly bought out four other power and streetcar firms.[15]

Richmond's telephone system was operated by a privately owned utility developed in the 1880s with the aid of northern capitalists. In 1879 Richmond got the country's third telephone exchange—a city switchboard operated by the Southern Bell Telephone Company (a lessee of American Bell Telephone Company), managed by Bostonian Charles E. McCluer, and financed by William H. Forbes and other Boston investors. In the 1880s almost all telephone customers were businesses, although the fire department had phone service by 1884. The city council initially granted Southern Bell a broad franchise such as local Bell affiliates received in other southern cities. At first the phone company hung its lines from private houses, but after it found that the costs of damages caused by its linesmen's climbing spikes were exceeding revenues, it asked for permission to erect telephone poles, and the council drew up a contract that was much more favorable to the city's interests. The agreement allowed the company to erect poles but stipulated that they also be used for Richmond's fire alarm and police telegraph system. In the face of opposition from the board of aldermen, the council failed to hold the phone company to other, even more restrictive, provisions. The American Bell Telephone Company absorbed Southern Bell late in the 1880s and linked Richmond with other cities before reorganizing into the American Telephone and Telegraph Corporation in 1899. Yet the council had not learned a lesson from its experience with competing power and streetcar companies: after receiving complaints about poor service from Southern Bell, the city allowed the Richmond Telephone Company to begin operations in the 1890s. The separate company was merged with the Bell System in 1903.[16]

The city gasworks continued to be the exception to the general rule about privately owned utilities in Richmond and the nation. The city gas plant was improved and enlarged in the 1880s. As a result, although complaints about the quantity and quality of gas persisted, in 1885 the works made a large profit—significantly higher than in earlier years. As in other southern cities, private firms attracted by the commercial potential of the municipal plant, and councilmen with interests in these various companies, proposed in 1888 that the gasworks be leased to a private corporation. Assertions that the city would derive even more revenue from leasing the works than it did from gas sales and that customers would get better service from a private contractor fell on deaf ears; a majority of the council suspected that a few of their colleagues were not acting in the public interest, and they voted against a private gas utility. Richmond's municipal gasworks remained a city-owned utility into the twentieth century—one of only five in the United States in 1902.[17]

A steady supply of good water proved more difficult to ensure than gas. New pumps upriver on the James were completed in 1883. They supplied a new waterworks, and the system was deemed adequate to keep the new reservoir full in any weather short of extreme drought. But the city's drinking water was still muddy, and efforts made in 1885 to devise a workable filter were unsuccessful. The various steam- and water-driven pumps needed almost constant repair or replacement. The council considered drilling for water to ensure a more reliable supply, and some areas went without city water. Eastern areas such as Fulton had no water mains as late as 1887.[18]

In December 1887 an accident endangered the water supply. Weakened by trains of the Richmond and Allegheny Railroad that ran atop the old towpath, the earthen bank of the old canal broke. Water and debris poured into the pump house, and the pumps and mains leading to the reservoir were broken. The city sued both the receivers of the ailing railroad and the Chesapeake and Ohio Railway, which controlled the line. Until repairs could be made, the city depended entirely on its new upriver pumps. If they had failed or if the level of the river had gone down, the reservoir would quickly have been drained. Fortunately neither disaster occurred, and after much argument the controversy between the city and the railroad was settled in 1890. Under a complicated agreement the C. & O. agreed to pay part of the cost of repair without admitting that it had inherited the old canal company's legal obligation to supply Richmond with drinking water.[19]

Residential sewer connections and large drainage culverts were constructed along with the new houses and streets throughout the 1880s. The work of enclosing Shockoe Creek, begun in the 1870s both as a sanitary measure and to prevent damage to streets and bridges in Shockoe Valley during the perennial freshets, continued. Like Jones Falls in Baltimore and other free-flowing urban creeks, Shockoe Creek had become a natural sewer fed by tributary culverts that drained most of the city. The council also enacted ordinances requiring home owners to connect flush toilets with the city sewer system and providing for proper traps and ventilation.[20]

Fire and police protection became increasingly important in the 1880s as the city expanded and as population increased. After two years of retrenchment, in 1882 the council's fire committee pleaded for new equipment on the grounds that the public safety was endangered: fire had destroyed the Richmond and Petersburg Railroad bridge, the Vulcan Iron Works, several of the largest tobacco factories, many houses, and caused half a million dollars in damage. The committee requested $12,215 for a new fire station, a hook and ladder truck, a steam fire engine, and hose. The council appropriated $9,000, referred the request for a firehouse to the building committee, and made no provision for the hook and ladder truck. But as the building boom continued, the council became more receptive to requests for increased fire protection. In 1885 it authorized one new hose company and reassigned another for duty in the congested area of docks and warehouses at Rocketts. It stiffened the building code, prohibiting any structure from being erected in the downtown area unless its walls were entirely of brick, stone, or other fireproof material. An 1890 clause required all buildings more than three stories high to have iron fire escapes, and another gave the fire department committee greater power over the approval of building permits. John Mitchell, Jr., the energetic black newspaper publisher from Jackson Ward, opposed the latter measure. He feared that blacks, who had but two representatives on the seven-man committee, might not be able to erect houses in conformity with the new building code and that the committee might favor permits requested by white realtors and contractors.[21]

Despite these advances, the council might have done far more for fire protection. Residents of the west end asked for a fire truck in 1888, but the council referred the matter to its finance committee, which took no action. A series of fires demonstrated the need for more firemen and equipment: a fire at the state penitentiary in 1888 threatened the lives of eight hundred convicts and caused twenty thousand dollars in damages at the prison shoe shop. Two years later fire destroyed a fertilizer

Table 17

Republican Presidential Voting in Richmond, 1872–1892

(In Percentage of Total Ballots Cast)

	1872	1876	1880	(1880 Readjuster)	(1880 Combined)*	1884	1888	1892
Marshall Ward	48.4	43.4	25.2	(6.5)	(31.7)	39.6	39.3	24.5
Jefferson Ward	43.0	35.9	20.5	(6.5)	(27.0)	33.6	35.0	20.4
Madison Ward	44.3	37.7	21.0	(4.1)	(25.1)	34.3	33.8	20.0
Monroe Ward	47.5	37.6	21.1	(5.1)	(26.2)	36.5	36.4	17.3
Clay Ward	44.2	32.7	20.8	(7.2)	(28.0)	35.7	35.8	17.0
Jackson Ward	74.6	70.1	63.8	(3.2)	(67.0)	74.4	79.0	62.4
City-wide percentage	50.3	42.9	28.7	(5.4)	(34.2)	42.4	43.2	26.9
Percentage for predominantly white wards	45.5	37.5	21.7	(5.9)	(27.6)	35.9	36.1	19.8

SOURCE: Official vote printed in postelection issues of the *Richmond Daily Dispatch*.

*Percentage indicates combined Republican and Readjuster voting.

company and two tobacco factories valued at a quarter of a million dollars. A fire at the locomotive works in 1891 put one hundred fifty men out of work and damaged the engines and boilers being built for the battleship *Texas*. When another quarter-million-dollar fire destroyed the cigarette factory of Allen and Ginter in 1893, a thousand women lost their jobs, but Lewis Ginter continued to pay their wages.[22]

Like the fire department, the Richmond Bureau of Police had inadequate staff and funds during the 1880s. It was also buffeted by political turmoil throughout the decade. False economy and city politics explain the council's failure to increase the size of the police force between 1870 and 1888. The salaries of other city workers had been restored to the level of 1877, before wages had been cut in an economy move, but not until 1888 were police salaries restored and the department enlarged. In 1884 the council remedied one long-standing grievance by relieving patrolmen of the strenuous additional duty of lighting and extinguishing gas streetlamps, but this was a meaningless concession as the city was switching to electric streetlights. Even during Reconstruction, blacks never served on the police force—a circumstance common to all southern cities except a few such as

Table 18

Property Holding by Registered Voters in Richmond, 1880–1890

	Number of Registered Voters		Property Valuation per Registered Voter			
			Real	Real	Personal	Personal
	1880	1890	1880	1890	1880	1890
Marshall Ward	1,795	2,568	$ 989	$ 952	$ 201	$ 224
Jefferson Ward	2,476	2,715	3,033	2,519	595	1,797
Madison Ward	1,612	1,925	4,875	4,674	1,609	3,945
Monroe Ward	2,145	2,691	2,736	2,771	1,145	1,013
Clay Ward	2,123	3,389	1,851	2,352	775	685
Jackson Ward	2,502	3,327	670	734	46	48
Total	12,653	16,616				
		Average	$2,359	$2,334	$ 729	$1,285

SOURCE: Richmond personal and real property tax books, 1880–1890, Archives Branch, Virginia State Library, Richmond; *Richmond Daily Dispatch*, 1 Jan. 1891.

Montgomery, Alabama, and Raleigh, North Carolina, which had Negro policemen. Because the force lacked black patrolmen and frequently had been charged with brutality, Councilman John Mitchell, Jr., opposed the 1888 police department bill, but he was alone in his opposition.[23]

While the common council had made some effort to expand and modernize city services in response to Richmond's growth, in general the *Richmond Dispatch*'s January 1888 indictment seems just: the editorial concluded that the council had failed to increase the police and fire departments in proportion to the city's population growth, failed to open and improve streets in the suburbs, and failed to maintain streets in the older areas.[24]

• 3 •

In politics the 1880s were years of tumult in which it seemed that Richmonders might embrace the two-party system. The Funders, conservatives who advocated paying the entire antebellum state debt, were challenged both by local Democratic factions and by Republicans. The Republican vote in Richmond's six wards increased from an average of 29 percent in 1880 to 43 percent in 1884 and 1888 (see table 17). The reasons for this increase are not entirely clear, but Republicans benefited from a continuing split in Democratic ranks, first between the

Funders and the Readjusters (who wanted to readjust the state debt), and later between the Funders and groups who supported unions and a local option on liquor sales.

Funder Democrats governed the city except for a brief period in 1886–1887 and had a majority in every ward except Jackson, where about three-quarters of the voters were black. There were only minor differences in the size of the Democratic majorities in the five white wards. Republicans always won in Jackson Ward; of the other wards, Marshall, with a large black population, always returned the most Republican votes. In the city as a whole, between a quarter and a third of the Republican voters were white. Ward organization as well as race may have affected party strength. Republican strength in Jackson and Marshall resulted in part from superior organization, for voter turnout was high in these wards (see table 18). Conversely, strong Democratic organizations in the city's central wards may have helped to reduce the size of the Republican vote, making a large Democratic turnout unnecessary.

It is clear that Republican strength increased in the mid-1880s, and that this change was not entirely a result of the Readjusters joining forces with the Republicans: the Republican vote increased by 14 percent between 1880 and 1884, but the Readjuster vote had been less than 6 percent. More than half of the Republican gain must have come either from new voters or from men who had abstained in 1880. A decline in Republican strength between 1888 and 1892 is also clear: while the Democrats united behind Grover Cleveland and increased their total vote by a quarter, the Republican party's total vote dropped by half, and Republicans lost ground in every ward (see table 17).[25]

This decline was the result of social pressure on white Republicans and widespread disfranchisement and intimidation of black voters. In the 1870s and 1880s conservative Democrats perfected tactics to reduce the black vote, particularly during city-wide elections for state and national office, while allowing the largely black population of Jackson Ward to elect Negro councilmen and aldermen. In 1876 petty larceny was added to the list of felonies that were grounds for disfranchisement in Virginia. About a thousand blacks were disfranchised in Richmond between 1870 and 1892 by conviction of petty larceny or felony in the city hustings court, while another thousand Negroes lost the vote after being convicted of petty larceny in the Richmond police court. Until the poll tax was abolished by the Readjusters in 1882, voters could also be disfranchised for failure to pay it. Despite appeals by the black *Virginia Star* and explanations of the intentionally complicated proce-

dure for paying the tax, thousands of Negroes in Richmond neglected
this duty. Such Democratic ploys had a cumulative effect, but the
strategy was not immediately successful because of party factionalism
in both the state and city. After 1888, however, the newly unified
Democrats increased their efforts to prevent or impede Negro voting:
thousands of blacks were kept waiting for hours at each election, even
though they may have stood in line throughout the previous night, and
election judges examined the black Republicans individually, asking
legalistic or insulting questions. The city police threatened black
voters, and white hoodlums tried to start riots so that black voters could
be arrested. Then, after the election, charges were dropped and the
blacks released. False ballots were issued to blacks, and eventually the
Democrats resorted to running candidates with names similar or identi-
cal to those of Republican nominees. Typically, when the polls closed,
hundreds of black Richmonders were still waiting to vote.[26]

White Republicans were subjected to almost universal scorn, even by
small boys like John A. Cutchins, who confessed to his father that one
of his playmates was the son of a Republican, "but he can't help that."
The city's leading Republican in the late 1880s, John S. Wise, had been
educated at the Virginia Military Institute and the University of
Virginia law school and was a son of former governor Henry A. Wise.
His attempt to organize Negro voters by walking through Jackson
Ward and visiting them in their shops and stores infuriated conservative
Democrats, who regarded him as a turncoat. Wise finally left
Richmond for New York about 1890, largely because of the vilification
of conservative newspapers and the threats made against him and his
family. Most men of Wise's class drifted back into the Democratic party
when the Readjusters disintegrated in the mid-1880s. White Republicans of the middle and lower classes who persisted in their affiliation
were usually either of northern or foreign birth, and they usually
adopted increasingly conservative racial views that reflected both the
policy of the national party and the prevailing sentiment of the city.[27]

At first the battle between Funders and Readjusters that had split the
Virginia Democratic party in the late 1870s had had little impact on
Richmond, a center of Funder strength. The Readjusters had not won a
majority in the General Assembly until 1879 and not until 1881 had
they managed to elect their gubernatorial candidate. Once William E.
Cameron had taken office in January 1882, however, the Readjusters
had the power to deal with their enemies in Richmond. The two bills
introduced to weaken Richmond's Funders were a metropolitan police
bill that would have given appointive power over the city police to the

state so that the Readjusters could remove conservatives on the Richmond police force as they had already done in Norfolk, and a bill to establish a state-owned gasworks in Richmond to compete with the city-owned utility. Both bills were defeated because of divisions among the leaders of the Readjuster party. Governor Cameron tried to remove Funders from the board of the Medical College so that he could install his own appointees, but the incumbents forcibly resisted the takeover attempt and called in the city police, who arrested one of the Readjusters. The Virginia Court of Appeals eventually ruled that the governor had exceeded his authority.[28]

The Readjusters had more success in other areas. Although George D. Wise, a Funder, was elected to represent the Richmond district in Congress in November 1882, his Readjuster cousin, John S. Wise, was elected as congressman-at-large. Readjusters won two municipal judgeships early in 1883, and in June the Readjuster-controlled State Board of Education used a technicality to remove Mayor William C. Carrington and other Funders from the city school board. Two blacks were among the Readjusters appointed to fill the vacancies.[29]

Outraged by these developments, the Funders allowed their opponents scant time to enjoy their triumph. Exploiting the deaths of several blacks and whites in a Danville race riot as evidence for the incompetence of the Readjuster government, Funder candidates won the election of November 1883 and brought a large majority to the General Assembly. The Funders removed the blacks and other Readjusters from Richmond's school board. A year later Grover Cleveland carried Richmond and the state against the opposition of the Readjusters, who supported Republican nominee Benjamin Harrison. The final blow to the Readjusters' power in Virginia came a year later, when Fitzhugh Lee defeated John S. Wise to succeed Governor Cameron.[30]

Funder control of Virginia at the state level was complete by the mid-1880s, but the conservatives in Richmond had to face new challenges. Organized labor had never been a force in city politics, but the national growth of the Knights of Labor stimulated a strong union movement. The first district assembly of the Knights in the South was founded in Richmond in 1885. Although estimates of their strength vary, the Richmond Knights eventually had several dozen locals in the two segregated district assemblies (the white number 84, and the black number 92), a cooperative soap factory, and plans for a building association and an underwear factory. The Knights claimed a city membership in 1886 of 7,692—more than three thousand whites and four thousand blacks—better than a third of the city's labor force in the late 1880s. Affiliation with the Knights of Labor, and the booming economy, encouraged Richmond unions to be more militant. More strikes occurred in Richmond in 1886 than in the previous five years combined. In 1886 and 1887 craftsmen staged nine strikes for higher pay or shorter hours. Seven succeeded.[31]

The oldest and perhaps the strongest of the city brotherhoods was the typographical union, which dated from 1856. It had conducted at least one successful strike during the Civil War, and in 1886 it blacklisted Baughman Brothers, the only nonunion printing firm in the city. The Knights supported the strike. They also organized a bitter, eight-month boycott of the Haxall-Crenshaw flour mills because the company used barrels made by penitentiary convicts rather than union coopers. Men of both races at the Old Dominion Iron and Nail Works staged a walkout that lasted for more than three months. The biracial stone quarrymen's strike in June 1886 was notable because white stonecutters in Richmond were regarded as particularly hostile to blacks.

Conservatives were naturally alarmed by this unusual degree of union activity, brought on in part by the failure of the Democratic machine to make overtures to labor leaders. City and state courts tried to crush the workers with injunctions and other legal actions, including conspiracy indictments, against organizers. The conservative press, in Richmond as in other cities, portrayed the local Knights as dangerous radicals unrepresentative of honest laborers. Either because they were trying to confuse the issue or because they were misled by the temperance policy of the national Knights of Labor, both the *Dispatch* and the *Richmond State* claimed that union men were receiving unexpected support from the city's growing number of prohibitionists. As the number of beer- and whiskey-drinking immigrants in Richmond declined, the advocates of prohibition had become relatively stronger, led by evangelical clergymen and even an Episcopal bishop. After the General Assembly passed a state local option law, Richmond's saloon-keepers formed the Liquor Dealers' Protective Association and collected 4,541 signatures on a petition requesting a referendum. The issue was decided in April 1886 with a voter turnout comparable to that of a presidential election. The wets defeated the drys, 8,940 to 3,260, partly because saloons, the headquarters of ward and precinct captains of both parties, were the indispensable focal points for political organization. At the same time, strong support for prohibition came from some conservative churchmen and wealthy whites who drank at home and did not frequent saloons. In an attempt to put the best face on the wet victory, the *Dispatch* argued that Negroes advocated prohibition and cited as evidence the Reverend John Jasper's dry stance. But it seems likely that most Richmond blacks followed state Republican boss William Mahone's instructions and voted with the wets. The wet victory aroused some resentment against the Democratic organization among drys, but more importantly it signaled the success of Mahone's plan to exploit at the city level a split among white Democrats over the labor and liquor questions.[32]

Shortly after the local option referendum, the white assemblies of the Knights of Labor organized a political party, nominated candidates for the common council and board of aldermen on a reform ticket (all but two of whom were longtime Democrats), and adopted a moderate labor platform. One issue in the 1886 campaign was the conservative council's failure to build a new city hall to replace the old structure, which had been demolished in 1874. Both skilled craftsmen and day laborers, eager for jobs, demanded that construction begin using only Richmond workers. The project had been delayed for years as the Democrats quarreled over architects and outside contractors. White and black Republicans, former Readjusters, and perhaps some angry temperance advocates aided the labor cause, and late in May 1886 the reform slate won the municipal election, electing its candidates in five of Richmond's six wards.

Although surprised by the results, the disappointed Democrats focused most of their ire on Republicans and Mahonites. Fearing to widen the split with the disaffected members of their party, the *Richmond Dispatch* merely referred to their "misguided" leaders, "captured by the reform idea," and argued that there was no justification for endangering party organization. There was no obvious attempt before or after the election to link the "Reformers" or "Workingmen's" party with the Haymarket riot of 4 May 1886, although the paper referred to "labor agitation" within the city as a factor in the election. The handing down of a decision in the locally sensational murder trial of Thomas J. Cluverius shortly after Haymarket overshadowed news of the Chicago troubles. The accounts of the riot carried in the *Dispatch* had a distinctly antilabor slant (as did some advertisements) but Terence Powderly's denunciation of the anarchists probably helped the Knights in the city.[33]

The labor candidates had been more liberal on many issues than the regular Democrats, but they proved just as conservative on racial matters. The biracial labor-Republican coalition broke down over the summer, leaving a mosaic of mutual distrust and suspicion, labor fear of association with blacks, petty bickering over the spoils of office, and white refusal to share patronage with black politicians. That fall, the three-way race for Richmond's district congressional seat ended in victory for George D. Wise, the conservative nominee, when labor candidate William Mullen, a Virginia native and district master workman for the Knights, withdrew and threw his support to the incumbent to deny victory to the Republican nominee, Edmund Waddill, Jr., whose backers were mostly black. After the November election, the reform councilmen announced that black workers would not be hired for the city hall project, but when the labor leaders lost their majority on the common council and board of aldermen, resurgent regular Democrats rejected their attempt to restrict construction jobs to local craftsmen and apprentices. By 1887 once prominent labor leaders were complaining that they and other union tradesmen had lost their jobs. The new city hall, begun during labor's brief control of the city government, was not completed until 1894. The total cost of the impressive granite structure was three times its original estimate, a fact that led to rumors of corruption but no formal charges, although conservatives boasted that it had been erected entirely by day laborers.[34]

Most Knights of Labor district assemblies were integrated, although some southern black locals were directly affiliated with the national general assembly. In Richmond, however, the black and white locals were segregated in the two district assemblies, largely because black workers wanted to elect their own leaders and control their own locals. Despite this policy of separation, the race issue undid the Knights of Labor in Richmond as elsewhere in the south. When the organization held its national convention in Richmond in October 1886, the delegation from New York's District Assembly 49 included a former Virginian, Frank J. Ferrell, who was the most prominent black leader in the Knights of Labor. Conservative Richmond whites were angered when the New Yorkers attended the Academy of Music in a body and were seated together in an obvious challenge to Richmond's policy of segregation. The following night a race riot almost occurred when the northerners sought admission to the Richmond Theater and were confronted by members of a white, antilabor group, the Law and Order Association.

At the grand session of the convention Governor Fitzhugh Lee refused to be introduced by Ferrell, whom the Knights had picked as a speaker in a show of biracial solidarity. The labor leaders reached a compromise with the governor. Ferrell introduced Knights president

Terence V. Powderly, and Powderly in turn presented Lee to the delegates. But Ferrell, who had been refused admission to Murphy's Hotel upon his arrival in Richmond, irritated white Richmonders by referring to southern "racial superstitions" in his opening speech. Many of the Knights had to stay in private boardinghouses and black hotels, and a ball scheduled for the end of the convention was canceled when the black delegates insisted on their right to attend on terms of social equality. Even without any racial problems, the union men would have had difficulty contending with large manufacturers and businessmen, who organized the Law and Order Association and used court injunctions, lockouts, and other tactics to intimidate workers. The Knights were excluded from the cornerstone-laying ceremony for the new city hall, a building that might never have been started without the impetus provided by the labor council. The speaker chosen for the occasion was a lawyer known for antiunion sentiments and poor oratory, the chief marshal of the parade was a judge known for his injunctions against the Knights, and other marshals were prominent leaders of the Law and Order Association.[35]

In time, however, larger political concerns, such as the restitution and maintenance of Democratic control of the city government, reunited the labor and conservative wings of the party in Richmond. In 1888, when William C. Carrington, mayor since 1876, decided to retire because of poor health, the labor and conservative leaders sought a compromise mayoral candidate to succeed Carrington. They chose J. Taylor Ellyson who had served as head of the school board and who was the son of former mayor Henry K. Ellyson. Ellyson held more progressive views of labor matters than his predecessor, but he was conservative on race and other political issues and was thus acceptable both to businessmen and to labor and conservative Democrats. The Democrats united to elect Ellyson, and black and white Republicans were removed from some city offices and denied city jobs. In the fall of 1888 the Democrats again carried the city for President Cleveland in his unsuccessful bid for reelection, and Republicans, particularly the blacks, began to lose what power they had enjoyed during the 1880s.[36]

Many more allegations of dishonesty in Richmond government were made during the 1880s than during the early period of Reconstruction, which is popularly regarded as a time of continuous scandal. Conservative Democrats brought corruption to city government. No municipal scandal surfaced during the brief tenure of the labor party. Most of the corruption involved the misuse of city funds. In 1882, for instance, a member of the board of aldermen charged that four councilmen,

Table 19
Richmond Males, Twenty-one Years of Age or Older, 1890

	Total	Percentage Registered to Vote	Native-born		Foreign-born		Black	
Marshall Ward	2,706	94.9	1,776	(65.6%)	163	(6.0%)	767	(28.3%)
Jefferson Ward	3,054	88.9	1,865	(61.0%)	372	(12.2%)	817	(26.8%)
Madison Ward	2,780	69.2	1,833	(65.9%)	303	(10.9%)	644	(23.2%)
Monroe Ward	4,232	63.6	2,343	(55.3%)	323	(7.6%)	1,566	(37.0%)
Clay Ward	4,642	73.0	3,355	(72.3%)	355	(7.6%)	932	(20.1%)
Jackson Ward	4,272	77.9	784	(18.3%)	214	(5.0%)	3,274	(76.6%)
City-wide total	21,686	77.9	11,956	(55.1%)	1,730	(8.0%)	8,000	(36.9%)
Total for predominantly white wards	17,414	76.6	11,172	(64.2%)	1,516	(8.7%)	4,726	(27.1%)

SOURCE: U.S., Bureau of the Census, *Compendium of the Eleventh Census, 1890, I* (Washington, D.C., 1896), 850.

including the former chairman of the poor committee and the longtime almshouse superintendent, had misappropriated funds paid the city by Henrico County for the use of Richmond's facilities for the poor. John M. Higgins, a member of the council for many years, called for a complete investigation but was ruled out of order. Higgins also charged that a member of the council had pocketed a commission on the sale of city bonds. An alderman charged that merchants on the council, some of whom allegedly spent hundreds or thousands of dollars to get elected, persuaded the city department heads to buy from their stores and prevented their competitors from getting city business. On a unanimous vote, the council finally authorized an investigation to be directed by the alderman who had made the initial charges. No report was ever made. Another scandal was the 1885 investigation of embezzlement in the city auditor's office, for which no report was ever released. When the local brick manufacturers' association charged that some councilmen had competed, in violation of law, to supply bricks for the city hall and for sewers, Lewis D. Crenshaw, a prominent civic leader, miller, alderman, and chairman of the investigating committee, declined to pursue the charges because the brick manufacturers, aware of the laws against slander, would not name those whom they suspected of wrongdoing.[37]

Perhaps the most spectacular case of dishonesty in Richmond's government—and one of the few in this period in which the city took action—was the embezzlement of at least $38,270 by Aylett R. Woodson, collector of city taxes from 1876 to 1887. The council approved the city attorney's recommendation that suit be brought against Woodson's estate. But among the items needed for the investigation was a special ledger kept by Woodson. It was the key to the whole affair, and it had been carried away after his death by an associate, who was also dead. The ledger was never found. Other ledgers revealed that Woodson's accounts for street paving were irregular between 1882 and 1887 and that he had stopped listing them at all from 1884 until his death in February 1887. No records could be found for delinquent gas bills or collections from 1884 and 1885. The main deficit appeared to be in tax collections from 1883 to 1887. Throughout the surviving records are systematic errors in addition, all against the city and all in Woodson's handwriting. The council minutes do not reveal the result of this case.[38] A careful student of Richmond politics in the 1890s concluded that

> the city's government was inefficient, tainted with corruption, and the object of countless investigations. . . . As the *Dispatch* admitted, "it is seldom that one hears a kind word spoken of the average councilman, . . . he is the object of constant criticism and the target of many idle and malicious shafts." . . . Although the corruption in Richmond was on a relatively petty scale, many citizens rightly suspected that the city was poorly managed and that the council dispensed contracts, franchises, and other favors for a price.[39]

This description of the nineties fits the eighties equally well.

• 4 •

Blacks in Richmond had considerable power during the early 1880s as a result of the Readjuster challenge to conservative Democrats. This was reflected in the number of Richmond blacks appointed to federal jobs by the Republican administration of Chester A. Arthur at the instigation of the Readjusters. A few blacks were appointed to office during Democratic administrations, and state and city Democrats occasionally chose black party members—as when they appointed Isaac Hunter to the board of directors of the state's Central Lunatic Asylum for Negroes—but patronage rewards for black politicians were always greatest when the Republicans were in power. In 1879, for example, there was only one black, Josiah Crump, among fourteen post office clerks, and of sixteen mailmen, five were black. Governor Cameron later appointed Crump to the asylum board. In 1882 all six clerks in the mailing department were black and two more were hired in 1883; three additional black mailmen were appointed in 1882, and by 1883 nine of the twenty carriers were black. That blacks comprised about half the workers in the Richmond post office—jobs that could easily have been filled with white Readjusters and Republicans—is the clearest indication of the black community's political power in Richmond. But in 1884 the Democrats elected Grover Cleveland and during the next four years regained control of both the state and city governments. They promptly cut the number of blacks in office, and by 1888 no mailmen and only two of seven mailing clerks were black. An exodus of blacks who left the city for better opportunities in the North also weakened their community's influence.[40]

Richmond was an exception to the population trends of the postwar urban South. Richmond and Atlanta were the only large southern cities in which the black percentage of the total population declined before 1900: in 1870 Richmond's population had been 45 percent black; in 1880, 44 percent; in 1890, 40 percent; and in 1900, 38 percent. The black population had been growing slowly—by 20 percent in the 1870s and by 16 percent in the 1880s—but the absolute number of blacks in Richmond dropped during the 1890s.

In terms of the ability to elect city officials, black political power in Richmond was confined to Jackson Ward, where the electorate was 77 percent black (see table 19) and where nearly half the city's black population resided. In some years, such as 1888 and 1889, the ward's five members of the common council and two of the three aldermen were black, but black councilmen or aldermen were not elected from any other ward, for the wards had been gerrymandered in 1871 and blacks comprised only 20 to 37 percent of the population in each of the others.[41]

The presence of black representatives from Jackson Ward on the common council did accomplish some things. Grave robbing, which was committed principally in black cemeteries, was ended in the early 1880s when, after a black janitor at the Medical College and several white medical students were arrested with cadavers, the state agreed to supply both the Medical College and the University of Virginia medical school with unclaimed bodies from the poorhouse and the city hospital.

In 1886 blacks on the council also secured the end of the chain gang in Richmond. Readjuster legislation had abolished the whipping post four years earlier. Black historian Luther P. Jackson cites "considerable gains for the Negroes in Richmond"—such as a new school, fuel for the poor, an armory for the black militia, street improvements, and better lighting in black neighborhoods—but concludes, in a realistic if perhaps contradictory vein, that the presence of blacks on the common council and the board of aldermen "had but little effect in changing the policies of the dominant race."[42]

Even at the peak of their representation in Richmond government—when the black council members included aggressive John Mitchell, Jr., publisher of the *Richmond Planet*, as well as the more diplomatic Joseph E. Farrar, a building contractor—the black community lacked political clout. This relative weakness showed in the attempts to secure a building for the First Colored Battalion of the Virginia State Militia. Blacks introduced resolutions for such an armory in 1882, in 1883, and again in every year from 1885 to 1890. The proposals were either summarily rejected by the white majority, or, more often, pigeonholed in committee. After thirteen years of agitation, the armory finally erected in 1895 was a pitifully small structure in comparison with the enormous buildings the city built for such white units as the Richmond Grays (1881), Howitzers (1895), and Light Infantry Blues (1910). The blacks on the council failed to obtain a city park for Jackson Ward. By the mid-1880s every ward in the city except Jackson had a tastefully decorated and landscaped park in which children played and adults strolled, relaxed, and listened to band concerts on hot summer evenings. Jackson Ward never shared in this municipal largess. The council refused even to select a site for a park, although the subject was discussed at a dozen council meetings between 1884 and 1890. A park was never laid out in the ward, which was itself gerrymandered out of existence in 1903.[43]

The white-controlled city government continued the practice, instituted by radical Republicans during Reconstruction, of segregation in social welfare. In theory the system promised separate but equal treatment, but in reality blacks normally received far less from city institutions such as hospitals and almshouses than whites of any class. The council did continue to support the Friends' Colored Orphan Asylum, established in 1869 on a lot donated by the city, but it contributed the same amount to each of four white orphanages. The crowded black hospital, almshouse, and orphan and insane asylums had higher mortality rates, poorer facilities, and less money to spend per

patient than the corresponding white institutions. Semipublic buildings, such as the separate YMCA founded because blacks were not
admitted to the white association, were refused the free gas and water
service that the council regularly voted to give white charitable and
recreational institutions.[44]

Blacks achieved their greatest success in independent enterprises that
they organized, supported, and controlled. The United Order of True
Reformers, founded late in the 1870s in Richmond, flourished into the
twentieth century. Its bank, founded in 1887, was the first black bank
in the United States, antedating the more successful and enduring Saint
Luke Penny Savings Bank administered by Maggie Lena Walker after
1900. The order ran groceries, clothing stores, and a one-hundred-
fifty-room hotel that competed with two other black hotels, Flagg's and
Harris's. The *Reformer*, the group's newspaper, had a circulation of five
thousand, and the order also operated a home for the aged, a building
and loan association, and a real estate firm. The city had, of course,
many black institutions in addition to those run by the True Reformers. In the press, both the weekly *Virginia Star* and the later daily
Richmond Planet spoke ably for the black community, and Joseph T.
Wilson's monthly *Industrial Day* became a weekly in 1889.[45]

Richmond blacks supported a number of private schools. The Moore
Street Industrial School, established in 1878 by members of a mission
organization of the Second Baptist Church, was operating as an incorporated institution by 1887. Among its trustees and instructors were the
most prominent blacks in the city, including John Oliver and Robert C.
Hobson, who had been leaders during Reconstruction. By 1891 the
school had sixty-two enrolled students: the boys learned carpentry and
printing, the girls learned to use sewing machines to make clothing for
women and children.[46]

The Reverend and Mrs. Joseph C. Hartshorn, of Rhode Island,
founded Hartshorn Memorial College in 1883 with a gift of twenty
thousand dollars for the education of young black women. By 1890 the
college was training school teachers, church workers, housewives, and
foreign missionaries. The school had no permanent endowment, but
was supported by donations from the American Baptist Home Mission
Society and the Woman's American Baptist Home Mission societies, of
New England and of Michigan. Most of the instruction was at the
normal-school level for teacher training, but the college offered
higher-level classes in English and boasted many successful graduates
including one who was appointed to the faculty of the Virginia Normal

and Collegiate Institute for Negroes (now Virginia State University) in Petersburg.[47]

The number of black businessmen and professionals—men trained at such institutions as the University of Michigan medical school and the law schools of Howard and of Yale universities—increased in the 1880s: in 1880 Richmond had only one black physician and two black lawyers; by 1889 the city had five black doctors, four lawyers, and a dentist. The proportion of blacks among the city's morticians increased, from one-third to one-half, and black barbers and hairdressers continued to dominate their profession. Nursing was another area in which blacks found jobs; an 1883–1884 city directory listed ten black and no white nurses. There were almost as many Negro blacksmiths, wheelwrights, watchmakers, and jewelers as white.[48]

Richmond's whites generally preferred nonthreatening black leaders, but some Richmond blacks, such as the lawyer Giles B. Jackson, both tactfully won the respect of whites and continued to work effectively behind the scenes for the advancement of black interests. Postal clerk Josiah Crump, who served several terms on the board of aldermen, was another leader of high standing in the black community who was also respected by whites. The board of aldermen attended his funeral in a body in 1890—as it would have done for any white colleague—invited members of the common council to join them, and draped Crump's desk and chair in mourning for thirty days, a customary sign of respect not always extended to blacks. The crusading publisher John Mitchell, Jr., on the other hand, was the kind of black leader that white Richmonders hated and feared. Mitchell had had the audacity to ridicule the Confederacy and to campaign openly against the brutal and increasingly frequent practice of lynching.[49]

Race relations in Richmond, as in much of the South and the nation, began to worsen in the late 1880s. Blacks were disqualified from working on the city hall and from other city jobs, both because of their race and because they were Republicans. None of those laid off were rehired, despite John Mitchell's demand for an investigation. On 15 March 1889 a white preacher from Brooklyn delivered a sermon to black congregations that the *Dispatch* branded as "negrophilist." Because of the tension that resulted, the sermon was not printed until seven months later. Black military units had once marched in Confederate memorial parades, sometimes over the protests of unreconstructed rebels like Jubal Early, but by the end of the decade they refused to take part even if invited. In October 1887, for instance, when the black companies were asked, almost as an afterthought, to participate in the cornerstone-laying ceremony for a monument to Robert E. Lee, the members met and formally voted to accept the invitation, but then in an informal session decided not to march because the tardy invitation was an insult that did not allow them time to practice their drills or clean their uniforms. City leaders showed a total lack of regard for black feelings in the fall of 1890 when they extended Seventh Street across Bacons Quarter Branch to the new real estate developments on the city's north side: the street and viaduct cut through and tore up Richmond's historic black cemetery, in which many of the city's most famous slaves and free Negroes had been buried. Where the displaced remains were reinterred is still uncertain.[50]

John W. ("Justice John") Crutchfield, who presided over Richmond's police court from 1888 through the early years of the twentieth century, attracted national attention by baiting black defendants who appeared before him on misdemeanor charges. Some whites regarded the judge's behavior as appalling. Yet, he amused others, who fondly remembered his paternal attitude toward Negro children. A Progressive-era account of proceedings in his courtroom, written by a northern white reporter attracted by Crutchfield's notoriety, shows clearly that his justice did not amuse Richmond blacks:

> All the benches were occupied and many persons, white and black, were standing up. . . . The performance is more like a vaudeville show with the judge as headliner than like a serious tribunal. . . . At the back of the room, in what appeared to be a sort of steel cage, were assembled the prisoners, all of them, on this occasion, negroes; while at the head of the chamber behind the usual police-court bulwark, sat the judge—a white-haired, hook-nosed man of more than seventy, peering over the top of his eyeglasses with a look of shrewd, merciless divination. . . .
>
> THE JUDGE (severely)—Was—you—*drunk?*
>
> THE PRISONER—No, suh, Jedge. Ah was n't drunk. Ah don't think no man's drunk s' long 's he can navigate, Jedge. I don't—
>
> THE JUDGE—Oh, yes, he can be! He can navigate and navigate mighty mean!—Ten dollars. . . .
>
> (While the next prisoner is being brought up, the judge entertains his audience with one of the humorous monologues for which he is famous, and which, together with the summary "justice" he metes out, keeps ripples of laughter running through the room): I'm

going to get drunk myself, some day, and see what it does to me. [Laughter.] Mebbe I'll take a little cocaine, too. . . .

THE JUDGE (inspecting the prisoner sharply)— You ain't a Richmond nigger. I can tell that to look at you.

THE PRISONER—No, suh, Jedge. That's right.

THE JUDGE—Where you from? You're from No'th Ca'lina, ain't you?

THE PRISONER—Yas, suh, Jedge.

THE JUDGE—Six months!

(A great laugh rises from the courtroom at this. On inquiry we learn that the "joke" depends upon the judge's well-known aversion for negroes from North Carolina.)[51]

The reporter, whose account was published in 1917, went on to say that when he later saw Walter C. Kelly's vaudeville performance of *The Virginia Judge*, he saw "a certain gentle side" in the vaudeville portrayal "of which I saw no signs in Judge Crutchfield."

White observers customarily attributed the high rate of infant and adult mortality among blacks to their innate weakness as a race and implied that they had been better cared for as slaves. They also blamed the city's large black population for Richmond's slow economic growth; the *Dispatch* thought it unfair to compare Richmond with northern cities because they had few Negroes and, therefore, almost all of their residents were productive members of society. The reverse of this argument was advanced in 1889 by Lewis Harvie Blair, an aristocratic Richmond reformer and critic of the prevailing social order in the South, in a book entitled *The Prosperity of the South Dependent Upon the Elevation of the Negro*. Blair argued, correctly, that racial discrimination prevented black southerners from making more significant contributions to the progress of their region, but Richmond's economic growth was slowed by other factors as well.[52]

• 5 •

The city's business leaders liked to say that Richmond's growth, although unspectacular, was steady and not subject to the instability of northern cities. They also claimed that Richmond suffered fewer economic fluctuations than most cities because its large tobacco industry was "depression proof." In fact, Richmond's economy followed national trends in the fourth quarter of the nineteenth century: recovery for several years after 1878, recession from 1882 to 1885, and then further expansion until the Panic of 1893.

Although Richmond continued to decline as an entrepôt, it briefly dominated the wholesale markets in eight southern states and even penetrated the Midwest. Richmond's jobbing firms sent out hundreds of drummers, or wholesale salesmen, on railroads throughout the South to dispose of large consignments of groceries and liquor, as well as smaller quantities of coffee, dry goods, notions, boots and shoes, hardware, and drugs. Annual jobbing sales increased from $17 million in 1885 to better than $36 million by 1891. In 1892 jobbing sales surpassed the value of Richmond's manufacturing production for the first time.[53]

Midway between southern consumers and northeastern manufacturers, Richmond's merchants had several advantages that helped them to enter new markets in the 1880s. Their drummers had good rail connections to the south and west over the Atlantic Coast Line, the Richmond and Danville, and the Chesapeake and Ohio. In 1880 Richmond was one of only ten southern cities with a population of twenty-five thousand. Then, as the South became more urban in the eighties, Richmond lost some of its advantages to rival towns such as Lynchburg; Charlotte, Greensboro, and Asheville, North Carolina; and Bristol and Knoxville, Tennessee. This new competition and the Panic of 1893 caused a 20 percent drop in Richmond's jobbing sales in the 1890s.[54]

Richmond was also the financial center of the upper South in the last decades of the nineteenth century. Its ten banks had a total capital of about $2 million in 1890 and handled transactions amounting to $83 million—a figure that represents a level of financial activity in the city far greater than that in cities of the same size such as Syracuse, New York; Columbus, Ohio; or New Haven, Connecticut. Insurance companies were another component of Richmond's financial power. Five large firms, including two that were founded before the war, had headquarters in the city. The relative newcomer was the Life Insurance Company of Virginia, established in Petersburg in 1871, which helped the city through depressions by cashing checks and making loans to manufacturers.[55]

In the 1880s Richmond industry became more diversified: in 1871 the tobacco, flour, and iron industries accounted for 89 percent of the city's total manufactured product; in 1880 they contributed only 63 percent; in 1890, only 43 percent. The secondary industries—wooden products, drugs and chemicals, and foodstuffs—each produced goods worth more than $1 million in 1880. The Richmond Cedar Works was the largest woodworking plant in the world, with twelve hundred workers and shops covering twelve acres. The Richmond Chemical Works employed fifty workers in the manufacture of acids and fertilizers. Five coffee and spice manufacturers produced goods worth $241,000. Twenty bakers made $238,000 worth of bread and crackers. Thirteen confectioners supplied Richmonders with $151,000 in sweets. The Valentine Meat Juice Company sold bottled steak sauce worth $52,000. Leather goods, printing and publishing, paper manufacturing, and clothing and textile firms formed a third group of industries, each of which contributed $400,000 to $500,000 to Richmond's 1880 production. By 1890 the value of manufactured leather goods had reached almost $2 million and of paper products almost $1 million. The clothing and textile industry did not grow as fast, primarily because after 1880 women's clothing was imported from the North rather than made in Richmond.[56]

Although the processing of grain, iron ore, and tobacco continued to dominate the city's economy, each of these industries had serious problems in the 1880s. The milling industry reached its postwar peak of $3 million per year between 1881 and 1883. Flour production then fell to half that level by 1887, increased again to $2.5 million by 1892, and then went into its final decline, dropping below the $1 million level in 1897.

Flour exports to South America, traditionally the city's largest market, declined steadily after 1883. Of the three major mills, only one survived the century. The Haxall-Crenshaw mill had sent almost all of its flour to Brazil. When it lost its South American markets the company suffered financial difficulties and failed in 1891, after a century of continuous operation. The Gallego mill, which had exported flour both to South America and to England, went into receivership in 1900. Only the Dunlop mill, which marketed most of its flour in the southern and southwestern states and a small amount locally, continued to operate without serious difficulty.[57]

Richmond's decline as a port had crippled its milling industry and grain trade. The president of the grain and cotton exchange reported in 1890 that no wheat or cotton had been exported from the city during the previous year—it all had been shipped from Newport News or West Point. Since export wheat, the highest grade, was not marketed in the city, Richmond attracted fewer buyers, less interest was shown in the available lower grades, and this grain brought lower prices than it had in the past. In turn, low prices induced sellers to market their grain in cities where higher bids could be expected.[58]

Richmond's iron industry continued a slow decline from its 1881 level of $5.25 million—a figure just $.25 million below the city's 1872 total. Iron production dropped to $4.25 million in 1890. Although the Virginia iron industry did not peak until 1900, Richmond's iron industry was declining. The city's manufacturers had adequate supplies of limestone, coke, iron ore, and cheap labor in the 1880s. But most of its products were sold only in the South, and pig iron was the chief product (Virginia's ore contained too much phosphorous to be converted to steel by the Bessemer process). The opening of vast coal deposits in West Virginia helped Richmond remain marginally competitive in the industry, but the discovery of rich ore deposits on the Mesabi range near Lake Superior gave Pittsburgh a decisive national advantage, and in the southern market Richmond suffered from competition with Birmingham and the booming iron industry in Alabama.[59]

New ironworks were started in Richmond in the 1880s, and the older companies' products became more varied. Tredegar was still the city's largest employer, with five or six thousand men working on its thirty-acre site until the early 1890s. The Old Dominion Iron and Nail Works on Belle Isle remained the largest nail factory in the South, and at the Southern Stove Works, founded in the 1870s, a hundred workers turned out a specialty line of heating and cooking stoves through the early nineties. Talbott and Sons, the oldest engine works in Richmond, had three hundred workers by 1883 and a plant occupying two city blocks, but it weakened in the Panic of 1893 and failed in 1895. At full capacity the Tanner and Delaney Engine Company, which became the Richmond Locomotive Works in 1888 following an enlargement of its plant, had two thousand workers and could turn out two hundred locomotives a year. Purchased in the late 1890s by northern interests that sought to reduce its competition with their other regional factories, it did not survive the first decade of the new century.[60]

Tobacco manufacturing in Richmond during the 1880s never reached the $13 million peak set in 1876: the industry's product fell to $8.75 million in 1881, and $7.75 million in 1883, then gradually increased to $9.25 million in 1887. With the largest supply of raw material of the city's three big industries and a long tradition of successful manufacturing and exporting, it represented Richmond's best chance for economic greatness in the modern United States. The failure of Richmond's conservative manufacturers to adopt new technology sealed the city's fate as the economic vassal of outside interests. The industry changed radically in the 1880s, particularly in the manufacture of cigarettes. Mechanization glutted the market for tobacco products, and fierce competition ensued between the major companies in New York, North Carolina, and Richmond, all of whom sought to expand sales with advertisements and attractive packaging. Consumer demand for tobacco continued to increase, but the industry's growth rate declined.[61]

The most significant technological development was a device to manufacture cigarettes that was invented by a Virginian, James Bonsack, who patented it in 1881 and improved it during the next two years. The inventor organized the Bonsack Machine Company in 1883 and sent his first machines to Allen and Ginter, the largest cigarette manufacturer in Richmond and the South. After a brief trial, however, the Richmond company discarded the machines, claiming that machine-made cigarettes would never sell and that the device did not work perfectly. Such objections did not deter James B. Duke, of North Carolina, whose company began manufacturing cigarettes in 1881, six years after Allen and Ginter. Duke leased some of Bonsack's machines in 1883, improved them, and signed a favorable contract with the inventor in 1885. By the time Allen and Ginter resumed use of the Bonsack machine in 1887, Bonsack and Duke were closely allied.[62]

In 1888 and 1889 Bonsack's company secured control of the patents for the other two cigarette-making machines then in use, and Duke began to organize his American Tobacco Company, one of the first great holding companies in the United States. Lewis Ginter's Richmond firm was one of the five—which together manufactured 90 percent of all the cigarettes made in the United States—that joined the holding company. The founders disagreed over the division of stock in the new company. Ginter thought his share should be slightly larger than Duke's, but the smaller partners sided with Duke, who was elected president. After the General Assembly of Virginia refused to issue a charter for the new tobacco giant, Duke easily secured a charter in New Jersey and moved company headquarters to New York. Richmond, the great tobacco manufacturing center, became merely a large appendage of the American Tobacco Company.[63]

• 6 •

Despite signs of modernity, conservative and reactionary values remained strong during the 1880s. The comte de Haussonville, perhaps a more perceptive observer of Richmond than the urban boosters quoted earlier, described the city as he saw it on his visit in 1887:

The view [of Richmond] has nothing that might be considered particularly original, and no longer presents that air of prosperity and excitement which always, at least to my eyes, gives a certain charm to American towns. There are almost no vessels anchored along the docks; the wooden breakwaters fall in ruins; the streets that can be seen are in bad condition, the houses appear equally awful; no factories, nothing that betrays activity and life, but rather an appearance of poverty and decadence. One feels that this unfortunate town . . . formerly so flourishing, has not recovered from the events whose theater it was. . . . The first view of the town is melancholy enough, and while looking at it, I cannot keep myself from deploring the fate of this old Virginia.

Haussonville had arrived at a steamship depot in Rocketts, one of the city's poor, unattractive neighborhoods, but after touring Richmond with local dignitaries his impression was somewhat more favorable. "The inhabitants . . . have in part repaired their ruins," he observed, "and today the town, without having entirely regained her former prosperity, is once again in the process of development and growth."[64]

Religious and ethnic tolerance seemed to continue in the 1880s. The council allowed the ladies of various Catholic churches to use the First Regiment Armory for their two-week-long charity fair. The *Richmond Dispatch* celebrated Pope Leo XIII's golden jubilee in a two-column article on the front page, and in 1885 Richmond Jews were routinely given permission to expand the Hebrew Cemetery north to Bacons Quarter Branch. By the end of the decade, however, conservative trends had become dominant again in Richmond. Religious fundamentalism and evangelism increased in the 1880s, among both whites and blacks. The Richmond Sabbath Association was organized in 1883, with Dr. J. L. M. Curry as president, and William Wirt Henry as vice-president, to secure a strict observance of Sunday, which Germans profaned by frequenting their beer gardens in the afternoon, and which Italian confectioners, Jewish merchants, and black barbers violated by opening their shops. Bishop John J. Keane, of the Roman Catholic Diocese of Richmond, disturbed the city's ecumenism and irritated Protestant divines by preaching to blacks and addressing them on terms of social and spiritual equality—something that Protestant ministers allegedly refused to do. In 1885 Dwight L. Moody launched a revival in Richmond that continued for months in the city's Baptist, Methodist, and Presbyterian churches. Moody's success was certain after he assured Moses D. Hoge, the city's most prominent minister, that he had never criticized Lee or Jackson. In 1890 Samuel P. Jones, another noted revivalist, and his choir of two hundred voices visited Richmond and claimed many converts. Advocates of prohibition grew ever stronger, and although they failed to close the saloons in the 1880s, they did secure passage of a law that provided a fine or a jail term for minors who drank in bars without parental consent.[65]

The council responded to the decline in the city's immigrant population by resolving to cease publication of municipal notices and advertisements in Richmond's German newspapers, but this action was vetoed by the board of aldermen in 1887. Cultural activities supported by the Germans and Irish, such as the weekly concerts of the Mozart Association, seemed to be at their peak in the late 1880s when the Academy of Music was completed. In the 1890s such entertainment began to decline in popularity, and music seemed of little importance in Richmond after 1900.[66]

Public schools gained popularity during the 1880s. Enrollments increased 78 percent, almost three times the rate of growth in the total population, and seven new schools were built to supplement the eleven in use in 1880. Sentiment against public education remained strong, however, and was reflected in the continued inadequacy of school facilities and in the council's apparently halfhearted commitment to public education. In 1885 the chairman of the school board told the councilmen that the schools were overcrowded, that many held half-day sessions, and that hundreds of white children and at least a thousand blacks had been denied admission. The council appropriated 80 percent of the chairman's funding request, but the amount proved insufficient. In the fall of 1886 the council again was told that eight hundred black and two hundred white children were still without schools. The council voted a small sum to provide temporary classrooms.[67]

Adherents of the New South creed held educational ideas unlike those of more traditional private school teachers in Richmond. John P. McGuire and W. Gordon McCabe, headmasters of the two most noted boys' schools in the postwar decades, emphasized character-building over intellectual training. The curricula of their schools were heavily weighted toward religion, ancient languages, and history—subjects that had been favored in the antebellum era—rather than economics, modern languages, and science.[68]

Beautiful young women continued to reign at the Virginia springs and at coastal resorts. Mary Triplett and Mattie Ould, the leading

belles of the 1870s, were succeeded in the 1880s by May Handy and
Irene Langhorne. Such women tended to marry rich—and even old or
divorced—northerners, rather than impecunious young Richmonders,
however long their family pedigree. Perceval Reniers observed that
"belles of such a stature weren't marrying poor journalists," such as
Page McCarty, who had fought a duel over Miss Triplett, "and sure
enough, Miss Mary soon betrothed herself to one of those rare Southerners of substance, Mr. Philip Haxall, a gentleman with mills." Miss
Ould wed wealthy northern-born editor Oliver J. Schoolcraft, while
May Handy married a divorced New York banker, James Brown
Potter. Irene Langhorne won the heart of Charles Dana Gibson and
became his Gibson girl. "A path was being worn to the North by the
feet of the premier belles, bound for the better marriages of bonanza
land," Reniers concluded. "Before the crest of belledom began to break
[in the mid–1890s] an exceptionally lovely lot was riding it. . . . Every
one of them made a brilliant match. Four of the seven followed a path to
the North; two of the four married millionaires."[69]

The renewed conservatism of Richmond society was evident not
only in the continued glorification of southern womanhood but also in
the hatred of Republicans, in the emigration of Richmond blacks, and
in the absence of new blood—whether immigrant or Yankee. The
atmosphere was changing, Richmond was becoming more like a city of
the Old South than of the New. Richmond had failed to become a
modern metropolis, and white Richmonders increasingly turned to the
only thing that was unique to the city, its past.[70]

Chief among the conservative trends that developed in the 1880s was
the cult of the Lost Cause. In the 1860s and 1870s Richmonders had
been too poor and too busy recovering from the war and Reconstruction to celebrate their Confederate experience. They were unable even
to care properly for the graves of Confederate dead in Hollywood and
Oakwood cemeteries. Expensive monuments and elaborate parades
during the depression of the 1870s had been out of the question. The
statue of Stonewall Jackson that was erected in Capitol Square in 1875
was gratefully accepted by Richmond's whites, but it had been paid for
by English gentlemen.

With the return of prosperity in the 1880s Confederate reunions
increased in frequency and popularity. The generation gap that had
separated old city politicians and young veterans during Reconstruction
had diminished. Civil War soldiers, in their forties or older, were in
their prime, holding positions of power in business and government.
They liked to read about the South's heroes, who were being glorified

in books and articles. The movement gained strength after the death of
Jefferson Davis in December 1889. The city school board had acquired
the Davis mansion in 1870 from a council that had no use for Confederate relics. After using and abusing the building for twenty years, the
board proposed to raze the structrue and build a new school on the site,
rather than buy another piece of property. The growth of Confederate
sentiment, bolstered by Davis's timely death, saved the building.
Organizations of veterans and ladies prevented its destruction, and it
was turned over to the Confederate Memorial Literary Society in the
1890s as a museum of the Lost Cause.[71]

In 1890 Richmonders erected an equestrian statue of Robert E. Lee,
the first of many Confederate monuments in the city that were paid for
by the people throughout the South. At the insistence of Governor
Fitzhugh Lee, the French sculptor Jean Antonin Mercié enlarged his
design to equal the size of the statue of Washington in Capitol Square.
Locating a site for the monument was another problem. To the
consternation of many, the Lee Monument Association eventually
chose a cornfield west of the city limits, which fell within a district
annexed in 1892. The statue, shipped from Paris addressed to "General
Lee" (an irony noted by Richmonders) arrived on the R. F. & P., and
was hauled from the Elba Station at Broad and Pine streets by
thousands of Richmonders, just as Thomas Crawford's statue of
Washington had been dragged from the dock at Rocketts to Capitol
Square in 1857.[72]

When the monument was unveiled before a huge crowd in May
1890, it was found that Lee's head rose more than sixteen inches higher
than Washington's. The antebellum statue celebrated a great, victori-
ous American who was venerated as the nation's principal hero by
citizens everywhere. The new and larger statue was a tribute to a great,
defeated Virginian who had not yet joined the American pantheon. At
the time, only southerners unreservedly admired the man who was
smaller in some ways than Washington, and who had taken Washington as his own model and yet fought to destroy his hero's creation. The
dedication ceremonies did not go unnoticed in the northern press.
Many papers, particularly the Republican ones, thought the statue
offensive, since it honored a "traitor." Some demanded that Congress
prohibit the erection of any additional monuments to former Confederates, and the *Boston Transcript* voiced especially virulent criticisms
because the thousands of Confederate flags used in the dedication
ceremony had been made by a Massachusetts company.[73]

For some prominent Richmonders the Lee statue became the object of a peculiar practice that epitomized sentiment in the city. The noted schoolmaster W. Gordon McCabe walked to the site at four each afternoon, winter and summer, to salute the equestrian figure. He taught his son to do the same thing. Decades later, the biographer and newspaper editor Douglas Southall Freeman saluted the statue each day on his way to work. Lee would not have approved of this idolatry.

It was the loyalty to the old over the new that young novelist Ellen Glasgow, born in Richmond in 1874, found stifling. The readiness to sentimentalize the past impeded development in the arts as surely as it retarded economic, social, and political growth. With the exception of the automobile, a white or black Richmonder of the 1890s would not have felt himself a stranger in Richmond during the Progressive era, the 1920s, or even the 1930s. Changes were of degree not kind. Statues of J. E. B. Stuart and Jefferson Davis were unveiled in 1907, during a week-long Confederate reunion attended by eighteen thousand veterans. A statue of Stonewall Jackson was put up in 1919, followed by one of Matthew Fontaine Maury in 1929. Not until 1932 was the final Richmond reunion held, attended by two thousand Confederate veterans who marched in the "The Last Parade."[74]

How was the sight of Richmond not to be a potent idea; how was the place not, presumably, to be interesting, to a restless analyst . . . to whose young imagination the Confederate capital had grown lurid, fuliginous, vividly tragic—especially under the process through which its fate was to close round it and overwhelm it, invest it with one of the great reverberating historic names? . . . I could not possibly have drawn near with an intelligence more respectfully and liberally prepared for hospitality to it.

Henry James

EPILOGUE

James on Richmond

WHEN Henry James visited Richmond in 1903 he was prepared to be a sympathetic observer. The city was legendary. After walking around Richmond, and after a visit to the Confederate museum, he posed the first of many questions. "What will they be . . . the Southern shrines of memory, on the day the last old Confederate soldier shall have been gathered to his fate?" The question was significant, but that day did not come until the last veteran in the city died in 1941.[1] James reluctantly concluded that

> Richmond . . . looked to me simply blank and void. . . . The great modern hotel, superfluously vast, was excellent; but it enjoyed as a feature, as a "value," an uncontested priority. It was a huge well-pitched tent . . . proclaiming in the desert the name of a new industry. . . . The wind was harsh, the sky sullen, the houses scarce emphasized at all as houses; the "Southern character," in fine, was nowhere. . . . Was it practically but a question then, deplorable thought, of a poor Northern city?—with the bare difference that a Northern city of such extent would, however stricken, have succeeded, by some Northern art in pretending to resources.[2]

The writer continued his self-interrogation.

> What was I tasting of, at that time of day, and with intensity, but the far consequences of things, made absolutely majestic by their weight and duration? I was tasting, mystically, of the very essence of the old Southern idea—the hugest fallacy . . . for which hundreds of thousands of men had ever laid down their lives. I was

tasting of the very bitterness of the immense, grotesque, defeated project—the project, extravagant, fantastic, and to-day pathetic in its folly, of a vast Slave State (as the old term ran) artfully, savingly isolated in the world that was to contain it and trade with it. This was what everything round me meant—that that absurdity had once flourished there; and nothing, immediately, could have been more interesting than the lesson that such may remain, for long years, the tell-tale face of things where such absurdities *have* flourished.[3]

After paying visits to the state Capitol, the public library, and other places of interest in Richmond, James came to the statue of Lee: "High aloft and extraordinarily by itself. . . . As some precious pearl of ocean washed up on a rude bare strand. . . . The place is the mere vague centre of two or three crossways, without form and void, with a circle half sketched by three or four small groups of small, new, mean houses." At last James felt that he was "solving the riddle of the historic poverty of Richmond. It is the poverty that *is*, exactly, historic. . . . The condition attested is the condition . . . of having worshipped false gods. As I looked back . . . at Lee's stranded, bereft image, . . . I recognized something more than the melancholy of a lost cause. The whole infelicity speaks of a cause that could never have been gained."[4]

Richmond inherited the worst of both the Old and the New South. The racism and the conservatism of life before the war became even more embedded in its society, but much of the antebellum gracious-ness, noblesse oblige, and disdain for money was gone, replaced by a materialism and a superficiality vividly perceived by Ellen Glasgow. The rights of workers, women, and blacks were little more respected, and the need for a good public school system, for libraries, and for other progressive features of modern urban life were scarcely more recognized in 1890 than in 1860. The tragedy of Richmond after the war was that its white leaders, after two decades of flirtation with progress, returned to a cause that they had all but abandoned and embraced the dead thing with a passion they had never felt while it lived.

Short Titles and Symbols

CCR	Records of the Richmond Common Council, City Clerk's Office, Richmond City Hall, Richmond, Virginia
CWH	*Civil War History*
JAH	*Journal of American History*
JSH	*Journal of Southern History*
MCC	Louis H. Manarin, ed., *Richmond At War: The Minutes of the City Council, 1861-1865* (Chapel Hill, N.C., 1966)
RD	*Richmond Daily Dispatch*
RE	*Richmond Enquirer*
REx	*Richmond Examiner*
RW	*Richmond Daily Whig*
VHS	Virginia Historical Society, Richmond, Virginia
VM	Valentine Museum, Richmond, Virginia
VMHB	*Virginia Magazine of History and Biography*
VSL	Archives Branch, Virginia State Library, Richmond, Virginia
W & M	Manuscripts Department, Earl Gregg Swem Library, College of William and Mary, Williamsburg, Virginia

Notes

Chapter 1: Richmond on the James

1. Virginius Dabney, *Virginia: The New Dominion* (Garden City, N.Y., 1971), 203–204; Charles Henry Ambler, *Thomas Ritchie: A Study in Virginia Politics* (Richmond, 1913), 17. *See also* Barbara J. Griffin, "Thomas Ritchie: Other Dimensions," *The Richmond Literature and History Quarterly* 2 (1979): 29–33, whose forthcoming study is based on Ritchie's previously unused personal papers in the Library of Congress, Washington, D.C.

2. Emory M. Thomas, *The Confederate State of Richmond: A Biography of the Capital* (Austin, 1971), 21; Bayrd Still, *Urban America: A History with Documents* (Boston, 1974), 89; Richard C. Wade, *Slavery in the Cities: The South 1820–1860* (New York, 1964), 12.

3. Richard B. Morton, *Colonial Virginia*, 2 vols. (Chapel Hill, N.C., 1960), 2:559; Andrew W. Morrison, ed., *The City on the James: Richmond, Virginia* (Richmond, 1893), 12; Jean Gottmann, *Virginia at Mid-Century* (New York, 1955), 104–105; M. Ethel Kelley Kern, *The Trail of the Three Notched Road* (Richmond, 1928), 7–9.

4. Virginius Dabney, *Richmond: The Story of a City* (Garden City, N.Y., 1976), 10–16; Raus McDill Hanson, ed., *Virginia Place Names: Derivations, Historical Uses* (Verona, Va., 1969), 228.

5. Samuel Mordecai, *Virginia, Especially Richmond, In By-Gone Days . . .* , 2d ed. (Richmond, 1860), 296–301; Mary Wingfield Scott, *Houses of Old Richmond* (Richmond, 1941), 179; Gottmann, *Virginia at Mid-Century*, 105–106; Robert McEwen, "Exploring the Kanawha Canal: Gateway to the Past," *Richmond Mercury*, 11 Sept. 1974.

6. W. Asbury Christian, *Richmond: Her Past and Present* (Richmond, 1912), 90, 93, 99–100; Ambler, *Ritchie*, 13–14; Clement Eaton, *The Growth of Southern Civilization, 1790–1860* (New York, 1961), 198–199.

7. George Rogers Taylor, *The Transportation Revolution, 1815–1860*, in Henry David, et al., eds., *The Economic History of the United States*, vol. 4 (New York, 1951), 15–24.

8. John B. Mordecai, *A Brief History of the Richmond, Fredericksburg and Potomac Railroad* (Richmond, 1940), 5–6, 8–10, 17–18, 20, 24–25, 44; Charles W. Turner, *Chessie's Road* (Richmond, 1956), 73; Maury Klein, *The Great Richmond Terminal: A Study in Businessmen and Business Strategy* (Charlottesville, 1970), 55; Stuart Bowe Medlin, "The York River Railroad: 1851–1881" (M.A. thesis, University of Richmond, 1968).

9. Frederick Law Olmsted, *The Cotton Kingdom . . .* , ed. Arthur M. Schlesinger (New York, 1953), 34, 44–45; Eugene Alvarez, *Travel on Southern Antebellum Railroads, 1828–1860* (University, Ala., 1974), 110; *RD*, 19 Dec. 1867.

10. Olmsted, *Cotton Kingdom*, 33; Eaton, *Southern Civilization*, 252–253; Christian, *Richmond*, 41, 46, 92, 326; Mordecai, *By-Gone Days*, 305–310; Thomas F. Hale and Louis H. Manarin, *Richmond: A Pictorial History From the Valentine Museum and Dementi Collections* (Richmond, [1974]), 3.

11. Allen M. Wakstein, *The Urbanization of America: An Historical Anthology* (Boston, 1970), 135–139; *RD*, 6 Dec. 1866, 30 Sept. 1869.

12. T. C. DeLeon, *Four Years in Rebel Capitals: An Inside View of Life in the Southern Confederacy, From Birth to Death* (Mobile, Ala., 1890), 85.

13. Mary Newton Stanard, *Richmond: Its People and Its Story* (Philadelphia, 1923), 25; *RD*, 17 Oct. 1866, 7 Sept., 10 Oct. 1867, 10 Aug. 1869.

14. Scott, *Houses*, 27, 135; Morrison, ed., *City on James*, 176–178.

15. Scott, *Houses*, 47, 187, 303; Christian, *Richmond*, 288. On the significance of family enterprises in southern urban development *see* Don H. Doyle, "Urbanization and Southern Culture: Economic Elites in Four New South Cities," (Paper presented at the Forty-fourth Annual Meeting of the Southern Historical Association, St. Louis, Mo., 11 Nov. 1978).

16. Fred A. Shannon, *The Farmer's Last Frontier: Agriculture, 1860–1897*, in David, et al., eds., *Economic History of the U.S.*, vol. 5 (New York, 1945), 148–149, 157–158; Stuart Bruchey, *The Roots of American Economic Growth, 1607–1861* (New York, 1965), 14–15; Edward King, *The Great South* (Hartford, Conn., 1875), 631–632; Charles B. Dew, *Ironmaker to the Confederacy: Joseph R. Anderson and the Tredegar Iron Works* (New Haven, Conn., 1966), 22, 32–39; Morrison, ed., *City on James*, 144–145; Scott, *Houses*, 230; Mordecai, *History of R. F. & P.*, 81–82; Moncure Robinson Papers, 1788–1889, W & M. There are frequent references to Richmond's old industrial families in Robert Beverley Munford, Jr., *Richmond Homes and Memories* (Richmond, 1936), and John A. Cutchins, *Memories of Old Richmond (1881–1944)*, (Verona, Va., 1973). *See also RD*, 9 Dec. 1865, 31 Jan. 1866, 7 Sept. 1867, 19 Feb., 30 Mar. 1869; and *RW*, 15 May 1865.

17. King, *Great South*, 631–632; Morrison, ed., *City on James*, 13–14; U.S., Bureau of the Census, Eighth Census, 1860, Industrial Schedule MSS, VSL. The figure for flour includes cornmeal.

18. *RD*, (David Currie's obituary) 4 Aug. 1866, 28 Oct. 1869; Eaton, *Southern Civilization*, 238.

19. Scott, *Houses*, 127, 163, 180, 283; Eaton, *Southern Civilization*, 229–230; Eighth Census, Industrial Schedule MSS.

20. Scott, *Houses*, 179, 283, 285; Thomas, *State of Richmond*, 23–24; Dew, *Ironmaker to Confederacy*; Christian, *Richmond*, 171, 179; Eaton, *Southern Civilization*, 207, 235–236. The Eighth Census lists 1,659 men in the iron and other metal shops, with sales of $2.3 million. The Tredegar employed half of these men and had $1 million in sales in 1860. Most of the other 59 shops and foundries were small operations, with only a few workers and a product of less than $25,000 each. The large flour mills, by contrast, were high volume, capital intensive operations, requiring expensive machinery but few workers to mill large quantities of grain. Antebellum tobacco factories were labor intensive, with many workers using mostly hand labor to process tobacco.

21. Stanard, *Richmond People*, 11, 39; Dabney, *Virginia*, 47, 228–229, 240–243; Wade, *Slavery in Cities*, 33–37, 202–203; Robert S. Starobin, *Industrial Slavery in the Old South* (New York, 1970), 15–16, 21–22; Herbert S. Klein, *Slavery in the Americas: A Comparative Study of Virginia and Cuba* (Chicago, 1967), 187–189; Ira Berlin, *Slaves Without Masters: The Free Negro in the Antebellum South* (New York, 1974), 219–220; Frederic Bancroft, *Slave-Trading in the Old South* (Baltimore, 1931), 94–119, 174, 237–238, 245–247, 273, 289; Robert Russell, *North America, Its Agriculture and Climate* (Edinburgh, 1857), 157; Mary Wingfield Scott, *Old Richmond Neighborhoods* (Richmond, 1950), 72; Christian, *Richmond*, 189; Clement Eaton, *A History of the Old South*, 3d ed. (New York, 1975), 234–236; Olmsted, *Cotton Kingdom*, 39–41, 593–600; Ernest Taylor Walthall, *Hidden Things Brought to Light* (Richmond, 1908), 42; John S. Wise, *The End of An Era*

(Boston, 1899), 78–88; David R. Goldfield, *Urban Growth in the Age of Sectionalism: Virginia, 1847–1861* (Baton Rouge, 1977), 120–121.

Robert W. Fogel and Stanley L. Engerman, in *Time on the Cross: The Economics of American Negro Slavery* (Boston, 1974), 52–55, 57–58, argue that Richmond's role in the general interstate slave trade was of limited significance. Fogel and Engerman refute Bancroft's work on two points—the alleged prevalence of the sales of slave children, and the question of whether slave breeding was practiced—but do not address themselves to Bancroft's evidence regarding the size of the Richmond slave trade. Evidence both from primary and secondary sources indicates that it was large, although the statement in the 5 Oct. 1865 *Daily New Nation* that weekly slave sales in the city at times totaled $2 million hardly can be credited, for such a figure would require the sale in one week of about two thousand prime field hands at top prices.

William Calderhead's "How Extensive Was the Border State Slave Trade? A New Look," *CWH* 18 (1972): 42–55, deals almost entirely with Maryland, but does serve as a useful corrective to Bancroft. Calderhead, following Kenneth Stampp's *The Peculiar Institution: Slavery in the Ante-Bellum South* (New York, 1956), recognizes Richmond's role in the largest slave exporting state, and finds that the 1830s were even busier for the trade than the 1850s.

22. Bancroft, *Slave-Trading*, 96–98, 276–277 n.26; Christian, *Richmond*, 274, 326, 467; Scott, *Houses*, 138–141, 175, 209, 228, and *Neighborhoods*, 198–200, 234, 275; Munford, *Homes and Memories*, 138–139; Wade, *Slavery in Cities*, 43; *MCC*, 5 Apr. 1862, 2 Apr. 1865 and pp. 628, 631–632; Edward V. Valentine's MS notes, "Traders (Negro)," VM; *RW*, 15 Apr. 1865; *RD*, 5 Feb., 4 Aug., 25 Oct. 1866, 22 Oct., 16 Nov. 1867, 7 May, 11 and 19 Aug., 10 Sept. 1869, 16 Mar. 1870; CCR, 27 July 1865, 7 Apr. 1866.

23. Mordecai, *By-Gone Days*, 274–280, 316–319; Thomas, *State of Richmond*, 21–22, 23; Richmond Chamber of Commerce, "List of firms 100 years old or more," typescript (Richmond, 1940).

24. Marvin Davis Evans, "The Richmond Press on the Eve of the Civil War," *The John P. Branch Historical Papers of Randolph-Macon College*, n.s., vol. 1 (January 1951). A fifth daily, the *Richmond Index*, published by Bennett M. De Witt and begun early in 1859, was the only city paper to support Stephen A. Douglas. It did not long survive the defeat of its candidate. The *Dispatch* was one of the new penny dailies that had become popular in antebellum America.

25. Eaton, *Southern Civilization*, 251–252; Thomas, *State of Richmond*, 29.

26. Margaret Meagher, *History of Education in Richmond* (Richmond, 1939), 66–90; Wise, *End of Era*, 57–58, 70; Munford, *Homes and Memories*, 79, 85–87, 122; Cutchins, *Old Richmond*, 33–37, 52–67; Stanard, *Richmond People*, 221.

27. Reuben E. Alley, *History of the University of Richmond, 1830–1971* (Charlottesville, 1977), 14, 21–23, 35, 54, 74, 90, 111; *RD*, 24 Nov. 1866, 27 Sept. 1869, 1 Jan. 1890.

28. Meagher, *Education in Richmond*, 65–66; Paul S. Dulaney, *The Architecture of Historic Richmond* (Charlottesville, 1968), 99–100; James O. Breedon, "Body Snatchers and Anatomy Professors: Medical Education in Nineteenth-Century Virginia," *VMHB* 83 (1975): 344. The University of Virginia medical school also remained open.

29. Thomas, *State of Richmond*, 30; Meagher, *Education in Richmond*, 72–75.

30. Dabney, *Richmond*, 33; Mordecai, *By-Gone Days*, 249–252; *RD*, 7 Mar., 30 Nov., 6 Dec. 1866, 29 Jan. 1868, 23 Feb. 1869; Cutchins, *Old Richmond*, 177–179; Hale and Manarin, *Pictorial History*, 38, 174; George Augustus Sala, *America Revisited . . .* , 2d ed., 2 vols. (London, 1882), 1:236, 243, 245–246; F. Barham Zincke, *Last Winter in the United States . . .* (London, 1868), 90.

31. Stanard, *Richmond People*, 146–148; Dabney, *Virginia*, 415–416; Wise, *End of Era*, 94–97; James T. Moore, "The Death of the Duel: The *Code Duello* in Readjuster Virginia, 1879–1883,"

VMHB 83 (1975): 259–276; Evan R. Chesterman, "Duels and Duelists of Bygone Days," clippings from the *Richmond Evening Journal* (Richmond, 1908–1909); Christian, *Richmond*, 51–52, 58.

32. John A. Cutchins, *A Famous Command: The Richmond Light Infantry Blues* (Richmond, 1934); *RD*, 19 Jan., 28 Feb., 9 and 22 May, 22 Aug. 1866.

33. Dabney, *Richmond*, 50–60; Wise, *End of Era*, 59, 74; Olmsted, *Cotton Kingdom*, 33–34; Wade, *Slavery in Cities*, 98, 100.

34. Louis B. Cei, "Law Enforcement in Richmond: A History of Police-Community Relations, 1737–1974" (Ph.D. diss., Florida State University, 1975), 7–11, 17–19, 21, 32, 36, 40–41, 43.

35. The best discussion of the mid-nineteenth century black community in Richmond is John T. O'Brien, "Factory, Church, and Community: Blacks in Antebellum Richmond," *JSH* 44 (1978): 509–536. *See also* Wade, *Slavery in Cities*, 12–13, 33–37; Starobin, *Industrial Slavery*, 21–22; Klein, *Slavery in Americas*, 189. Starobin disputes Wade's thesis that slavery was weakening in the cities, as does much other recent scholarship; but Wade clearly felt that Richmond was an exception to his thesis. Fogel and Engerman (*Time on the Cross*, 38–39) argue that slaves held most of the skilled jobs not just in cities but also in the rural areas, where the great majority of them lived.

36. Eighth Census, Industrial Schedule MSS; Leslie Winston Smith, "Richmond During Presidential Reconstruction, 1865–1867" (Ph.D. diss., University of Virginia, 1974), 6. Although the taxes were only levied on a few items (and thus were not paid by everyone), the articles taxed were luxuries and those who paid the taxes were more likely to own slaves (Wade, *Slavery in Cities*, 21, 36–37, 46–47, 139–140).

37. *RE*, 17 Aug. 1859 and Wade, *Slavery in Cities*, 260. For Wade's reasoning about the female imbalance of the slave sex ratio, *see* page 23 and tables for ten large southern cities at page 330. Fogel and Engerman disagree (*Time on the Cross*, 156). The character of the domestic life of urban slaves is also hotly argued. Herbert G. Gutman (in *The Black Family in Slavery and Freedom, 1750–1925* [New York, 1976], 564–565) has attacked Wade's description of the married life of urban slaves (*Slavery in Cities*, 119) as "weak at best." Yet both Fogel and Engerman (*Time on the Cross*, 132) and Eugene B. Genovese (*Roll, Jordan, Roll: The World the Slaves Made* [New York, 1974], 415) have presented evidence that indicates that the majority of mulattoes were in southern towns and cities, and that miscegenation most frequently took place there. Genovese states that "most of the miscegenation in the South occurred in the towns and cities . . . [which] provided the favored setting and housed the larger numbers of the mulattoes. . . . Sexual ratios in the towns and cities propelled interracial concubinage, for white males usually outnumbered white females, whereas black females usually outnumbered black males." Genovese's argument seems to follow Wade's very closely. Even if these arguments are correct, they do not prove that urban slave marriages were unstable. In Richmond the larger number of free black women may have worked to offset the unequal number of female slaves, but the total number of black males in Richmond compared to black females increased steadily from 4 percent in 1840 to 16 percent in 1860. While free Negro males could and did marry slave women, hoping to buy their freedom, there seems to have been far less incentive for a free female to marry a male slave. She was not as capable of freeing him, since her income as a laborer was far lower than a man's. A free black husband had more to offer: protection, status, and a more conventional family life. Historians do not agree about the nature of the domestic institutions of urban slaves, but there is evidence of interracial sexual liasons in Richmond (*see*

Wade, *Slavery in Cities*, 258–260; Cei, "Law Enforcement," 52; and Berlin, *Slaves Without Masters*, 55, 220–221).

38. Wade, *Slavery in Cities*, 60–61, 64, 68, 71–73, 75–79, 106–107, 117, 275–277; Walthall, *Hidden Things*, 36–37; Scott, *Neighborhoods*, 17–18, 20, 203–204, 211; Klein, *Slavery in Americas*, 188–189.

39. Wade, *Slavery in Cities*, 84–87, 89, 108–109, 133, 155–156, 159–160; Berlin, *Slaves Without Masters*, 241–243.

40. Olmsted, *Cotton Kingdom*, 37–38; Mordecai, *By-Gone Days*, 356–357; Berlin, *Slaves Without Masters*, 345.

41. Berlin, *Slaves Without Masters*, 76–78, 287, 290–291, 295, 297–302, 311–312, 335–338; Wade, *Slavery in Cities*, 166–167, 169, 171–172; Scott, *Neighborhoods*, 96–98, 202–204; *RD*, 9 Aug. 1866.

42. Thomas, *State of Richmond*, 30 and n.63; Scott, *Neighborhoods*, 229, 283; James H. Bailey, *History of St. Peter's Church, Richmond, Virginia* (Richmond, [1959]), 11–12; [Father Joseph Magri], *The Catholic Church in the City and Diocese of Richmond* (Richmond, 1906), 50–51, 57–68, 78–79, 83, 85–86; Lester J. Cappon, *Virginia Newspapers, 1821–1935: A Bibliography with Historical Introduction and Notes* (New York, 1936), 165–166, ·182, 191–192; Meagher, *Education in Richmond*, 123, 128–129. The best study of the local Jewish community is Myron Berman, *Richmond's Jewry, 1769–1976: Shabbat in Shockoe* (Charlottesville, 1979). *See also* Herbert T. Ezekiel and Gaston Lichtenstein, *The History of the Jews of Richmond From 1769 to 1917* (Richmond, 1917), 14, 35, 225–227, 236; Olmsted, *Cotton Kingdom*, 38; Mordecai, *By-Gone Days*, 155–156; Scott, *Houses*, 242; *RD*, 19 May, 5 Nov. 1866, 1 Jan. 1870.

43. Howard N. Rabinowitz, "From Exclusion to Segregation: Health and Welfare Services for Southern Blacks, 1865–1890," *Social Service Review* 48 (1974): 331; Olmsted, *Cotton Kingdom*, 34–45; Wade, *Slavery in Cities*, 169–170; Berlin, *Slaves Without Masters*, 307–309; *RD*, 12 Oct. 1866, 22 May 1867; Walthall, *Hidden Things*, 32–33.

44. Alice Böhmer Rudd, *Shockoe Hill Cemetery, Richmond, Virginia*, 2 vols. (Washington, D.C., 1960–1962); Christian, *Richmond*, 143; Scott, *Neighborhoods*, 285–290; *Map of Richmond, Manchester, and Suburbs, From Surveys by Jas. T. Redd, County Surveyor* (Richmond, 1877); *see also* Ezekiel and Lichtenstein, *Jews of Richmond*, 283–284; *RD*, 22 May 1867; Mordecai, *By-Gone Days*, 165.

45. Christian, *Richmond*, 163–165; Scott, *Neighborhoods*, 216; Mordecai, *By-Gone Days*, 165; Wise, *End of Era*, 104–111; *RD*, 6 Sept. 1869. On the social and symbolic importance of urban graveyards *see* W. Lloyd Warner, *The Living and the Dead: A Study of the Symbolic Life of Americans* (New Haven, Conn., 1959), 31–33, 248–320; and David E. Stannard, *The Puritan Way of Death* (New York, 1977), 156–161, 177–181, 184–185. On the nineteenth-century rural cemetery movement in the American city *see* Stanley French, "The Cemetery as Cultural Institution: The Establishment of Mount Auburn and the 'Rural Cemetery' Movement," *American Quarterly* 26 (1974): 37–59; and R. Kent Lancaster, "Green Mount: The Introduction of the Rural Cemetery Into Baltimore," *Maryland Historical Magazine* 74 (1979): 62–79.

46. Harry M. Ward and Harold E. Greer, Jr., *Richmond during the Revolution, 1775–83* (Charlottesville, 1977), 8; Gottmann, *Virginia at Mid-Century*, 484; Scott, *Houses*, 5–6, 27, 30, and *Neighborhoods*, 91; Dulaney, *Architecture of Richmond*, 44; Christian, *Richmond*, 21–23, 27, 41, 44, 64; *RD*, 1 Jan. 1885; Giles Cromwell, *The Virginia Manufactory of Arms* (Charlottesville, 1975), 22–23, 148–152.

47. Christian, *Richmond*, 28; Alexander W. Weddell, *Richmond, Virginia, in Old Prints*,

1737–1887 (Richmond, 1932), 35–36, 68–69; Eaton, *Southern Civilization*, 279–281; Scott, *Neighborhoods*, 202–206; *RD*, 5 June, 17 Oct., 1, 5, 11 and 12 Dec. 1866, 9 Aug. 1867, 1 Jan. 1874 and 1878.

48. Christian, *Richmond*, 56–57; Marianne Patricia Buroff Sheldon, "Richmond, Virginia: The Town and Henrico County to 1820" (Ph.D. diss., University of Michigan, 1975), 131, 141–142; Smith, "Presidential Reconstruction," 13; Wise, *End of Era*, 55–56.

49. CCR, Apr. 1865 to Dec. 1870.

50. *MCC*, pp. 627–636; Thomas, *State of Richmond*, 19–20.

51. Harry Ammon, "The Richmond Junto, 1800–1824," *VMHB* 61 (1953): 395–418; Joseph H. Harrison, Jr., "Oligarchs and Democrats—The Richmond Junto," *VMHB* 78 (1970): 184–198; Cappon, *Virginia Newspapers*, 171–173; Dabney, *Virginia*, 196, 203–204.

52. W. Dean Burnham, *Presidential Ballots, 1836–1892* (Baltimore, 1955), 842; Ella Lonn, *Foreigners in the Confederacy* (Chapel Hill, N.C., 1940), 2–3, 481.

53. Wise, *End of Era*, 58.

54. Dabney, *Virginia*, 211–223, 226–227; Henry T. Shanks, *The Secession Movement in Virginia, 1847–1861* (Richmond, 1934), 1–17; Goldfield, *Urban Growth*, 205–225, 267–269; Dabney, *Virginia*, 220–223; Gottmann, *Virginia at Mid-Century*, 113–114; Eaton, *Southern Civilization*, 182, 198–199.

55. William H. Gaines, Jr., *Biographical Register of Members, Virginia State Convention of 1861 First Session* (Richmond, 1969), 49–50, 53–54, 65–66, 79.

56. Christian, *Richmond*, 221; Thomas, *State of Richmond*, 13–14.

57. *RD*, 1 Aug. 1866, 18 Oct. 1869; Meriwether Stuart, "Samuel Ruth and General R. E. Lee," *VMHB* 71 (1963): 35–109, and "Colonel Ulric Dahlgren and Richmond's Union Underground, April 1864," *VMHB* 72 (1964): 152–204; Bailey, *St. Peter's Church*, 47.

58. Frederick Law Olmsted, *A Journey in the Back Country (New York, 1860)*, 279–280.

Chapter 2: The Conservative Citadel, 1861–1865

1. *See* Alfred Hoyt Bill, *The Beleaguered City: Richmond, 1861–1865* (New York, 1946); and Emory M. Thomas, *The Confederate State of Richmond: A Biography of the Capital* (Austin, 1971).

2. *MCC*, 9 and 25 May, 8 and 13 July 1861; *RD*, 9 July 1861; *REx*, 17 June 1861.

3. *MCC*, 9 Dec. 1861.

4. Ibid., 15 Apr. 1861, 12 May 1862; Margaret Carey, "Richmond In April 1865," *Yale Review* 20 (1931): 645–648; James H. Brewer, *The Confederate Negro: Virginia's Craftsmen and Military Laborers, 1861–1865* (Durham, N.C., 1969), 137–160; Louis H. Manarin and Lee A. Wallace, Jr., *Richmond Volunteers: The Volunteer Companies of the City of Richmond and Henrico County, Virginia, 1861–1865* (Richmond, 1969); W. Dean Burnham, *Presidential Ballots, 1836–1892* (Baltimore, 1955), 842.

For a rough proportion of adult males in Richmond who served in the war, compare the number of volunteers (about 3,000) with the number voting in the 1860 presidential election (4,322). The actual number of men was greater, both because viva voce voting was used in antebellum Richmond, and because many who were eligible did not vote. On the other hand, some men of military age fled to the North in 1861.

5. *MCC*, 8 and 16 July, 1861; *REx*, 30 Aug. 1861.

6. *MCC*, 12, 15, 28 and 29 May, 3 June, 11 July 1862, 9 and 26 Mar. 1863.

7. Ibid., 18 and 19 May, 13 July 1863; J. B. Jones, *A Rebel War Clerk's Diary at the Confederate States Capital*, 2 vols. (Philadelphia, 1866), 1:347–348.

8. Virgil Carrington Jones, *Eight Hours Before Richmond* (New York, 1957), 77–78, 165. There

is no adequate history of the city battalion in its various forms; articles in the *Examiner*, 6 and 20 Apr. 1863, contradict some of the material drawn from Jones and the city council minutes.

9. *MCC*, 11 Jan., 13 June 1864, 15 Mar. 1865.

10. David R. Goldfield, *Urban Growth in the Age of Sectionalism* (Baton Rouge, 1977), 147; *MCC*, 12 Jan., 13 July 1863, 10 Oct. 1864.

11. *MCC*, 4 Nov. 1861, 23 May 1862.

12. Alfred D. Chandler, Jr., *The Visible Hand: The Managerial Revolution in American Business* (Cambridge, Mass., 1977), 122–124. *MCC*, 26 Apr. 1861, 26 May 1862, 23 Feb. 1863; Robert C. Black III, *The Railroads of the Confederacy* (Chapel Hill, N.C., 1952), 9, 73.

13. *MCC*, 3, 5, 8, and 10 June, 14 Oct. 1861; *REx*, 19 Oct. 1861. Extra meals, carriage hire, and fine wines accounted for two-thirds of the bill, although the *Examiner*, while hostile to Davis, admitted that he was a teetotaler. Evidently his hungry associates were not.

14. *MCC*, 22 and 24 Apr., 13 May, 8 July 1861.

15. Ibid., 1 Mar., 24 Apr. 1862, 5 Jan., 23 Mar. 1864; Jones, *Clerk's Diary, 1:178; RW*, 8 Oct. 1863.

16. *MCC*, 24 Mar., 23 Oct. 1862; *REx*, 25 Mar. 1862.

17. *MCC*, 14 June 1862, 14 and 26 Jan., 9 Feb. 1863, 3 Dec. 1864, 9 Jan. 1865.

18. Ibid., 12 Jan., 9 and 23 Feb., 8 June, 2 Oct. 1863, and p. 209; *REx*, 10 Feb., 5 Oct. 1863.

19. *MCC*, 15 Feb., 14 Mar. 1864; *REx*, 16 Feb. 1864.

20. *MCC*, 15 Feb., 13 June, 30 Aug., 12 Sept., 14 Nov., 3 and 12 Dec. 1864; *REx*, 31 Aug. 1864; *RW*, 5 Dec. 1864.

21. *MCC*, 11 and 28 July 1862, 8, 15, and 22 June, 12 Oct., 9 Nov. 1863.

22. Ibid., 3, 14, 15, and 19 May 1862, 9 Jan., 24 and 27 Feb. 1865; *REx*, 19 and 20 May 1862.

23. *MCC*, p. 629. At least one councilman was a Union Democrat who opposed secession but was reelected during the war.

24. Ibid., 9 and 16 Dec. 1861.

25. Ibid., 10 Nov. 1862, 17 Apr., 18 May 1863, 8 and 30 Aug., 12 Sept. 1864, 3, 13, 20, and 23 Feb., 13 Mar. 1865.

26. *MCC*, 9 June, 28 July, 11 Aug., 24 Nov. 1862, 9 and 26 Mar., 20 July, 9 Nov. 1863, 20 Sept. 1864, 9 Jan. 1865; *REx*, 27 Mar. 1863; Jones, *Clerk's Diary*, 1:246.

27. *MCC*, 23 Oct. 1862, 5 and 11 Jan., 8 Feb. 1864; Thomas, *State of Richmond*, 156.

28. *MCC*, 19 and 22 Apr., 8 July 1861, 24 Apr., 8 Sept. 1862; *REx*, 13 May 1862; *RE*, 26 Apr., 12 May 1862.

29. *MCC*, 11 July 1862, 13 Apr. 1863, 22 Feb. 1864; *RW, REx*, and *RD*, 5 May 1864.

30. *MCC*, 8 Dec. 1862, 9 Feb., 18 May, 22 June, 23 Dec. 1863, 11 and 18 Jan., 21 Apr., 31 May, 30 Aug., 6 Sept. 1864; *REx*, 19 Jan., 7 Sept. 1864.

31. *MCC*, 22 Apr. 1861, 5 and 24 Apr., 24 Nov. 1862, 9 Jan., 13 Mar. 1865; *REx*, 25 Nov. 1862, 19 Dec. 1863.

32. *MCC*, 28 July 1862, 26 Mar. 1863, 8 Feb., 11 July 1864, 1 and 13 Feb. 1865.

33. Ibid., 13 May 1861, 8 Sept. 1862, 9 Mar. 1863, 24 Oct., 11 Nov., 12 Dec. 1864; *RE*, 25 Oct. 1864. The twelve thousand dollar figure included harness and other equipment, and the stabling and feeding of the extra horses.

34. *MCC*, 12 Oct., 3 Dec. 1863, 5 May, 24 Oct. 1864; *REx*, 13 Oct., 4 Dec. 1863; *RE*, 4 Dec. 1863.

35. *MCC*, 24 Feb., 8 Sept., 10 Nov. 1862, 12 Jan., 17 Feb., 9 and 13 Mar., 15 June, 10 and 15 Aug. 1863, 4 May 1864.

36. Ibid., 23 Feb. 1865.

37. Ibid., 3 and 5 June, 12 Aug., 9 Sept., 14 Oct. 1861, 20 Feb., 24 Apr., 14, 23, and 29 May, 6 June, 28 July, 13 and 23 Oct., 10 Nov. 1862, 12 Jan., 9 Feb., 12 Oct., 9 Nov., 3 and 23 Dec. 1863, 5 and 21 Jan., 8 and 12 Dec. 1864; *REx*, 13 Nov. 1862, 5 and 13 Dec. 1864, 2 Jan. 1865; *RD*, 20 Sept. 1862.

38. *MCC*, 10 Nov., 8 Dec. 1862, 23 Feb., 10 May, 13 July 1863, 30 Aug., 15 Nov. 1864.

39. Ibid., 14 Dec. 1863, 5 Jan. 1864, 20 Mar. 1865; *RE*, 14 June 1864; *REx*, 21 Mar. 1865.

40. *MCC*, 23 Feb. 1863, 11 Jan., 8 Feb. 1864, 27 Feb. 1865.

41. Robert Garlick Hill Kean, *Inside the Confederate Government: The Diary of Robert Garlick Hill Kean*, ed. Edward Younger (New York, 1957), 41, 45–47; F. N. Boney, *John Letcher of Virginia: The Story of Virginia's Civil War Governor* (University, Ala., 1966), 188–190; Jones, *Clerk's Diary*, 1:196, 277, 2:184.

42. The brief summary of the bread riot in this and the following eight paragraphs is based on files of the *Richmond Daily Examiner*, 3–29 Apr. 1863, and the *Richmond Daily Dispatch*, May-June 1863, in the American Antiquarian Society, Worcester, Mass. All quotations are from the *Examiner*, except that from Fred Fleet's letter to his father, Dr. Benjamin Fleet, which appears in Betsy Fleet and John D. P. Fuller, eds., *Green Mount, A Virginia Plantation Family during the War: Being the Journal of Benjamin Robert Fleet and Letters of His Family* (Lexington, Ky., 1962), 216–217.

43. Various accounts differ in substance and detail. For traditional versions *see* Bill, *Beleaguered City*, 165–166; Thomas, *State of Richmond*, 119–122; and Virginius Dabney, *Richmond: The Story of a City* (Garden City, N. Y., 1976), 181–182.

44. Mrs. Roger A. Pryor [Sara Agnes Rice Pryor], *Reminiscences of Peace and War* (New York, 1904), 237–239; Jones, *Clerk's Diary*, 1:284–287; [Judith W. McGuire], *Diary of a Southern Refugee, During the War* (New York, 1867), 202–203; Ernest Taylor Walthall, *Hidden Things Brought to Light* (Richmond, 1908), 24; *REx*, 4 and 6 Apr. 1863.

45. *REx*, 4 and 6 Apr. 1863.

46. *MCC*, 2, 13, and 18 Apr., 18 May 1863.

47. Ibid., 14 June, 28 July, 18 Aug., 8 Sept. 1862, 13 Apr., 18 May, 8 June, 10 Aug. 1863; Stephen E. Ambrose, "Yeoman Discontent in the Confederacy," *CWH* 8 (1962): 259–268.

48. *MCC*, 12, 15, and 19 Oct. 1863, 11 and 20 Apr. 1864.

49. Ibid., 23 June, 11, 19, and 21 July, 12 Sept. 1864.

50. Ibid., 11 July, 8 and 24 Aug. 1864.

51. Ibid., 6 and 20 Sept. 1864, 1 and 20 Feb., 13 and 15 Mar. 1865.

52. Ibid., 10 Nov. 1862, 26 Mar., 12 Oct., 9 Nov. 1863, 14 Mar. 1864.

53. *RD*, 11 Dec. 1861; Ludwell H. Johnson, "Commerce Between Northeastern Ports and the Confederacy, 1861–1865," *JAH* 54 (1967): 30–42; Jones, *Clerk's Diary*, 1:92, 343; T. C. DeLeon, *Four Years in Rebel Capitals: An Inside View of Life in the Southern Confederacy From Birth to Death* (Mobile, Ala., 1890), 147; *REx*, 21 Apr. 1863.

54. Thomas, *State of Richmond*, 70–71; John S. Wise, *The End of an Era* (Boston, 1899), 370.

55. Mark M. Boatner III, ed., *The Civil War Dictionary* (New York, 1959), 699, 847; DeLeon, *Rebel Capitals*, 92.

56. J. Malcolm Bridges, "Industry and Trade," in *Richmond, Capital of Virginia: Approaches to Its History*, ed. [Hamilton J. Eckenrode] (Richmond, 1938), 74.

57. DeLeon, *Rebel Capitals*, 86, 95–97; [Sallie A. Brock Putnam], *Richmond During the War; Four Years of Personal Observations* (New York, 1867), 30–31, 36; Mary Boykin Chesnut, *A Diary From Dixie*, ed. Ben Ames Williams (Boston, 1949), 75.

58. W. Asbury Christian, *Richmond: Her Past and Present* (Richmond, 1912), 346; Bill, *Beleaguered City*, 4; Bell Irvin Wiley, *The Life of Johnny Reb: The Common Soldier of the Confederacy* (New York, 1943), 53–58; Ben Ames Williams, *House Divided* (Boston, 1947), 1145; Fleet and Fuller, eds., *Green Mount*, 96, 157.

59. *MCC*, 18 Jan., 22 Feb., 14 Mar. 1864; *REx*, 4 and 21 Apr. 1863.

60. Thomas, *State of Richmond*, 138–139; Dabney, *Richmond*, 182.

61. I am indebted to National Park Service historian Hyman Schwartzberg, of the Richmond National Battlefield Park, for the most recent estimate of the mortality rate at Chimborazo. Winder had a larger capacity, but Chimborazo may have had more total patients; each has been referred to as the biggest hospital in the Confederacy.

62. Phoebe Yates Pember, *A Southern Woman's Story: Life in Confederate Richmond*, ed. Bell Irvin Wiley (Jackson, Tenn., 1959), 100; Mrs. William Mason Smith, Richmond, to J. J. Pringle, Charleston, 4 July 1864, in Katherine M. Jones, *Ladies of Richmond, Confederate Capital* (New York, 1962), 227–228.

63. Brewer, *Confederate Negro*, 96–99.

64. *MCC*, 22 June, 13 July, 14 Dec. 1863, 11 and 18 Jan., 10 Oct. 1864, 9 Jan., 13 Feb. 1865; *REx*, 12 Jan. 1864; Chesnut, *Diary From Dixie*, 363–365, 368; Jones, *Clerk's Diary*, 1:291.

65. Thomas Jefferson to Nathaniel Burwell, 14 Mar. 1818, in Thomas Jefferson, *The Life and Selected Writings of Thomas Jefferson*, ed. Adrienne Koch and William Peden (New York, 1944), 689.

66. DeLeon, *Rebel Capitals*, 105–106, 146–149, 351–353; Chesnut, *Diary From Dixie*, 367; Pryor, *Peace and War*, 263–264; [Putnam], *Richmond During War*, 210; Dabney, *Richmond*, 182; Jones, *Clerk's Diary*, 2:290; Bill, *Beleaguered City*, 86, 186–187.

67. Jones, *Clerk's Diary*, 1:104, 119–120, 164, 185–186, 202, 320, 2:211, 389; [Putnam], *Richmond During War*, 106, 271; Wise, *End of Era*, 176–177, 401–402; Thomas, *State of Richmond*, 151–152; Myrta Lockett Avary, ed., *A Virginia Girl in the Civil War, 1861–1865* (New York, 1903), 126, 139, 144; Myron Berman, *Richmond's Jewry, 1769–1976: Shabbat in Shockoe* (Charlottesville, 1979), 176–193; Bertram Wallace Korn, *American Jewry and the Civil War* (Philadelphia, 1951).

68. Chesnut, *Diary From Dixie*, 306.

69. [McGuire], *Southern Refugee*, 328–329; Pember, *Woman's Story*, 187; Mrs. Burton Harrison [Constance Cary Harrison], *Recollections Grave and Gay* (New York, 1911), 150–151, 201–208. The admonition is a recurring theme in Ben Ames Williams's novel *House Divided*.

70. Meriwether Stuart, "Samuel Ruth and General R. E. Lee: Disloyalty and the Line of Supply to Fredericksburg, 1862–1863," *VMHB* 71 (1963): 35–109, and "Colonel Ulric Dahlgren and Richmond's Union Underground, April 1864," *VMHB* 72 (1964): 152–204; [Putnam], *Richmond During War*, 101–102; *Richmond New Nation*, 20 Sept. 1866; James D. Horan, *Desperate Women* (New York, 1952), 124–168.

71. Bill, *Beleaguered City*, 262; Jones, *Clerk's Diary*, 2:388; Philip Whitlock, MS recollections, 1843–1913, VHS.

72. Harry M. Ward and Harold E. Greer, Jr., *Richmond During the Revolution, 1775–83* (Charlottesville, 1977), 82; *RW*, Apr. 1865 quoted in E. Merton Coulter, *The Confederate States of America, 1861–1865* in Wendell Holmes Stephenson and E. Merton Coulter, eds., *A History of the South*, vol. 7 ([Baton Rouge], 1950), 559. Ironically, today most Virginians believe that General Grant burned Richmond. Articles to this effect regularly appear in Virginia newspapers and magazines, and similar statements are made by otherwise well-informed people.

Chapter 3: The Desolate City, 1865–1870

1. *RW*, 6 and 18 Apr., 23 and 29 May 1865.

2. The most convenient summary of the evacuation is Rembert W. Patrick's *The Fall of Richmond* (Baton Rouge, 1960).

3. CCR, 2 Apr. 1865.

4. George L. Christian, *Confederate Memories and Experiences* ([Richmond, 1914]), 33; interviews with Phyllis Fentress Coleman in *Richmond News Leader*, 3 Apr. 1937, and *Richmond Times-Dispatch*, 5 Apr. 1942; Ernest Taylor Walthall, *Hidden Things Brought to Light* (Richmond, 1908), 32; Philip Whitlock, MS recollections, 1843–1913, VHS.

5. *RW*, 2 May 1865; Patrick, *Fall of Richmond*, 61; reminiscences by Mrs. Laura J. Allen Sutherland on the burning of Richmond, 3 Apr. 1865, Accession 23964, Personal Papers Collection, VSL. Samuel J. T. Moore, Jr., *Moore's Complete Civil War Guide to Richmond*, rev. ed. (n.p., 1978), 99, states that Mrs. Stanard's house was not destroyed; however, both the map of the Burnt District and a list of residential property losses (*RW*, 10 Apr. 1865) indicate that it did burn.

6. George Anson Bruce, *The Capture and Occupation of Richmond* (n.p., [1918?]), 8–9, 12.

7. Ibid., 12; Patrick, *Fall of Richmond*, 72; *RW*, 28 June 1865.

8. *RW*, 15 and 18 Apr., 26 May, 1 June 1865; Mary Wingfield Scott, *Houses of Old Richmond* (Richmond, 1941), 224–226; James K. Sanford, ed., *A Century of Commerce* (Richmond, [1967]), 27. Sanford's book has been reprinted, with additional material, as James K. Sanford, ed., *Richmond: Her Triumphs, Tragedies and Growth* (Richmond, [1975]).

9. Patrick, *Fall of Richmond*, 71, 102; W. Asbury Christian, *Richmond: Her Past and Present* (Richmond, 1912), 273.

10. *RW*, 4 and 10 Apr. 1865.

11. Ibid., 15 Apr. 1865.

12. Ibid.; Patrick, *Fall of Richmond*, 102.

13. *RW*, 15 Apr. 1865.

14. Ibid.; Patrick, *Fall of Richmond*, 102.

15. *RD*, 14 Dec. 1865. I compiled my figures by checking the names in the *Whig*, 15 Apr. 1865, against those in [B. W. Gillis, comp.], *Richmond City Directory . . . , 1871–2* (Richmond, 1871).

16. *RW*, 18 Apr., 31 May 1865; *RD*, 11 Jan. 1866.

17. *RW*, 4, 13, and 14 Apr., 8 May 1865.

18. *RW*, 6 and 13 Apr., 18 and 26 May, 14 June 1865.

19. [John B. Purcell, comp.], *Fiftieth Anniversary of the First National Bank, Richmond, Virginia* (n.p., [1915]), 4–5; Sanford, ed., *Century of Commerce*, 57, 63; Benjamin P. Thomas, *Abraham Lincoln: A Biography* (New York, 1952), 413; Abraham Lincoln, *The Collected Works of Abraham Lincoln*, ed. Roy P. Basler, 10 vols. (New Brunswick, N. J., 1953), 8:558; *RD*, 1 Aug. 1866, 18 Oct. 1869; *RW*, 15 Apr. 1865; *Richmond Mercury*, 10 Oct. 1973; *REx*, 5 Feb. 1866; Herbert T. Ezekiel, *The Recollections of a Virginia Newspaper Man* (Richmond, 1920); Meriwether Stuart, "Colonel Ulric Dahlgren and Richmond's Union Underground, April, 1864," *VMHB* 72 (1964): 189–190; Scott, *Houses*, 235. Despite Hamilton G. Fant's Republican connections, Fants from northern Virginia, who probably were related to the financier, figured prominently in the social life of Confederate Richmond (*see* Mary Boykin Chesnut, *A Diary From Dixie, passim*).

20. *RW*, 15 May, 12 June 1865; *RD*, 5 and 19 Feb. 1865, 8, 9, 10, and 17 Jan. 1866; [Purcell, comp.], *First National Bank*, *11–12*.

21. *RD*, 9 Jan., 9 July, 18 Dec. 1867; [Purcell, comp.], *First National Bank*, 7, 8, 11–12; Sanford, ed., *Century of Commerce*, 61.

22. *RW*, 22 and 23 June 1865.

23. Ibid.; Christian, *Richmond*, 272–273; Virginius Dabney, *Richmond: The Story of a City* (Garden City, N.Y., 1976), 201–202.

24. Dabney, *Richmond*, 203–204.

25. *RD*, 1 Jan. 1866.

26. *RW*, 10 Apr. 1865.

27. *RD*, 10 and 19 Jan., 6 and 7 Feb. 1866.

28. Turpin to George, 25 Feb. 1867, George Family Papers, 1724–1869, Accession 24642, Richmond City Chancery Court Papers, VSL.

29. CCR, 6 Nov. 1865; *RW*, 26 May, 27 July 1865; *RD*, 6 Sept. 1867; Anne Carter Lee, "Architectural Ironwork in Main Street, Richmond, Virginia" (M.A. thesis, University of Virginia, 1970), 8–9, 25, 101–102; A. Lawrence Kocher and Howard Dearstyne, *Shadows in Silver: A Record of Virginia, 1850–1900 in Contemporary Photographs* . . . (New York, 1954), 21; Paul S. Dulaney, *The Architecture of Historic Richmond* (Charlottesville, 1968), 117–118, 120–124.

30. Lee, "Architectural Ironwork," 8–9, 21, 25, 101–102; Alexander W. Weddell, *Richmond, Virginia, in Old Prints, 1737–1887* (Richmond, 1932), xxx–xxxi; *RD*, 9 Dec. 1865; Thomas F. Hale and Louis H. Manarin, *Richmond: A Pictorial History From the Valentine Museum and Dementi Collections* (Richmond, [1974]), 107, 112, 116, 137.

31. *RW*, 27 July 1865; *RD*, 2, 9, and 11 Jan., 2 Aug. 1866; Christian, *Richmond*, 302; CCR, 18 Feb. 1869.

32. *RD*, 15 May 1869.

33. *RW*, 18 May 1869.

34. *RD*, 1866–1870; *RW*, Apr.–Dec. 1865, 18 May 1869.

35. Quoted in Weddell, *Richmond Prints*, 215.

36. Patrick, *Fall of Richmond*, 106; Mark M. Boatner III, ed., *The Civil War Dictionary* (New York, 1959), 658; *RW*, 19 May, 13 and 29 June, 3 July 1865; Weddell, *Richmond Prints*, 221–222.

37. *RW*, 7, 8, 10, and 12 Apr. 1865; Patrick, *Fall of Richmond*, 75; CCR, 19 May 1866.

38. *RD*, 6 July, 17 Aug. 1866.

39. The James froze in the winter of 1866–1867 and December 1867; CCR, 12 Aug. 1867, 12 July 1869; *RD*, 22 May 1866, 20 Apr., 15 May 1868.

40. *RW*, 29 Apr. 1865.

41. Ibid., 18 May, 4 July 1865; *RD*, 7 Mar. 1867, 11 Feb. 1868, 23 June 1869; Scott, *Houses*, 179; Chandler, *Visible Hand*, 83, 86.

42. *RW*, 28 Apr., 8 May 1865; *RD*, 17 Feb., 20 Mar. 1866.

43. Stuart Bowe Medlin, "The York River Railroad; 1851–1881" (M.A. thesis, University of Richmond, 1968), 52–60; *RD*, 30 Jan. 1869.

44. *RW*, 5 June 1865; *RD*, 4 and 10 Jan. 1866; John B. Mordecai, *A Brief History of the Richmond, Fredericksburg and Potomac Railroad* (Richmond, 1940), 38, 44.

45. *RW*, 20 May, 25 July 1865; *RD*, 22 June 1869; Charles W. Turner, *Chessie's Road* (Richmond, 1956), 62–64, 73.

46. Weddell, *Richmond Prints*, 202; Christian, *Richmond*, 327–328; Mordecai, *History of R. F.*

& P., 47; *RD*, 1 Oct., 30 Nov. 1866, 25 Feb., 6 Apr., 19 Aug., 19 and 20 Dec. 1867, 19 May 1870; CCR, 14 Oct., 4 Nov., 16 Dec. 1867, 12 July 1869; Chandler, *Visible Hand*, 122–123.

47. *RW*, 13 Apr. 1865; *RD*, 14 Mar., 28 July 1866, 13 Mar., 2 Sept. 1867, 29 Jan., 14 Nov., 12 Dec. 1868, 11 and 12 Feb., 8 June, 16 Sept., 11 Nov., 1869.

48. *RW*, 14 June 1865; *RD*, 16 Dec. 1865; Leslie Winston Smith, "Richmond During Presidential Reconstruction, 1865–1867" (Ph.D. diss., University of Virginia, 1974), 345.

49. Smith, "Presidential Reconstruction," 346.

50. *RW*, 12 and 15 Apr. 1865; Smith, "Presidential Reconstruction," 349; John Thomas O'Brien, Jr., "From Bondage to Citizenship: The Richmond Black Community, 1865–1867" (Ph.D. diss., University of Rochester, 1975), 114–115.

51. Smith, "Presidential Reconstruction," 48, 69, 82–85, 347.

52. Ibid., 350–351.

53. Ibid., 352–353.

54. Ibid., 68, 82, 88, 354

55. Ibid., 354–355.

56. *RW*, 27 and 28 Apr., 16 and 19 May, 19 June 1865; CCR, 27 and 29 Nov. 1865.

57. Smith, "Presidential Reconstruction," 84; O'Brien, "Bondage to Citizenship," 5–7, 9, 119.

58. Smith, "Presidential Reconstruction," 352, 376–377; *RD*, 16 Dec. 1865.

59. Emory M. Thomas, *The Confederate State of Richmond: A Biography of the Capital* (Austin, 1971), 24; *RD*, 2 Sept. 1867.

60. U.S., Bureau of the Census, Ninth Census, 1870, Social Statistics for City of Richmond MSS, VSL.

61. Weddell, *Richmond Prints*, 236–240.

62. Richard M. Duggan, "The Military Occupation of Richmond, 1865–1870" (M.A. thesis, University of Richmond, 1965), 32, 59, 86.

63. Clement Eaton, *The Growth of Southern Civilization* (New York, 1961), 254; Christian, *Richmond*, 115–116; *RD*, 19 July 1866.

64. *RD*, 18 Mar. 1867, 2 Jan. 1868, 2 Apr., 16 July, 10 Aug. 1869; Christian, *Richmond*, 343; CCR, 17 Aug. 1867.

65. *RW*, 4, 13, and 14 Apr., 18 May 1865; CCR, 22 Apr. 1867.

66. *RD*, 14, 18, 19, 21, and 28 Dec. 1865, 15 Jan., 3 Feb. 1866.

67. Ibid., 9 Dec. 1865, 12 Jan., 2 Feb., 18 July, 24 Aug., 25 Dec. 1866, 28 Nov. 1867, 13 Nov. 1869; Christian, *Richmond*, 313–314.

68. *RW*, 7 Apr., 25 and 31 May, 15 June 1866; *RD*, 4 May 1866; Edward V. Valentine, MS notes, "Neighborhoods," VM.

69. *RW*, 20 May 1865; *RD*, 21 May 1869; CCR, 29 Nov., 11 Dec. 1865, 11 Feb. 1867.

70. *RD*, 1, 5, 11, and 12 Dec. 1866, 9 Aug. 1867; CCR, 14 Oct. 1867, 13 June 1870; Robert Skipwith Diary, 8, 10, and 20 Dec. 1869, W & M.

71. *RD*, 15 Jan., 16 Aug., 17 Nov. 1866. Arrest figures in the *Dispatch*, 18 Dec. 1865, 22 Mar., and 15 Oct. 1866 cover the three months preceding each date. The arrests in these nine months were: 1,423 white civilians, 1,484 black civilians, 428 soldiers, and 51 policemen.

72. *RW*, 2 and 9 May 1865.

73. Ibid., 23 June 1865; *RD*, 8 and 11 Jan., 2 and 17 Feb. 1866; *New York Times*, 24 Jan. 1866.

74. *RD*, 8 Sept., 5 Nov. 1866.

75. Ibid., 16 Feb., 19 Dec. 1865, 7 Mar., 16 and 20 Aug. 1866, 2 Sept. 1867; *RW*, 7 July 1865.

76. *RD*, 15 Mar. 1866, 8 June 1867, 14 May 1869; CCR, 18 Feb. 1867; *RW*, 8 and 29 May 1865.

77. *RW*, 6, 8, and 27 Apr. 1865; James H. Dorman, "Thespis in Dixie: Professional Theater in Confederate Richmond," *Virginia Cavalcade* 28 (1978): 13.

78. Mrs. Christian to Richard Christian, 29 Mar. 1866, Christian Family Papers, W & M; *RD*, 14 and 20 Mar. 1866, 1 Oct. 1868.

79. *RD*, 9 May, 12 July, 15 Aug., 18 Oct., 6 Dec. 1866, and *passim* in fall 1866, 2 Apr. 1869; *RW*, 9 and 11 May 1865.

80. *RW*, 1 and 27 May, 12 June 1865; *RD*, 12 Feb., 23 Apr., 17 July 1866, 4 Feb. 1868.

81. George Harvey Clarke Diary, 20 Jan. 1871, VHS. Clarke (1852–1931) was a student at Richmond College and clerked in the family hardware store after the war. The entries in his diary between 1867 and 1870 show that he regularly attended a variety of Protestant churches and compared the styles of the various ministers. In 1870, for example, Clarke heard 130 different sermons and went to seventeen churches a total of 217 times, accompanied by his male and female friends.

Henry Lee Curry III, "The Confederate Careers of James Armstrong Duncan, Moses Drury Hoge, and Charles Frederick Ernest Minnegerode" (Ph.D. diss., Emory University, 1971); Christian, *Richmond*, 265–267; *RD*, 18 Aug., 21 Nov. 1866, 16 Apr. 1867, 29 Jan. 1874; John Jasper folder, VM; E[dward] A. Randolph, *The Life of Reverend John Jasper* . . . (Richmond, 1884); Charles E. Wynes, *Race Relations in Virginia, 1870–1902* (Charlottesville, 1961), 9.

Chapter 4: The City Reconstructed, 1865–1870

1. John A. Cutchins, *Memories of Old Richmond (1881–1944)* (Verona, Va., 1973), 3; Alfred Hoyt Bill, *The Beleaguered City: Richmond, 1861–1865* (New York, 1946), 293; Mary Newton Stannard, *Richmond: Its People and Its Story* (Philadelphia, 1923), 216. *See also* W. Asbury Christian, *Richmond: Her Past and Present* (Richmond, 1912), 279, 312; and Virginius Dabney, *Richmond: The Story of a City* (Garden City, N.Y., 1976), 199–219.

2. Jack P. Maddex, Jr., *The Virginia Conservatives, 1867–1879: A Study in Reconstruction Politics* (Chapel Hill, N.C., 1970), 35–90; John Thomas O'Brien, Jr., "From Bondage to Citizenship: The Richmond Black Community, 1865–1867" (Ph.D. diss., University of Rochester, 1974); Leslie Winston Smith, "Richmond During Presidential Reconstruction, 1865–1867" (Ph.D. diss., University of Virginia, 1974).

3. The governor spelled his name several different ways, as have historians. He spelled it Peirpoint while in Richmond (*see* William T. Alderson, Jr., "The Influence of Military Rule and the Freedmen's Bureau on Reconstruction in Virginia, 1865–1870" [Ph.D. diss., Vanderbilt University, 1952], 12 n.29; Hamilton James Eckenrode, *The Political History of Virginia During the Reconstruction*, Johns Hopkins University Studies in Historical and Political Science, vol. 22 [Baltimore, 1904], 297–300, 308–309; J. G. Randall, *Constitutional Problems Under Lincoln*, rev. ed. [Urbana, Ill., 1951], 445 n.16 and 17).

4. Christian, *Richmond*, 229, 233, 266–267; James E. Sefton, *The United States Army and Reconstruction, 1865–1877* (Baton Rouge, 1967), 50; Herndon to James Minor, 26 Apr. 1865, Dr. Brodie S. Herndon Letters, Accession 25837, Personal Papers Collection, VSL.

5. Thomas to Dr. William DeJarnette Quesenberry, 5 May 1865, Thomas Family Papers, VHS.

6. Christian, *Richmond*, 267, 272; Halleck to Secretary of War Edwin M. Stanton, quoted in

Sefton, *Army and Reconstruction*, 9; oath taken by Miss Fannie A. Holdsworth to become Mrs. Aylett R. Woodson, Richmond, 19 Oct. 1865, Accession 20698, Personal Papers Collection, VSL.

7. Sefton, *Army and Reconstruction*, 53; O'Brien, "Bondage to Citizenship," 106, 381. Patrick (West Point class of 1835) privately indicated his Southern sympathies as early as 1862 (*see* Marsena Rudolph Patrick, *Inside Lincoln's Army: The Diary of Marsena Rudolph Patrick . . .* ed. David S. Sparks [New York, 1964], 120). Ord and Halleck had been West Point classmates (1839) and perhaps shared viewpoints on racial and political matters as well.

8. O'Brien, "Bondage to Citizenship," 148–151, 162–166; Dabney, *Richmond*, 202; *RW*, 19 May, 9 June 1865.

9. O'Brien, "Bondage to Citizenship," 82–85, 180–181, 186, 189–190; Sefton, *Army and Reconstruction*, 9, 17–18, 20–21; Alderson, "Military Rule," 18–23, 149–150, 309.

Michael C. C. Adams, in *Our Masters the Rebels: A Speculation on Union Military Failure in the East, 1861–1865* (Cambridge, Mass., 1978), argues that many Northerners, particularly West Pointers of the old army, regarded upper-class Southerners, especially Virginians, as their social and military superiors, and that they continued to do so even after Confederate defeat.

Terry, a Yale graduate, was the only non-West Pointer among the nine most prominent generals in command at Richmond from 1865 to 1870. Such a small sample cannot prove or disprove Adams's provocative thesis. Col. Orlando Brown, head of the Freedmen's Bureau in Virginia and a native of Connecticut, like Terry, was another non-West Pointer. Academy graduate Weitzel (1855) held command only briefly, but Schofield (1853), Stoneman (1846), and Turner (1855) were all regarded more favorably by white conservatives than Terry. Canby (1839) interfered in the Municipal War, however, and his death at the hands of the Modoc Indians in 1873 was not mourned by the city's former rebels.

10. *RD*, 4 June 1866, 30 Jan. 1867.

11. Eckenrode, *History of Virginia*, 29–30; CCR, 7 June 1865.

12. Eckenrode, *History of Virginia*, 30–34.

13. Smith, "Presidential Reconstruction," 70–83; O'Brien, "Bondage to Citizenship," 162, 172–180.

14. CCR, 27 July 1865; Smith, "Presidential Reconstruction," 163.

15. CCR, 13 Feb. 1865; *RD*, 10 Aug. 1869; *RW*, 8 and 27 July 1865; Smith, "Presidential Reconstruction," 153–162; O'Brien, "Bondage to Citizenship," 284–289. Figures for councilmen and aldermen are derived from wartime and postwar council records and the biographies of members in *MCC*, pp. 627–636.

16. Smith, "Presidential Reconstruction," 163–164; O'Brien, "Bondage to Citizenship," 110.

17. CCR, 28 and 29 July, 5 and 25 Aug., 2, 3, and 21 Oct. 1865; *RW*, 27 July 1865; Alderson, "Military Rule," 23–25.

18. CCR, 21 and 25 Oct., 27 and 29 Nov., 1 and 8 Dec. 1865; *RD*, 12, 14, 18, 19, 21, and 28 Dec. 1865.

19. U.S., *Statutes at Large*, vol. 14, 428–429, and vol. 15, 14–15, 344; Sefton, *Army and Reconstruction*, 29–30, 167–168; CCR, 7 Apr. 1866.

20. Smith, "Presidential Reconstruction," 102–111. On Cook *see RD*, 31 Dec. 1867, 16 May 1868, 25 Jan., 11 Aug. 1869; CCR, 1 Feb., 23 Aug. 1869; *RD*, 27 Jan. 1881. On Hambrick *see RD*, 18 July 1866, 11 Feb. 1868. On Merrell *see RD*, 1 Oct. 1867; CCR, 14 and 21 May 1868; O'Brien, "Bondage to Citizenship," 309.

21. CCR, 27 and 29 Nov. 1865, 29 Mar., 14 May 1866, 17 Aug., 9 Sept., 30 Oct. 1867, 13 Jan., 10 Feb., 31 Mar. 1868; Smith, "Presidential Reconstruction," 441.

22. CCR, 7 and 14 July, 1, 28, and 30 Dec. 1868.

23. Ibid., 31 Dec. 1868, 13 Jan., 8 and 27 Feb., 12 Apr., 10 May 1869.

24. Ibid., 27 June 1870.

25. There were 6,021 registered black voters in 1867, a black majority of 961. Only 34 whites voted for the biracial slate of radical Republican delegates to the 1867 constitutional convention; only 22 blacks voted for the conservative Republican ticket. At the end of May 1870 there were 6,800 registered white voters and 6,200 blacks (see *RD*, 22 and 25 Oct. 1867, 28 May 1870).

Neither Maddex, *Virginia Conservatives*, 45–86, nor Christian, *Richmond*, 281–311, lists any black officeholders in city government, nor does the *Dispatch* mention any from Dec. 1865 through May 1870. For black protests over the removal of black candidates, and for all-white Republican tickets *see RD*, 7 May, 25 and 26 June 1869, 24 May 1870.

General Canby did suggest that if a black was qualified for lieutenant governor (a reference to Dr. J. D. Harris, Wells's running mate) blacks were certainly fit to be city police (*RD*, 25 Mar. 1869). And, during the Municipal War in 1870 Chahoon did appoint Capt. Ben Scott, who twice had tried to integrate the streetcars, as the head of his special twenty-five-man black police force. Scott had acquired his military title through service as a noncommissioned officer in the Negro company that was organized for the Confederate army in Richmond in March 1865, but which never saw action. He was still an active figure in Jackson Ward in the 1880s (*see* Peter Rachleff, "Black, White, and Gray: The Rise and Decline of Working Class Activity in Richmond, Va., 1865–1890" [M.A. thesis, University of Pittsburgh, 1976], 51; this study is an excellent account of the Richmond laboring community).

26. *RD*, 17 and 18 Apr., 1 May, 1 Aug. 1867, 4 May 1868, 8 Oct., 22 Nov. 1869; Eckenrode, *History of Virginia*, 87, 125; Luther Porter Jackson, *Negro Office-Holders in Virginia 1865–1895* (Norfolk, 1945), 9; Richard L. Morton, *The Negro in Virginia Politics, 1865–1902* (Charlottesville, 1919), 36 n.19; O'Brien, "Bondage to Citizenship," 166; Robert Francis Engs, *Freedom's First Generation: Black Hampton, Virginia, 1861–1890* (Philadelphia, 1979), 33–34, 48–49, 64, 91; U.S., Bureau of the Census, Ninth and Tenth Census, 1870 and 1880, Population MSS, VSL.

27. *RD*, 21 Nov. 1867, 13 July, 11 Aug. 1869.

28. It is easier to identify than to define a leader. Those black leaders described here were identified through research in a variety of primary and secondary sources (including those cited above in this chapter). The fact that these black men were even mentioned in sources written predominantly by whites, indicates that the white community recognized that they were men of some importance among the general black population. Newspaper accounts of black ward meetings and conventions mention only those persons who made motions or spoke, or who were nominated or elected to office. *Richmond Dispatch* reports of such meetings usually list the number of votes cast for each nominee. The freedmen in attendance at political, religious, and fraternal meetings were not listed by name; they were followers, not leaders. Blacks killed in saloon brawls, or as innocent bystanders to fights between soldiers and other blacks, were not necessarily leaders (even though their names may be known); however, those who were described as starting riots, initiating attempts to integrate the streetcars, or leading black rallies, are counted as leaders.

Other blacks are classed as leaders by virtue of their businesses or professions. Laborers were not necessarily leaders (although some black leaders were unskilled workers), but black ministers, doctors, barbers, and other successful businessmen have been counted as leaders. No comprehensive research in census records has yet been done to determine the antebellum status, occupations, wards of residence, and birthplaces of all of these men, although most of this information has been gathered for the more prominent blacks. Unfortunately, antebellum Richmond city directory listings did not include slaves or free blacks.

In general, then, some black Richmonders are identified as leaders because of their actions and others because of their occupations or social status. Further research, to identify leaders, trace their life histories, and measure their individual influence, is needed, but one cannot maintain that because no black served in the city government before 1871 Richmond's black community had no leaders in the immediate postwar years. Obviously, black leaders were not exclusively male politicians (officeholders or otherwise). Often, just as the most staunch Confederates were white women, the strongest Republicans were black women. The elected black leaders who served on the common council and board of aldermen in the generation after 1871 are the subject of my paper, "Black Leadership Patterns in Richmond, Virginia: 1850–1890," (Paper presented at the Seventy-second Annual Meeting of the Organization of American Historians, New Orleans, La., 13 Apr. 1979), which will appear in a revised version in Howard N. Rabinowitz, ed., *Southern Black Political Leaders During Reconstruction* (Champaign, Ill., forthcoming).

29. *RW*, 18 Apr., 1 June 1865; *RD*, 21 July, 16 Aug. 1866, 23 and 25 Oct., 21 and 22 Nov. 1867, 7 May, 3 and 13 July, 2 Aug. 1869, 8 June 1870, 19 and 21 Jan. 1881; *Richmond News Leader*, 15 Apr. 1938; Jackson, *Negro Office-Holders*, 57; Robert Skipwith Diary, 13 Feb. 1869, W & M; Smith, "Presidential Reconstruction," 133; Dabney, *Richmond*, 209.

30. Dabney, *Richmond*, 208; *RD*, 25 Apr., 18 Aug. 1879; Smith, "Presidential Reconstruction," 136–137.

31. *RD*, 5 and 9 Mar., 10 and 13 July, 13 Dec. 1866, 30 Jan., 24 Apr., 8 May, 2 and 6 July 1867, 7 Apr. 1868, 30 Mar., 9 June 1869, 22 Mar. 1870.

32. Ibid., 18 Apr., 27 July, 15 and 17 Oct. 1867, 7 May, 7 and 25 June, 22 Nov. 1869; Dabney, *Richmond*, 210; Jackson, *Negro Office-Holders*, 9, 25; Morton, *Negro in Virginia Politics*, 37–38 n; Smith, "Presidential Reconstruction," 141–144. Lindsay's career also may have declined because he broke with the carpetbaggers who continued to control the local Republican party, and because he advocated reconciliation with native whites—but these developments occurred in 1874, two years after he had left office (*see* Rachleff, "Black, White, and Gray," 141).

33. *RD*, 4 Apr., 6 June, 1 and 15 Oct. 1867, 7 May, 25 June 1869; O'Brien, "Bondage to Citizenship," 373, 426.

34. *RD*, 15 July, 9 Sept. 1867; U.S., Bureau of the Census, *Compendium of the Ninth Census of the United States, 1870* (Washington, D.C., 1872), 472–473; Alderson, "Military Rule," 198–199. In the 1867 election, 58.7 percent of the registered blacks and 59 percent of the registered whites voted. But more than 3 percent of the whites voted for the convention, thereby increasing the margin for the Republicans and blacks, while only 0.6 percent of the black voters opposed the convention or supported conservative candidates. Hundreds of apathetic whites failed to register or vote.

35. *RD*, 20 Oct. 1866, 11 June, 19 July 1867, 27 Oct. 1868, 25 June, 6 Aug. 1869; O'Brien, "Bondage to Citizenship," 78 ff. For evidence of the growing class divisions in black society and examples of hostility between conservative Negro leaders and the more radical black masses, *see* Rachleff, "Black, White, and Gray," 150, 151–153.

36. *RD*, 1 Oct. 1867; Luther Porter Jackson, *Free Negro Labor and Property Holding in Virginia, 1830–1860* (New York, 1942), 77, 179; Morton, *Negro in Virginia Politics*, 37 n.21; Smith, "Presidential Reconstruction," 144–145.

37. Alderson, "Military Rule," 104; O'Brien, "Bondage to Citizenship," 383–408.

38. CCR, 27 Apr., 8 and 12 June, 1 and 14 July 1868, 9 June 1869, 22 Feb., 30 June 1870; *RD*, 25, 27, and 29 Aug., 10 Sept. 1866, 22 and 25 Jan., 6 Feb., 16 and 22 Apr., 24 May, 18 June, 25 Nov. 1867, 8 and 9 Apr. 1868, 11 Aug. 1869; Eckenrode, *History of Virginia*, 93–94.

39. *RD*, 18 June, 23 Oct. 1867, 22 Mar. 1870; CCR, 9 June 1866. Stanley Engerman has reminded me that segregation (even if not generally called Jim Crow) existed before 1865 for free blacks, especially in cities, as is shown by the work of Ira Berlin and other historians. On the origin of the term Jim Crow, *see also* C. Vann Woodward, *The Strange Career of Jim Crow*, 3d rev. ed. (New York, 1974), 7.

40. Dabney, *Richmond*, 208; *RW*, 1 May, 5 and 17 June 1865; *RD*, 1 Aug., 20 Nov. 1867, 6 and 7 Jan. 1868, 19 July 1869.

41. Richard M. Duggan, "The Military Occupation of Richmond, 1865–1870" (M.A. thesis, University of Richmond, 1965), 59; *RD*, 4, 20, 24, and 25 Apr., 1 and 9 May, 29 Aug., 2 Sept., 21 Nov. 1867; Smith, "Presidential Reconstruction," 448–449; Rachleff, "Black, White, and Gray," 51. My findings differ somewhat from those in Woodward, *Jim Crow*, 27; and Charles E. Wynes, *Race Relations in Virginia, 1870–1902* (Charlottesville, 1961), 69, Richmond's streetcars continued to be segregated through 1870. The black leader, Ben Scott, who caused one of the streetcar riots in May 1867 led another in March 1870 during the Municipal War.

42. *RD*, 5, 6, 9, 10, and 24 Mar., 10 July 1866; O'Brien, "Bondage to Citizenship," 367.

43. *RD*, 10 and 13 May, 26 June, 2, 3, and 6 July 1867.

44. Ibid., 22, 23, and 25 Oct. 1867.

45. O'Brien, "Bondage to Citizenship," 487 n.

46. CCR, 8 Mar. 1869; *RD*, 3 and 8 Apr. 1867, 7 May 1868, 15 Feb., 23 and 24 Mar. 1869; *Richmond News Leader*, 30 July 1934; Christian, *Richmond*, 302; Alderson, "Military Rule," 216–218, 221–222.

47. Maddex, *Virginia Conservatives*, 3–4, 40–42, 50, 53, 55, 72–73, 105; *RD*, 8 Mar., 3, 16, 18, and 19 Apr., 2 Aug., 16 Oct. 1867.

48. Maddex, *Virginia Conservatives*, xiii–xv, 47, 54–57; *RD*, 8 and 16 Nov. 1867.

49. Maddex, *Virginia Conservatives*, 61; *RD*, 13 July 1868.

50. On the troublesome question of the political and social background of the scalawags, *see* David Donald, "The Scalawag in Mississippi Reconstruction," *JSH* 10 (1944): 447–460; Allen W. Trelease, "Who Were the Scalawags?," *JSH* 29 (1963): 445–468; and Warren A. Ellem, "Who Were the Mississippi Scalawags?" *JSH* 38 (1972): 217–240; Otto H. Olsen, "Reconsidering the Scalawags," *CWH* 12 (1966): 304–320. The methodology, criteria, and sources for identifying Republican leaders are similar to those used for black leaders (*see* note 28). In addition to those men known to have been either carpetbaggers or scalawags, I found 103 Republicans of unknown origins. The figures for both white and black leaders are estimates (rather than precise measurements) of factional strength and affiliation, based on evidence about each individual that is not always complete. Many of the most prominent Republicans switched factions one or more times during the first five years of Reconstruction; I have identified each man's affiliation on the basis of his factional association during the period of his greatest apparent prominence and influence. Men for whom I have found no evidence of factional allegiance have been excluded from these figures.

51. *RD*, 30 Aug. 1866, 18 Oct. 1869, 7 Feb. 1888; Maddex, *Virginia Conservatives*, 36, 70–71, 74, 100.

52. CCR, 13 Apr., 31 July 1868, 1 and 27 Feb. 1869, 16 Mar., 27 June 1870; *REx*, 5 Feb. 1866; *RD*, 19 Sept. 1867, 6 and 13 Apr. 1868, 18 Oct. 1869, 23 May 1870; Mary Wingfield Scott, *Houses of Old Richmond* (Richmond, 1941), 235. The Ferrets included: *Whig* editor William Ira Smith; Joseph M. Humphreys, who headed one of the four Union leagues in the city, served on the council for part of 1868 (when he was described as one of four "extreme radicals" on the body by the *Richmond Dispatch*), and apparently left the city the same year; R. F. & P. superintendent Samuel Ruth; and, George N. Gwathmey, an alderman from 1862 to 1865.

53. *RD*, 12 and 17 Apr. 1867, 27 Oct., 30 Nov. 1868, 30 June, 12 July 1869; Maddex, *Virginia Conservatives*, 58; Alderson, "Military Rule," 136, 170, 222, 234–235. For a highly partisan sketch of Hunnicutt, who has yet to find an objective biographer, *see* Claude G. Bowers, *The Tragic Era* (Cambridge, Mass., 1929), 199–200.

54. *REx*, 5 Feb. 1866; *RD*, 30 Aug., 21 Sept. 1866, 8 Mar., 27 July, 15 and 22 Oct. 1867, 16 and 21 Apr. 1868, 3 June, 11 Aug., 22 Nov. 1869; Alderson, "Military Rule," 195–196, 198–200; Smith, "Presidential Reconstruction," 125–127, 129.

55. CCR, 13 Apr., 10 Aug., 12 Oct. 1868; *RD*, 6 Apr., 25 July 1868, 9 and 25 June, 6 Aug., 22 Nov. 1869; *RW*, 27 June 1865; *REx*, 5 Feb. 1866; Maddex, *Virginia Conservatives*, 87; Edward Craige Pelouze, comp., *History of the Pelouze Families* . . . (n.p., 1952), 25–26; Smith, "Presidential Reconstruction," 127–128.

56. CCR, 11 May, 8 June, 14 July, 12 Oct. 1868, 28 June, 13 Sept., 8 Nov. 1869, 10 Jan., 14 Feb. 1870.

57. CCR, 14 Dec. 1868, 24 May, 30 June, 12 July 1869.

58. Ibid., 2 Apr. 1865, 14 Dec. 1868, 11 Jan., 28 June, 12 July 1869, 18 Feb., 3 and 14 Mar. 1870; *RD*, 11 and 18 Aug. 1869; Christian, *Richmond*, 313–314.

59. CCR, 22 Mar., 23 Aug., 13 Dec. 1869; 10 Jan., 14 and 18 Feb., 30 Apr. 1870; *RD*, 16 Mar. 1870.

60. CCR, 16, 18, 19, and 22 Mar. 1870; Ellyson Family file, VM; *RW*, 27 July 1865; Eckenrode, *History of Virginia*, 86; *RD*, 17, 18, 19, and 23 through 31 Mar., 1 Apr. 1870. The verse is quoted in M. Ethel Kelley Kern, *The Trail of the Three Notched Road* (Richmond, 1928), 16.

61. George Harvey Clarke Diary, 18 Mar. 1870, VHS.

62. *RD*, 4, 5, 6, 8, 9, 28, and 30 Apr., 19, 27, 28, and 31 May, 25 June 1870; Christian, *Richmond*, 317–325; Dabney, *Richmond*, 216–218; Maddex, *Virginia Conservatives*, 89–90; James Tice Moore, *Two Paths to the New South: The Virginia Debt Controversy, 1870–1883* (Lexington, Ky., 1974), 134.

63. John S. Wise, *The Lion's Skin: A Historical Novel and a Novel History* (New York, 1905), 283.

Chapter 5: A Miniature Metropolis, 1865–1870

1. Alfred Hoyt Bill, *The Beleaguered City: Richmond, 1861–1865* (New York, 1946), 191; Emory M. Thomas, *The Confederate State of Richmond: A Biography of the Capital* (Austin, 1971), 128; Leslie Winston Smith, "Richmond During Presidential Reconstruction, 1865–1867" (Ph.D. diss., University of Virginia, 1974), 69, 84.

2. Ella Lonn, *Foreigners in the Confederacy* (Chapel Hill, N.C., 1940), 3; David Ward, *Cities and Immigrants: A Geography of Change in Nineteenth-Century America* (New York, 1971), 76–77.

3. Thomas, *State of Richmond*, 25–26; "Selected Occupations, With Age and Sex, and

Nativity," in U.S., Bureau of the Census, *Ninth Census of the United States, 1870, I, Population and Social Statistics* (Washington, D.C., 1872), 797.

4. Thomas, *State of Richmond*, 25–26; Clement Eaton, *The Growth of Southern Civilization, 1790–1860* (New York, 1961), 250; Michael Chesson, "Henry A. Wise and the Fight for Virginia Democracy" (Colloquium paper in history, Harvard University, 1973). *See* Myron Berman, *Richmond's Jewry, 1769–1976: Shabbat in Shockoe* (Charlottesville, 1979), 184–188, for a summary of anti-Semitism in wartime Richmond.

5. Thomas, *State of Richmond*, 151–152; Herbert T. Ezekiel and Gaston Lichtenstein, *The History of the Jews of Richmond From 1769 to 1917* (Richmond, 1917), 148–195; John S. Wise, *The End of An Era* (Boston, 1899), 176–178, 401–402; Charles M. Wallace, *The Boy Gangs of Richmond in the Dear Old Days* (Richmond, 1938); and John B. Jones, *A Rebel War Clerk's Diary*, ed. Earl Schenck Miers (New York, 1958), xi, xiii. Many of the anti-Semitic remarks made by Jones in the 1866 edition of the diary have been omitted in this edition. *See also RD*, 27 Jan. 1866, 28 Mar. 1867, 11 Dec. 1868.

6. Thomas, *State of Richmond*, 12; *RW*, 18 May, 15 June, 1, 6, and 10 July 1865; *RD*, 17 Mar., 24 July 1866, 8 Mar., 22 Apr., 12 July, 28 Oct., 20 Nov. 1867, 13 Mar., 1 July 1868, 5 Apr., 5 and 10 June, 15 Sept., 8 Dec. 1869, 18 Mar. 1870. *See also* Wallace, *Boy Gangs*, 88.

On Anthony M. Keiley *see* James Tice Moore, *Two Paths to the New South: The Virginia Debt Controversy, 1870–1883* (Lexington, Ky., 1974), 134; Ezekiel and Lichtenstein, *Jews of Richmond*, 215–218; Joseph P. O'Grady, "Anthony M. Keiley (1832–1905): Virginia's Catholic Politician," *Catholic Historical Review* 54 (1969): 613–635.

7. Joseph P. O'Grady, "Immigrants and the Politics of Reconstruction in Richmond, Virginia," *Records of the American Catholic Historical Society of Philadelphia* 83 (1972): 89–92, 97–98.

8. Wallace, *Boy Gangs*; Smith, "Presidential Reconstruction," 5; Thomas, *State of Richmond*, 25; *RD*, 4 June 1867, 11 Jan. 1869; Robert Beverley Munford, Jr., *Richmond Homes and Memories* (Richmond, 1936), 60–61.

9. Mary Wingfield Scott, *Old Richmond Neighborhoods* (Richmond, 1950), 91, and *Houses of Old Richmond* (Richmond, 1941), 30; Paul S. Dulaney, *The Architecture of Historic Richmond*, 44; *RD*, 2 Sept. 1867, 24 Jan. 1876; and Munford, *Homes and Memories*, 60–64. Not every American city, of course, expanded toward the west. Muncie, Ind. (the "Middletown" of Helen and Robert Lynd's classic study), Springfield, Mass., and, Montgomery, Ala., for example, expanded to the east.

The process of westward expansion is the subject of bitter satire in several of Ellen Glasgow's novels about Richmond, including *The Sheltered Life* (Garden City, N.Y., 1932) and *In This Our Life* (New York, 1941).

10. The *Richmond Dispatch*, 5 May 1869, printed the list of the forty-eight Richmonders with incomes over $5,000 in 1868. Residences for all but one of these persons are found in the 1869 and 1870 editions of [William H. Boyd, comp.], *Boyd's Directory of Richmond City . . .* (Richmond, 1869 and 1870). Forty of the forty-eight are also found in W. Eugene Ferslew, comp., *Second Annual Directory for the City of Richmond . . .* (Richmond, 1860). *See also* Munford, *Homes and Memories*, 103. For many pictures and much information on the houses of Richmonders of various classes, *see* Scott, *Houses*.

11. Smith, "Presidential Reconstruction," 4–5; Thomas, *State of Richmond*, 25; *RD*, 29 May 1867.

12. Scott, *Neighborhoods*; Dulaney, *Architecture of Richmond*; Wallace, *Boy Gangs*, 7; Ernest Taylor Walthall, *Hidden Things Brought to Light* (Richmond, 1908), 36–37, 41, 46; Robert Shields Crump, "Yesterdays: Memories of An Earlier Richmond," typescript, VM, 36–37.

13. Walthall, *Hidden Things*, 37; *RW*, 5 June 1865; Edward V. Valentine, MS notes, "Richmond Suburbs," VM; Scott, *Neighborhoods*, 279–284, 297; M. Ethel Kelley Kern, *The Trail of the Three Notched Road* (Richmond, 1928), 34–35. 'Postletown acquired its name because several streets in the area were named after apostles. Navy Hill was the site proposed for a monument to naval victories; the name stuck, though the monument was never built.

14. *RD*, 2 Oct. 1866; U.S., Bureau of the Census, *Compendium of the Ninth Census of the United States, 1870*, (Washington, D.C., 1872), 543.

15. Smith, "Presidential Reconstruction," 84; Dulaney, *Architecture of Richmond*, 73. Many blacks continued to live in alleys behind white-occupied houses, whether as squatters in makeshift housing or as servants.

16. CCR, 1 Feb., 17 Aug., 30 Dec. 1867; *RD*, 22 Mar. 1866, 18 and 19 Jan., 19 June, 31 Dec. 1867; and map of city annexations in Scott, *Houses*, 28–30.

17. *RD*, 18 Jan. 1867; an earlier annexation attempt in 1866 had been defeated.

18. CCR, 8 July, 12 and 17 Aug., 14 Oct. 1867.

19. *RD*, 15 Mar. 1866, 17 June 1867; Alexander W. Weddell, *Richmond, Virginia, in Old Prints, 1737–1887* (Richmond, 1932), 190–192. Weddell quotes the lines, which were written by John R. Thompson, a local literary figure, parodying Thomas Campbell's "Ye Mariners of England."

20. On Van Lew *see* Meriwether Stuart, "Colonel Ulric Dahlgren and Richmond's Union Underground, April 1864," *VMHB* 72 (1964): 159–160. *See also* CCR, 9 Nov. 1868, 13 Jan. 1869; and *RD*, 23 Jan. 1866.

21. *RD*, 22 Oct. 1868, 22 Jan., 1 and 4 Feb. 1869; CCR, 31 Jan. 1869.

22. *Compendium of Ninth Census*, 618–619; U.S., Bureau of the Census, Ninth Census, 1870, Agricultural Production in Richmond MSS, VSL.

23. Richard J. Hopkins, "Status, Mobility, and the Dimensions cf Change in a Southern City, Atlanta, 1870–1910," in *Cities in American History*, ed. Kenneth T. Jackson and Stanley K. Schultz (New York, 1972), 219.

24. *Compendium of Ninth Census*, 844. The nine cities comparable in size to Richmond in 1870 were: Worcester, Mass.; Providence, R.I.; New Haven, Conn.; Rochester, Syracuse, and Troy, N.Y.; Allegheny, Pa.; Indianapolis, Ind.; and Charleston, S.C.

25. Eighth and Ninth Census, Industrial Schedule MSS, VSL. Unfortunately the industrial schedules have data for only one category, manufacturing. Figures from the published census, which appear to be arranged differently in categories, show a 14 percent decrease in the number of workers employed in manufacturing (from 7,589 in 1860 to 6,520 in 1870). (*See* U.S., Bureau of the Census, *Manufactures of the United States in 1860* [Washington, D.C., 1860], 216–217; and *Compendium of Ninth Census*, 618–619).

26. Eighth and Ninth Census, Industrial Schedule MSS.

27. Thomas F. Hale and Louis H. Manarin, *Richmond: A Pictorial History From the Valentine Museum and Dementi Collections* (Richmond, [1974]), 48, 51–53; Bill, *Beleaguered City*, 85, 183, 191, 248. I am indebted to Ira Berlin for information on the slave census.

28. [Alex Rivington and Harris Rivington], *Reminiscences of America in 1869, by Two Englishmen* (London, 1870), 306; Edward King, *The Great South* (Hartford, Conn., 1875), 632–633; *RD*, 15 Mar., 17 Oct. 1866; Ninth Census, Industrial Schedule MSS, and Social Statistics for City of Richmond MSS. Wages in 1860 were $1.25 for a day laborer, presumably without board (Thomas, *State of Richmond*, 24).

29. Eighth and Ninth Census, Industrial Schedule MSS; Thomas, *State of Richmond*, 22, for map of the city; CCR, 8 Nov. 1869, 30 May 1870; *RD*, 3 Jan. 1867.

30. Wilbur R. Thompson, *A Preface to Urban Economics* (Baltimore, 1965), 15–16.

31. Ninth Census, Industrial Schedule MSS; Benjamin W. Arnold, "History of the Tobacco Industry in Virginia from 1860 to 1894," *Johns Hopkins University Studies in Historical and Political Science* 15, nos. 1 and 2 (1897), 58–59.

32. Arnold, "Tobacco Industry," 14, 31, 33–36, 58–59; Nannie May Tilley, *The Bright-Tobacco Industry, 1860–1929* (Chapel Hill, N.C., 1948), 24–25; *RD*, 9 Sept. 1867, 28 Oct. 1869. In 1867 the paper noted the receipt in the city of a shipment of bright tobacco from Caswell County, N.C., where it had first been developed in the 1850s. The editors reported that several experts who had examined it said it was the best bright they had ever seen. Despite this, conservative interests operating through the Richmond Tobacco Exchange tried to keep bright and burley out of the city's markets. One of the paper's civic-booster editorials in 1869 condemned this attitude and suggested that closer ties with western tobacco-growing areas such as Kentucky might be what the city's tobacco industry needed to revitalize itself.

33. *RD*, 17 May, 4 and 7 Aug. 1867, 25 June 1868; King, *Great South*, 631–632.

34. *RD*, 20 Apr., 28 July, 3 Aug., 28 Oct., 8 Nov. 1869.

35. Ibid., 17 Sept. 1868, 1 Jan. 1871; Fred A. Shannon, *The Farmer's Last Frontier: Agriculture, 1860–1897* in Henry David, et al., eds., *The Economic History of the U. S.*, vol. 5 (New York, 1945), 157–158; Allen W. Moger, "Industrial and Urban Progress in Virginia From 1880 to 1900," *VMHB* 66 (1948): 314–315.

36. Walthall, *Hidden Things*, 23; Weddell, *Richmond Prints*, 151–153; Ninth Census, Industrial Schedule MSS.

37. Eighth and Ninth Census, Industrial Schedule MSS; *RD*, 30 Mar. 1866.

38. Charles B. Dew, *Ironmaker to the Confederacy: Joseph R. Anderson and the Tredegar Iron Works* (New Haven, Conn., 1966), 22, 32–33, 34–39; James Ford Rhodes, *History of the United States From the Compromise of 1850*, 9 vols. (New York, 1904), 5:390–393; *RD*, 6 Dec. 1866; Weddell, *Richmond Prints*, 144; Alfred D. Chandler, Jr., *The Visible Hand: The Managerial Revolution in American Business* (Cambridge, Mass., 1977), 52, 76.

39. Transportation problems are discussed in chapter 6.

40. *RD*, 29 May, 23 July 1867.

41. Ibid., 26 Aug., 1 Oct. 1868, 3 June 1869; CCR, 17 Aug., 14 Oct. 1867, 7 Feb., 11 May, 12 Oct. 1868, 13 Dec. 1869, 14 Feb. 1870.

42. *RD*, 29 June 1865.

43. Ibid., 26 Sept., 4, 6, and 10 Dec. 1866.

44. Ibid., 26 May, 28 July, 18 Aug., 28 and 30 Sept., 13, 14, 21, and 26 Oct. 1869, 1 Apr. 1870; CCR, 30 June 1868, 25 May, 30 Aug. 1869; Virginius Dabney, *Richmond: The Story of a City* (Garden City, N.Y., 1976), 237.

45. Sam Bass Warner, Jr., *Streetcar Suburbs: The Process of Growth in Boston, 1870–1900* (Cambridge, Mass., 1962), 21–23. The valley of Bacons Quarter Branch north of nineteenth-century Richmond was not bridged by pedestrian and electric streetcar viaducts until after 1888. These improvements allowed the development of Richmond's north side with real estate ventures like Barton Heights (*see* chapter 7). *See also* Munford, *Homes and Memories*, 65; *RD*, 1 Jan. 1891; James K. Sanford, ed., *A Century of Commerce* (Richmond, [1967]), 51–56; CCR, 25 May 1869; *RD*, 26 May 1869.

46. Rembert Patrick, *The Fall of Richmond* (Baton Rouge, 1960), 40, 42, 45, 50, 100; Mark M. Boatner III, ed., *The Civil War Dictionary* (New York, 1959), 658; *RW*, 13 and 29 June 1865.

47. *RD*, 24 May 1869; Dabney, *Richmond*, 224.

Chapter 6: The Decline of the Entrepôt, 1871–1881

1. G. M. Bowers, "Transportation on the James River," *Marine News* 26 (December 1939): 40–43, 51; Virginius Dabney, *Richmond: The Story of A City* (Garden City, N.Y., 1976), 226–227.

2. John A. Hain, *Side Wheel Steamers of the Chesapeake Bay, 1880–1947*, rev. ed. ([Glen Burnie, Md., 1951]); Samuel Ward Stanton, *Steam Navigation on the Carolina Sounds and the Chesapeake in 1892*, Steamship Historical Society of America, Reprint Series no. 4 (Salem, Mass., 1947), 20.

3. Alexander Crosby Brown, *The Old Bay Line* (Richmond, 1940), 75–78.

4. *Journal of Industry*, Dec. 1873; *RD*, 12 Jan. 1874; John Diedrich Couper Diary, 30 Oct. and 4 Nov. 1877, VHS.

5. Bowers, "Transportation on James River"; CCR, 6 Dec. 1877, 4 Feb. and 7 Oct. 1878, 3 Feb. 1879; *RD*, 11 Jan. 1881.

6. CCR, 1 Feb. 1869, 15 June 1870; Bowers, "Transportation on James River"; U. S. Army, Corps of Engineers, *Index to the Reports of the Chief of Engineers, U. S. Army . . . 1866–1912: I, Rivers and Harbors* (Washington, D.C., 1915), 419–422.

7. Bowers, "Transportation on James River"; *RD*, 17 Jan. 1876, 1 Jan. 1890; CCR, 1 Nov. 1875.

8. Brown, *Old Bay Line*, 79–80, and *Steam Packets on the Chesapeake: A History* (Cambridge, Md., 1961), 72–74.

9. Thomas J. Wertenbaker, *Norfolk: Historic Southern Port* (Durham, N.C., 1931), 255–330.

10. Richmond customhouse figures in *RD*, 1 Jan. 1871 through 1 Jan. 1901; U. S., Bureau of Statistics, *Statistical Abstract of the United States* (Washington, D.C., 1892 and 1900).

11. Robert McEwen, "Exploring the Kanawha Canal: Gateway to the Past," *Richmond Mercury*, 11 Sept. 1874.

12. U. S. Army, Corps of Engineers, *Report on James River . . .* (Washington, D.C., 1932), 10–11; U. S., Congress, House, *A Report . . . on the James River*, 87th Cong., 2d sess., 1962, H. Doc. 586, 13; Virginia, Department of Conservation and Economic Development, Water Resources Division, *James River Comprehensive Water Resources Plan, III* (Richmond, 1969), 125–126; U.S., Department of Agriculture, Soil Conservation Service, *Atlas of River Basins of the United States* (Washington, D.C., 1963), maps 5 and 6; Jean Gottman, *Virginia at Mid-Century* (New York, 1955), 303.
Unlike watersheds in most South Atlantic states, in which surface runoff into mountain tributaries supplies two-thirds of a river's total annual flow, the James River collects nearly half its total flow as it passes through the lower piedmont and tidewater.

13. CCR, 3 Dec. 1877; W. Asbury Christian, *Richmond: Her Past and Present* (Richmond, 1912), 313.

14. CCR, 3 and 6 Dec. 1877, 17 and 25 Jan. 1878.

15. Ibid., 26 Nov. 1879, 28 Feb., 6 July 1880; *RD*, 1 Jan. 1880, 13, 18, 21, and 29 Jan., 26 May 1881, 1 May, 5 and 19 June 1882.

16. *RW*, 10 and 23 Mar. 1870, quoted in Nelson Morehouse Blake, *William Mahone of Virginia: Soldier and Political Insurgent* (Richmond, 1935), 113–114. For the best description of the process of postwar railroad consolidation into giant rail systems *see* Alfred D. Chandler, Jr., *The Visible Hand: The Managerial Revolution in American Business* (Cambridge, Mass., 1977), 122–205.

17. Allen W. Moger, *From Bourbonism to Byrd, 1870–1925* (Charlottesville, 1968), 14.

18. James Tice Moore, *Two Paths to the New South: The Virginia Debt Controversy, 1870–1883*

(Lexington, Ky., 1974), 14–19; Dabney, *Richmond*, 227–229; Moger, *Bourbonism to Byrd*, 15.

19. Moger, *Bourbonism to Byrd*, 16; *Journal of Industry*, Jan. 1873; *RD*, 10 July 1874, 26 Jan., 9 Feb. 1881.

20. Blake, *Mahone*, 20–134.

21. Moger, *Bourbonism to Byrd*, 14–15, and "Railroad Practices and Policies in Virginia After the Civil War," *VMHB* 59 (1951): 432; Blake, *Mahone*, 113–114, 129–134; *RD*, 22 Feb. 1868; Thomas Bruce, *Southwest Virginia and Shenandoah Valley* (Richmond, 1891), 97; Francis Butler Simkins, et al., *Virginia: History, Government, Geography* (New York, 1957), 478–479.

22. *First Annual Report of the President and Directors of the Chesapeake and Ohio Railroad Company . . .* (Richmond, 1868), 14; *RD*, 1 Feb. 1866; Charles W. Turner, *Chessie's Road* (Richmond, 1956), 73–74, 92–93, 104; CCR, 16 Nov. 1871, 10 Feb., 13 Oct., 22 Dec. 1873; Christian, *Richmond*, 329.

23. [Isaac M. St. John], *Notes on the Coal Trade of the Chesapeake and Ohio Railroad . . .* (Richmond, 1878), 3–8; Turner, *Chessie's Road*, 107.

24. Turner, *Chessie's Road*, 106, 112–113, 122; CCR, 8 Dec. 1881; Maury Klein, *The Great Richmond Terminal: A Study in Businessmen and Business Strategy* (Charlottesville, 1970), 56, 59.

25. Klein, *Richmond Terminal*, 87–88, 93–94; Moger, "Railroad Practices and Policies," 437–441; CCR, 18 June, 2 and 3 July 1877.

26. John B. Mordecai, *A Brief History of the Richmond, Fredericksburg and Potomac Railroad* (Richmond, 1940), 43–44.

27. Ibid., 44–46.

28. Ibid., 47; Dabney, *Richmond*, 226; *RD*, 19 and 20 Dec. 1867, 19 May 1870; CCR, 20 and 30 Apr., 12 Dec. 1866, 14 Oct., 4 Nov., 16 Dec. 1867, 12 and 13 July 1869, 16 Jan., 6 Feb., 1 May, 18 Sept., 23 Oct. 1871, 12 Feb., 11 Mar. 1872, 10 Mar., 14 July, 8 and 22 Sept., 22 Dec. 1873, 26 Jan., 5 Apr., 7 Sept., 16 Nov. 1874, 21 Feb., 20 Mar. 1876, 15 Jan., 19 Feb. 1877.

29. Mordecai, *History of R. F. & P.*, 49; Chandler, *Visible Hand*, 122–124, 217–218.

30. For the wartime members, *see MCC*, pp. 627–636. Information about postwar members comes from CCR, 1865–1881 (particularly the minutes for 1 July of each year, when the new councilmen were sworn in); the Richmond city directories published by W. Eugene Ferslew in 1860, J. L. Hill in 1871–1872, and J. H. Chataigne in 1881; and the *Richmond Dispatch* (which published a complete list of city officials each New Year's Day).

31. Samuel Mordecai, *Virginia, Especially Richmond, In By-Gone Days . . .*, 2d ed. (Richmond, 1860), 222–223; Mary W. Scott, *Houses of Old Richmond* (Richmond, 1941), 43, and *Old Richmond Neighborhoods* (Richmond, 1950), 244, 255, 266; *Richmond News Leader*, 16 Oct. 1975; *Washington Post*, 25 Sept. 1976; *New York Times*, 27 Jan. 1980; and interviews with Margaret T. Peters, research historian with the Virginia Historic Landmarks Commission in May-August 1979.

The name Jackson had been associated with the area since the 1790s, when Joseph Jackson, a contractor, built a house there. His son operated a resort area, known as Jackson's Garden, in the vicinity. I have been unable to find any contemporary evidence, either in Richmond papers or the common council minutes, to support the traditional claim that the ward was named at the direction of President Grant for Giles B. Jackson, who was an adolescent in 1871 but who became a prominent black leader in the city in later years. If such an event had taken place, it would surely have caused comment in the conservative white press, but both the newspapers and the council records are silent on the matter. Others have suggested that the ward was named for Stonewall Jackson, again, without any contemporary evidence. Since the other wards were named for Democratic presidents (Jefferson, Madison, and Monroe), and for a prominent Federalist and a leading Whig (Marshall and Clay), it seems plausible that the sixth ward was named after a southern but strongly nationalist president, who would have been acceptable both to white conservatives and to Union-loving Republicans, despite Andrew Jackson's affiliation with the Democratic party.

32. Dabney, *Richmond*, 237; CCR, 17 Apr. 1871; *RD*, 8 July 1869; Jack P. Maddex, Jr., *The Virginia Conservatives, 1867–1879: A Study in Reconstruction Politics* (Chapel Hill, N.C., 1970), 89–90; Ann Field Alexander, "Black Protest in the New South: John Mitchell, Jr., and the Richmond *Planet*" (Ph.D. diss., Duke University, 1973), 192–194.

33. *RD*, 9 Nov. 1872, 25 and 30 May, 5 Nov. 1874, 10 Nov. 1876, 23 and 24 May 1878, 5 Nov. 1880, 12 and 13 Jan. 1881.

34. Alexander, "Black Protest," 194–197; C. A. Bryce, "Good Old Days When Jackson Ward Was Political Battleground," *Richmond Times-Dispatch*, 8 May 1921; Frank Ruffin to Lewis Edwin Harvie, 10 Nov. 1876, Lewis Edwin Harvie Letters, Accession 25365, Personal Papers Collection, VSL; V. O. Key, Jr., *Southern Politics in State and Nation* (New York, 1949), 536; *Virginia Star*, 11 May 1878. An undated, unidentified newspaper clipping in the George W. Bagby Scrapbooks (VHS) gives the report of the auditor of public accounts for 1873, listing capitation tax delinquents. Of 6,186 registered black voters, 5,483 had not paid the tax.

35. *RD*, 12 and 16 Jan. 1874, 5 Jan. 1876, 6 and 19 Feb., 19 Mar. 1877, 1, 19, 23, 25, 28, and 29 Jan., 3, 4, and 5 Feb. 1881, 3 Apr., 1 May 1882; CCR, 7 and 21 Aug., 2 Oct. 1871, 12 Feb., 25 Mar., 15 Aug., 9 and 16 Sept., 14 Oct., 11 Nov. 1872, 27 May 1873, 13 Jan., 9 Feb. 1874, 19 Apr., 5 July, 20 Sept. 1875, 6 Mar. 1876, 6 Oct. 1879, 2 Feb., 1 Nov. 1880, 7 and 23 Feb., 4 Apr., 24 Aug., 1 and 8 Sept., 3 Oct. 1881. On the middle-class takeover of Richmond, *see* C. Vann Woodward, *Origins of the New South, 1877–1913* in Wendell Holmes Stephenson and E. Merton Coulter, eds., *A History of the South*, vol. 9 ([Baton Rouge], 1951), 150–151.

36. CCR, 22 Sept. 1873; *RD*, 28 and 29 Aug. 1876; on the uncertain identity of Attucks, *see* Hiller B. Zobel, *The Boston Massacre* (New York, 1970), 191, 214, 303.

37. *RD*, 1 Jan. 1880, 26 and 29 Jan. 1881; August Meier and Elliott Rudwick, *From Plantation to Ghetto* (New York, 1976), 215–216; William P. Burrell and D. E. Johnson, *Twenty-Five years history of the Grand Fountain of the United Order of True Reformers, 1881–1905* (Richmond, 1909), 32–45; William Saunders, *Through the Light Continent; or, the United States in 1877–8* (New York, 1879), 78; Alrutheus Ambush Taylor, *The Negro in the Reconstruction of Virginia* (Washington, D.C., 1926), 131; *Virginia Star*, 11 May 1878.

38. *Richmond News Leader*, 15 Apr. 1938; *Richmond Times-Dispatch*, 12 Aug. 1934; Richard Ellsworth Day, *Rhapsody in Black: The Life Story of John Jasper* (Philadelphia, 1953), 89–121; [William] Wells Brown, *My Southern Home; or, The South and Its People* (Boston, 1880), 203–206.

39. Saunders, *Through the Light Continent*, 77–79.

40. Christian, *Richmond*, 345; *RD*, 13, 14, and 23 Jan. 1876.

41. *RD*, 22 Mar. 1870, 8 Jan. 1876; CCR, 19 and 22 Feb., 16 Apr., 18 June 1877; Noble L. Prentis, *Southern Letters* (Topeka, Kans., 1881), 153; August Meier, *Negro Thought In America, 1880–1915* (Ann Arbor, Mich., 1963), 133.

42. Thomas P. Baer, "A History of the Richmond Bureau of Police" (B.A. thesis, University of Richmond, 1961), 14–16; Louis B. Cei, "Law Enforcement in Richmond: A History of Police-Community Relations, 1737–1974" (Ph.D. diss., Florida State University, 1975), 91–93; *Virginia Star*, 16 Dec. 1882; George Augustus Sala, *America Revisited . . .* , 2d ed., 2 vols. (London, 1882), 1:240–242; Saunders, *Through the Light Continent*, 78; CCR, 4 Feb. 1878; Robert Skipwith Diary, 23 Jan. 1872, W & M; Charles E. Wynes, *Race Relations in Virginia, 1870–1902* (Charlottesville, 1961), 22, 25, 28, 46, 137–138, 145.

43. Christian, *Richmond*, 341–342, 350–351; *see RD*, 1871–1901, for figures on manufactured goods.

44. Clement Eaton, *A History of the Old South*, 3d ed. (New York, 1975), 432; E. Merton Coulter, *The South During Reconstruction, 1865–1877* in Wendell Holmes Stephenson and E. Merton Coulter, eds., *A History of the South*, vol. 8 ([Baton Rouge], 1947), 255–256.

45. Nannie May Tilley, *The Bright-Tobacco Industry, 1860–1929* (Chapel Hill, N.C., 1948), 214, 545–546, 563–564. All figures computed are from the industrial schedule of the manuscript census.

46. Ibid., 150–152, 212–213, 253–255, 325–327, 365, 403–404; *RD*, 14 Jan. 1881; Benjamin W. Arnold, "History of the Tobacco Industry in Virginia from 1860 to 1894," *Johns Hopkins University Studies in Historical and Political Science* 15, nos. 1 and 2 (1897), 35.

47. Tilley, *Bright-Tobacco*, 491, 492, 494, 499, 500, 504.

48. Ibid., 504, 508–510, 515–516; James K. Sanford, ed., *A Century of Commerce* (Richmond, [1967]), 26.

49. U.S., Bureau of the Census, Eighth, Ninth, and Tenth Census, 1860–1880, Industrial Schedule MSS, VSL; Fred A. Shannon, *The Farmer's Last Frontier, 1860–1897* in Henry David, et al., eds., *The Economic History of the United States*, vol. 5 (New York, 1945), 148–149; Allen W. Moger, "Industrial and Urban Progress in Virginia from 1880 to 1900," *VMHB* 66 (1958): 314–315.

50. *RD*, 17 May 1866, 28 July, 28 Oct., 8 Nov. 1869, 1 Sept. 1874, 8 Feb., 1 Nov. 1881; *see* 1 Jan. 1871 through 1 Jan. 1898 for figures on annual production. Also, Shannon, *Farmer's Last Frontier*, 157–158; Turner, *Chessie's Road*, 106, 122.

51. *RD*, 1872–1881; *Journal of Industry*, Feb. 1873; Eighth, Ninth, and Tenth Census, Industrial Schedule MSS; Charles B. Dew, *Ironmaker to the Confederacy: Joseph R. Anderson and the Tredegar Iron Works* (New Haven, Conn., 1966).

52. Eighth, Ninth, and Tenth Census, Industrial Schedule MSS; Dabney, *Richmond*, 225.

53. Edward King, *The Great South* (Hartford, Conn., 1875), 637–638.

54. Frederick Myron Colby to the *Manchester* (N.H.) *Union Democrat*, reprinted in *RD*, 20 Jan. 1876; Brown, *My Southern Home*, 202; Sala, *America Revisited*, 1:248–251; Thomas R. Wilkinson, *Holiday Rambles* (Manchester, Eng., 1881), 30.

55. Willard Glazier, *Peculiarities of American Cities* (Philadelphia, 1883), 430–432.

56. CCR, 7 and 21 June 1875, 17 July 1876; Perceval Reniers, *The Springs of Virginia: Life, Love, and Death at the Waters 1775–1900* (Chapel Hill, N.C., 1941), 222, 225, 259, 261; *RD*, 1 July 1876; Blair Burwell to Jenny Burwell, 14 Sept. 1874, Burwell Family Papers, W & M.

57. Eda C. Williams, *The Richmond German, 1866–1966* (Richmond, 1966); Dabney, *Richmond*, 221; John A. Cutchins, *Memories of Old Richmond (1881–1944)* (Verona, Va., 1973), 151–176; Herbert T. Ezekiel and Gaston Lichtenstein, *The History of the Jews of Richmond From 1769 to 1917* (Richmond, 1917), 232; CCR, 9 Sept. 1872, 22 Sept., 8 Dec. 1873, 24 May, 6 July, 5 Oct. 1874, 3 Apr. 1876, 7 Feb., 7 July, 3 Oct. 1881; *RD*, 26 Jan., 27 June 1876, 2 Feb. 1881.

58. James H. Bailey, "A Bouquet of Beauties: Some Noted Virginia Belles of the Nineteenth Century," *Virginia Cavalcade* 2 (Winter 1952): 17–21; Evan R. Chesterman, "Duels and Duelists of Bygone Days," clippings from the *Richmond Evening Journal* (Richmond, 1908–1909).

59. Richmond, Va., School Board, *Annual Report of the Superintendent of Public Schools* (Richmond, 1870–1900); Ninth and Tenth Census, Industrial Schedule MSS; *RD*, 11 Jan.

1881. There were 6,781 white students and 4,968 black students enrolled for the school year of 1889–1890, or 11,749 total students. U.S., Bureau of the Census, *Compendium of the Eleventh Census of the United States* (Washington, D.C., 1896), 755, shows a total school age population of 27,575, or 16,423 whites and 11,152 blacks.

60. Margaret Meagher, *History of Education in Richmond* (Richmond, 1939), 66–89.

61. CCR, 13 Nov. 1871, 14 Apr. 1873, 21 June 1875; Christian, *Richmond*, 328–329, 331–332, 347–350, 354, 356, 369; *RD*, 6 and 15 Jan., 23 Feb. 1876.

62. Christian, *Richmond*, 344; CCR, 3 July 1871; Paul H. Buck, *The Road to Reunion, 1865–1900* (Boston, 1937), 199; Robert Skipwith Diary, 4 July 1872; *RD*, 3 and 4 July 1876; but cf. Dabney, *Richmond*, 220.

The continued strength of rebel sentiment in Richmond until the post–World War II era is well known to local historians, but it has surprised some strangers. For instance, as a young army officer from California visiting the city on Memorial Day in 1918, Earl Warren was shocked by the profusion of Confederate flags: "Not an American flag was to be seen." (*See, The Memoirs of Earl Warren* (Garden City, N.Y., 1977), 50).

63. CCR, 17 Jan. 1876, 6 Oct. 1879, 16 Nov. 1880, 10 Mar., 4 Apr., 2 May, 7 and 21 July 1881.

Chapter 7: Old City of the New South, 1882–1890

1. Virginius Dabney, *Richmond: The Story of a City* (Garden City, N.Y., 1976), 247; *Harper's Weekly* 15 Jan. 1887.

2. *RD*, 2 Jan. 1885; CCR, 3 Aug. 1885; W. Asbury Christian, *Richmond: Her Past and Present* (Richmond, 1912), 396, 400–401, 403; Dabney, *Richmond*, 243, 259, 266. An 1886 reception for Jefferson Davis in Montgomery, Ala., for example, provoked much sectional rhetoric (*see RD*, 4 May 1886).

3. *New York Times*, 14 Jan. 1887, quoted in Louis B. Cei, "Law Enforcement in Richmond: A History of Police-Community Relations, 1737–1974" (Ph.D. diss., Florida State University, 1975), 114; CCR, 1 Sept., 1 Dec. 1884, 6 Apr. 1885, 8 June, 7 Nov. 1887, 4 June 1888, 6 Oct., 3 Nov. 1890; Emily Clark, *Stuffed Peacocks* (New York, 1927), 11.

4. James Tice Moore, "The Death of the Duel: The *Code Duello* in Readjuster Virginia, 1879–1883," *VMHB* 83 (1975): 259–276; *RD* 1 Jan. 1891.

5. *RD*, 1 Jan. 1890; CCR, 7 May 1883; James K. Sanford, ed., *Richmond: Her Triumphs, Tragedies, and Growth* (Richmond, [1975]), 50.

6. CCR, Apr. 1885, 19 Apr. 1886, 3 Mar. 1890; *RD*, 1 Dec. 1884.

7. U.S., Bureau of the Census, *Compendium of the Eleventh Census of the United States, 1890, I* (Washington, 1896), 742–743; *RD*, 1 Jan. 1890.

8. *RD*, 1 Jan. 1891.

9. *RD*, 5 Jan. 1881; CCR, 7 Jan. 1884, 2 Mar. 1885, 11 Feb., 5 July 1887, 1 Oct. 1888, 7 Jan. 1889.

10. CCR, 10 Mar. 1881, 5 Mar. 1883, 6 Apr. 1885, 10 Dec. 1886, 10 Mar., 5 July, 5 and 8 Sept. 1887.

11. Ibid., 6 June 1887, 21 June 1888; Sanford, ed., *Richmond*, 51–54. The following biographical information about the directors of the Richmond Union Passenger Railway is found in William L. Montague, comp., *Richmond Directory and Business Advertiser* (Richmond, 1850–1851); W. Eugene Ferslew, comp., *Second Annual Directory for the City of Richmond . . .*

(Richmond, 1860); J. H. Chataigne, comp., *Directory of Richmond, Virginia* . . . (Richmond, 1881 and 1891); Christian, *Richmond*, and additional sources as cited below.

Two of the directors of the Richmond Union Passenger Railway, Frederick C. Brauer and Valentine Hechler, Jr., were members of the city's German community. Brauer had been nominated as a Republican candidate for the hustings court in 1870 but declined to run (*RD*, 23 and 24 May 1870). In the 1880s he was a cattle broker; nearly all of the Brauers and Hechlers in Richmond were involved in some sector of the meat business. Brauer may have been related to Dr. D. R. Brauer, who worked at Howard's Grove hospital and who participated in Republican politics (*RD*, 16 Apr., 29 July, 2 Aug. 1867).

Valentine Hechler, Jr., and his brother William T. Hechler were Main Street pork packers. They had butcher stalls in the Old Market during the 1870s and 1880s, when they gradually expanded their business. Their father, a butcher in the city since at least 1850, was imprisoned during the war as a Unionist along with John Minor Botts, Franklin Stearns, John M. Higgins, and others. He died 21 June 1880 (Christian, *Richmond*, 368).

Charles L. Todd served in the 1st Co., Richmond Howitzers, for part of the war, but later went into business as a grocer, claiming payment for flour left at the almshouse in February 1865 (CCR, 8 and 29 Jan. 1866). He was elected to the common council in 1870, serving one term (CCR, 1 July 1870). Todd was a leader in the free-bridge movement and helped organize the city's centennial observance in 1881. During the 1880s he was a wholesale grocer and commission merchant.

William H. Scott, a wealthy druggist, prospered during the war and was one of the interim councilmen appointed by Governor Walker in March 1870 (*RD*, 16 Mar. 1870). He was elected to a regular term from Clay Ward in 1871, replacing Todd. In the 1880s Scott owned two drugstores (Mary Wingfield Scott, *Old Richmond Neighborhoods* [Richmond, 1950], 84; *MCC*, 18 May 1863; CCR, 3 July 1871).

J. Thompson Brown, captain of the 2d Co., Richmond Howitzers, failed in his bids to get appointed to public office in 1867 and 1870, lacking support from the council (CCR, 19 Dec. 1867, 6 May 1870). He prospered as an auctioneer, headed a large real estate firm, and also published a trade paper, the *Richmond Progress*. As president of the Union Passenger Railway, Brown played a leading role in bringing Sprague's electric streetcars to the city. After the turn of the century Brown assisted historian Frederic Bancroft by identifying some of the most prominent men in antebellum Richmond as slave traders (Frederic Bancroft, *Slave-Trading in the Old South* [Baltimore, 1931], 96 n.23).

Whitmell S. Forbes listed himself as a manager in 1881; by 1891 he was the head of W. S. Forbes and Company, provision and commission merchants. He helped put down the Richmond streetcar strike in 1903 and later served as president of an interurban line.

John F. Barry is not listed in city directories for 1881 and 1891. He may have been an outsider, representing northern interests. He may also have been related to W. H. Barry, clerk of the U. S. Circuit Court in 1866–1867 under Judge John C. Underwood.

John S. Wise, the noted Readjuster and Republican, who had failed in Richmond politics and suffered social ostracism because of his beliefs, succeeded in New York as a corporation lawyer and served as counsel for the Union Passenger Railway. He may have been brought into the operation by the New Yorker Sprague, but Wise undoubtedly relished the idea of stealing a march on the conservatives who headed the competing lines, and he would not have served as attorney for a firm dominated by Democrats (Leon Fink, " 'Irrespective of Party, Color or Social Standing': The Knights of Labor and Opposition Politics in Richmond, Virginia," *Labor History* 19 [1978]: 347).

12. CCR, 3 Sept., 1 Oct. 1888, 5 Aug., 2 Sept., 7 Oct. 1889, 15 Jan., 16 Sept. 1890; *RD*, 1 Jan. 1891; Howard N. Rabinowitz, "Southern Urban Development, 1860–1900," in Blaine A. Brownell and David R. Goldfield, eds., *The City in Southern History: The Growth of Urban Civilization in the South* (Port Washington, N.Y., 1977), 119. Streetcars in Richmond were segregated as late as 1875, but the practice stopped sometime before 1890 (*see* Rabinowitz, *Race Relations in the Urban South, 1865–1890* [New York, 1978], 192). By the early 1890s, whites already were demanding a return to Jim Crow cars (*Richmond Labor News*, 16 July 1892, reprinted in *Richmond Planet*, 23 July 1892).

13. CCR, 1 Sept., 6 Oct. 1890.

14. Ibid., 13 Nov. 1871, 3 Feb. 1879, 4 Oct. 1886, 3 Mar. 1887; *RD*, 1 Jan. 1890; Rabinowitz, "Urban Development," 115; Christian, *Richmond*, 525–526.

15. Sanford, ed., *Richmond*, 47–48, 52–55; *RD*, 26 May 1881; CCR, 1 May 1882, 5 July, 8 Nov. 1883, 4 Aug. 1884, 5 Jan., 12 June, 3 Aug. 1885, 4 Jan., 2 Feb. 1886, 21 Feb. 1887, 14 Feb., 4 June 1888, 7 Apr., 5 May, 1 Sept. 1890.

16. Sanford, ed., *Richmond*, 42–46, 97; CCR, 1 Oct., 5 and 8 Nov. 1883, 15 Jan., 4 Feb., 3 Mar. 1884; *RD*, 1 Jan. 1886 and 1891; Rabinowitz, "Urban Development," 112–113; Blake McKelvey, *The Urbanization of America [1860–1915]* (New Brunswick, N.J., 1963), 107–108; Alfred D. Chandler, Jr., *The Visible Hand: The Managerial Revolution in American Business* (Cambridge, Mass., 1977), 200–201.

17. CCR, 6 Mar. 1882, 18 Jan., 2 Mar. 1884, 1 Feb. 1886, 19 Mar., 7 May 1888; Rabinowitz, "Urban Development," 112–113.

18. CCR, 4 Dec. 1883, 6 Apr., 3 Aug., 4 Nov. 1885, 11 Feb., 4 Apr. 1887; *RD*, 1 Jan. 1885; Rabinowitz, "Urban Development," 110–111.

19. CCR, 21 Dec. 1887, 4 and 25 Mar. 1890.

20. Ibid., 2 Jan. 1882, 18 July 1884, 2 Feb. 1885, 6 Sept. 1886, 3 June 1889; Hamilton Owens, *Baltimore on the Chesapeake* (Garden City, N.Y., 1941), 301.

21. CCR, 3 Apr., 1 May 1882, 5 Jan., 3 Aug. 1885, 5 July 1888, 7 Apr., 5 May, 2 June 1890; 5 July 1888, Board of Aldermen journal, City Clerk's Office, Richmond City Hall, Richmond, Va.; Christian, *Richmond*, 376–377.

22. CCR, 3 Jan. 1888; Christian, *Richmond*, 407, 416–417, 421, 428.

23. CCR, 3 Nov. 1884; Cei, "Law Enforcement," 109–119; Rabinowitz, "Urban Development," 101, 120.

24. *RD*, 1 Jan. 1888.

25. W. Dean Burnham, *Presidential Ballots, 1836–1892* (Baltimore, 1955), 843.

26. For the argument that these measures were not aimed at blacks, *see* Robert R. Jones, "James L. Kemper and the Virginia Redeemers Face the Race Question: A Reconsideration," *JSH* 38 (1972): 393–414; and Ralph Clipman McDanel, *The Virginia Constitutional Convention of 1901–1902* (1928; reprint ed., New York, 1972), 38. But *see also* Charles E. Wynes, *Race Relations in Virginia, 1870–1902* (Charlottesville, 1961), 22–25, 45–46, 136; James Hugo Johnston, "The Participation of Negroes in the Government of Virginia from 1877 to 1888," *Journal of Negro History* 14 (1929): 262–266; C. A. Bryce, "Good Old Days When Jackson Ward Was Political Battleground," *Richmond Times-Dispatch*, 8 May 1921; Ann Field Alexander, "Black Protest in the New South: John Mitchell, Jr., and the Richmond *Planet*" (Ph. D. diss., Duke University, 1973), 179, 188–190, 194–197; Peter Rachleff, "Black, White, and Gray: The Rise and Decline of Working Class Activity in Richmond, Va., 1865–1890" (M.A. thesis, University of Pittsburgh, 1976), 158; *Virginia Star*, 11 May 1878. An unidentified and undated newspaper clipping, with the report of the auditor for public accounts for 1873 (which listed capitation tax

delinquents), states that of 6,186 registered black voters in Richmond, 5,483 had not paid the tax (*see* George W. Bagby Scrapbooks, VHS).

27. John A. Cutchins, *Memories of Old Richmond, (1881–1944)* (Verona, Va., 1973), 16; Robert Beverley Munford, Jr., *Richmond Homes and Memories* (Richmond, 1936), 37–38; John S. Wise, *The Lion's Skin: A Historical Novel and a Novel History* (New York, 1905), 372–376, 378; Curtis Carroll Davis, "Very Well-Rounded Republican: The Several Lives of John S. Wise," *VMHB* 71 (1963): 461–487.

28. Christian, *Richmond*, 374–376, 378–379; Cei, "Law Enforcement," 109–110; James Tice Moore, *Two Paths to the New South: The Virginia Debt Controversy, 1870–1883* (Lexington, Ky., 1974), 105,111.

29. CCR, 4 June 1883; Christian, *Richmond*, 380–383.

30. Moore, *Two Paths*, 116–117; Christian, *Richmond*, 387–388, 396; Dabney, *Richmond*, 240.

31. Allen W. Moger, "Industrial and Urban Progress in Virginia From 1880 to 1900," *VMHB* 66 (1958): 323–325. Clipping of letter by anonymous Knight in the *Richmond State*, 20 Apr. 1885; boycott notice of Richmond Typographical Union No. 90, dated 14 Apr. 1885; undated notice of District Assembly No. 84 of the Richmond Knights of Labor; letter of the Haxall-Crenshaw Company in the *Richmond State*, 18 Apr. 1885; published letter from Philip Haxall (president of the company) to William H. Mullen (chairman of the boycott committee of the Knights of Labor, of Richmond) in an undated newspaper clipping, 30 Dec. 1885—all in the George A. Barksdale Scrapbook, VHS. Rabinowitz, "Urban Development," 117; Fink, "Knights of Labor," 328–329; Kenneth Kann, "The Knights of Labor and the Southern Black Worker," *Labor History* 18 (1977): 54–56; Melton Alonza McLaurin, *The Knights of Labor in the South* (Westport, Conn., 1978), 41–42, 48–50.

32. New York *Journal of Commerce*, 18 Feb. 1886; Barksdale Scrapbook, VHS; Fink, "Knights of Labor," 330, 334–335; Christian, *Richmond*, 397–398; Dabney, *Richmond*, 221; *RD* and *Richmond State*, cited in Cei, "Law Enforcement," 113–114, 116; cf. Rabinowitz, *Race Relations*, 318. On blacks and prohibition elsewhere in the South, *see* Hanes Walton, Jr. and James E. Taylor, "Blacks and the Southern Prohibition Movement," *Phylon* 32 (1971): 247–259.

33. *RD*, 5, 6, 7, 8, 11, 27, and 28 May 1886. *See RD*, 4 May 1886 for "Brown's Iron Bitters," which "strike" at various ailments.

34. CCR, 3 Jan., 21 Feb., 7 Mar. 1887; *RD*, 1 Jan. 1890; Dabney, *Richmond*, 253–254; Cei, "Law Enforcement," 115–116; Kann, "Southern Black Worker," 63–64; Fink, "Knights of Labor," 331–332, 335–340, 345–348; McLaurin, *Knights of Labor in the South*, 86–88.

35. *Richmond State*, 6 Oct. 1886; Dabney, *Richmond*, 238; Thomas E. Walton, "The Negro in Richmond, 1880–1890" (M.A. thesis, Howard University, 1950), 38–44; Kann, "Southern Black Worker," 60–62, Fink, "Knights of Labor," 341–345; *RD*, 3 Apr. 1887; Barksdale Scrapbook, VHS; McLaurin, *Knights of Labor in the South*, 135, 143–147.

36. CCR, 7 Jan., 4 Feb. 1889; Cei, "Law Enforcement," 117–119.

37. CCR, 7 Aug. 1882, 7 Jan., 6 Feb. 1885, 1 Oct., 3 Dec. 1888.

38. Ibid., 2 Dec. 1889, 6 Jan. 1890; *RD*, 4 June 1890.

39. Alexander, "Black Protest," 209.

40. Walton, "Negro in Richmond," 14, 28–29; Rabinowitz, *Race Relations*, 278–279; *Richmond Planet*, 22 Feb. 1890.

41. Walton, "Negro in Richmond," 14, 28–29; *Compendium of Eleventh Census, I*, 742–743; Bryce, "Good Old Days"; Rabinowitz, "Urban Development," 117; Reynolds Farley, "The Urbanization of Negroes in the United States," *Journal of Social History* 1 (1968): 241–258.

42. *Virginia Star*, 16 Dec. 1882; Luther Porter Jackson, *Negro Office-Holders in Virginia,*

1865–1895 (Norfolk, 1945), 83–84; Walton, "Negro in Richmond," 20–21; CCR, 1 Feb. 1886; James O. Breeden, "Body Snatchers and Anatomy Professors: Medical Education in Nineteenth-Century Virginia," *VMHB* 83 (1975): 321–345.

43. CCR, 26 May 1882, 5 Feb. 1883, 7 Apr., 5 May, 4 Aug. 1884, 7 Sept. 1885, 2 Feb., 6 Sept. 1886, 6 June, 5 July, 5 Sept., 3 Oct., 5 Dec. 1887, 3 Jan., 6 Feb., 7 May, 6 Aug., 3 Sept. 1888, 1 Apr., 2 Dec. 1889, 7 Apr. 1890; Thomas F. Hale and Louis H. Manarin, *Richmond: A Pictorial History From the Valentine Museum and Dementi Collections* (Richmond, [1974]), 126, 129; Paul S. Dulaney, *The Architecture of Historic Richmond* (Charlottesville, 1968), 104, 111; Christian, *Richmond*, 371, 442; John A. Cutchins, *A Famous Command: The Richmond Light Infantry Blues* (Richmond, 1934), 209–210, 214; Andrew Buni, *The Negro in Virginia Politics, 1902–1965* (Charlottesville, 1967), 24–25. On Farrar *see* Jackson, *Negro Office-Holders*, 57, and CCR, 22 Mar., 6 Dec. 1886. On Mitchell *see* Alexander, "Black Protest."

44. Howard N. Raboniwitz, "From Exclusion to Segregation: Health and Welfare Services for Southern Blacks, 1865–1890," *Social Service Review* 48 (1974): 327–354; CCR, 3 June, 5 Aug. 1889.

45. William P. Burrell and D. E. Johnson, *Twenty-Five Years History of the Grand Fountain of the United Order of True Reformers, 1881–1905* (Richmond, 1909), 32–45, 66–69, 84, 95–99, 116–119, 122–123, 128; Writers' Program of Works Progress Administration in Virginia, comp., *The Negro in Virginia* (New York, 1940), 293, 296; Walton, "Negro in Richmond," 41, 52, 59.

46. *RD*, 1 Jan. 1890–1891.

47. Ibid.; *Richmond Guide Book* (Richmond, 1909), 55; Dabney, *Richmond*, 253.

48. Walton, "Negro in Richmond," 47–50.

49. On Giles B. Jackson *see* W.P.A., comp., *Negro in Virginia*, 297, and Burrell, *True Reformers*, 47. On Crump *see* Jackson, *Negro Office-Holders*, 27, 57, 84, and *Richmond Planet*, 22 Feb. 1890 (Crump's obituary). *See also* 10 and 31 May 1890 for Mitchell's ridicule of noncombatant rebels and comments on the erection of the Lee statue.

50. *RD*, 28 Oct. 1887, 1 Jan. 1890; Dabney, *Richmond*, 232–233; CCR, 3 Jan. 1887, 7 Jan., 4 Feb. 1889, 1 Sept. 1890.

51. Dabney, *Richmond*, 269–270; Cutchins, *Old Richmond*, 146–147; James Meehan, "Bojangles of Richmond: 'His Dancing Feet Brought Joy to the World,' " *Virginia Cavalcade* 27 (1978): 103; Julian Street, *American Adventures: A Second Trip "Abroad At Home"* (New York, 1917), 243–247; author's interview with Mrs. Jesse H. Crouch, of Richmond, who visited Crutchfield's court after the turn of the century. Perceptions of Crutchfield were affected by class as well as race. Shortly after the judge took office, militant editor John Mitchell praised him. Although Mitchell was a crusader for black rights, he was also solidly middle class and apparently approved of Crutchfield's treatment of blacks who reflected discredit upon the race (*see Richmond Planet*, 14 June and 5 July 1890).

52. *RD*, 30 July 1882; Lewis Harvie Blair, *A Southern Prophecy: The Prosperity of the South Dependent upon the Elevation of the Negro*, ed. C. Vann Woodward (Boston, 1964), 89.

53. *RD*, 1 Jan. 1885, 1888, 1890; Moger, "Progress in Virginia," 322; Sanford, ed., *Richmond*, 47–66.

54. Arthur M. Schlesinger, *The Rise of the City, 1878–1898*, in Arthur M. Schlesinger and Dixon Ryan Fox, eds., *A History of American Life*, vol. 10 (New York, 1933), 14; *RD*, 1 Jan. 1884–1901.

55. U.S., Bureau of Statistics, *Statistical Abstract of the United States* (Washington, D.C., 1892 and 1900); *RD*, 3 Feb. 1881, 1 Jan. 1890; Sanford, ed., *Richmond*, 37.

56. U.S., Bureau of the Census, Ninth and Tenth Census, 1870 and 1880, Industrial Schedule MSS, VSL; *RD*, 1 Jan. 1872–1901; *Compendium of Eleventh Census, II*, 708–709, 956–959; note of special agent J. Alston Cabell on industrial schedule of manuscript census regarding letter written to him in July 1881, which reported that no women's clothing, except underwear, was made in Richmond.

57. *RD*, 1 Jan. 1872–1901; Sanford, ed., *Richmond*, 19–21.

58. *RD*, 1 Jan. 1890.

59. Ibid., 1 Jan. 1872–1901; Sanford, ed., *Richmond*, 15–18, 84; Moger, "Progress in Virginia," 316–319.

60. *The Advantages of Richmond, Virginia, as a Manufactory and Trading Centre* . . . (Richmond, 1882), 32–33; Moger, "Progress in Virginia," 323; Andrew W. Morrison, ed., *The City on the James: Richmond, Virginia* (Richmond, 1893), 14; Sanford, ed., *Richmond*, 16–18; Hale and Manarin, *Pictorial History*, 142.

61. *RD*, 1 Jan. 1872–1901; Patrick G. Porter, "Origins of the American Tobacco Company," *Business History Review* 43 (1969): 59–76.

62. Porter, "American Tobacco Company," 67–70.

63. Ibid., 61, 65, 72–74.

64. Gabriel Paul Othein de Cleron (le comte d'Haussonville), *A Travers les Etats Unis, notes et impressions* (Paris, 1888), 145–146. English translation by Mrs. Flora Stith Lowe.

65. Christian, *Richmond*, 365, 384, 389, 417, 420; Cei, "Law Enforcement," 103–104; CCR, 6 Jan. 1879, 4 Nov. 1885, 6 Sept., 4 Oct. 1886, 17 Oct. 1889; *RD*, 3 and 6 Jan. 1885, 3 Jan. 1888; [William] Wells Brown, *My Southern Home; or, The South and Its People* (Boston, 1880), 207–208. *See* William Joel Ernst III, "Urban Leaders and Social Change: The Urbanization Process in Richmond, Virginia, 1840-1880" (Ph.D. diss., University of Virginia, 1978), 277–278, for evidence of anti-Catholic sentiment involving former mayor Anthony M. Keiley and the use of the Protestant Bible in public schools in the 1870s.

66. CCR, 3 Jan., 7 Mar. 1887; Dabney, *Richmond*, 335–336.

67. CCR, 4 May, 1 June 1885, 4 Oct. 1886; Rabinowitz, "Urban Development," 111.

68. Paul M. Gaston, *The New South Creed: A Study in Southern Mythmaking* (New York, 1970), 107; Cutchins, *Old Richmond*, 52–67; Dabney, *Richmond*, 214, 261–262, 280.

69. Perceval Reniers, *The Springs of Virginia: Life, Love, and Death at the Waters 1775–1900* (Chapel Hill, N.C., 1941), 253, 259, 266.

70. Munford, *Homes and Memories*, 37–38; Cutchins, *Old Richmond*, 9; Moore, *Two Paths*, 119.

71. Munford, *Homes and Memories*, 42; Christian, *Richmond*, 347–350; Dabney, *Richmond*, 244; Edward King, *The Great South* (Hartford, 1875), 631; *RD*, 14 and 27 Mar., 17 Apr. 1866, 6 Sept. 1869, 26 May 1881; CCR, 7 May 1880, 5 May 1884, 5 Dec. 1887, 9 Dec. 1889, 7 Apr., 5 May, 2 June 1890; Charles Reagan Wilson, "The Religion of the Lost Cause: Ritual and Organization of the Southern Civil Religion, 1865–1920," *JSH* 46 (1980): 219–238.

72. *RD*, 6–8 May 1890; John S. Wise, *The End of An Era* (Boston, 1900), 98–100.

73. Munford, *Homes and Memories*, 44; *RD*, May 1890, particularly *Boston Transcript* editorial quoted on 31 May 1890; Guy Friddell, *What Is It About Virginia?* (Richmond, 1966), 39–42.

74. Dabney, *Richmond*, 275, 298, 304; Douglas Southall Freeman, *The Last Parade* (Richmond, 1932). A reunion, attended by three Confederate veterans, was held in Norfolk early in the 1950s.

Epilogue: James on Richmond

1. Henry James, *The American Scene* (New York, 1907), 377; Dabney, *Richmond*, 317.
2. James, *American Scene*, 355–356.
3. Ibid., 357.
4. Ibid., 378–379.

Index

The text of *Richmond After the War* was set in 11 on 13 Janson by Coghill Composition Company, of Richmond; the display faces are Garamond. This book was printed by Spencer Printing Company, of Richmond, on acid-free, permanent/durable papers: text on Warren Olde Style Wove, 60 lb., and plates on Warren Lustro Offset Enamel Dull Cream, 80 lb. The book has been bound both in Kennett Joanna 67350 with Canfield Colortext crimson end-papers (case-bound) and in Warren Lustro Offset Enamel Gloss, 100 lb. (paperbound).